מסורה

ArtScroll Mesorah Series®

Rabbis Nosson Scherman / Meir Zlotowitz
General Editors

A SEDER COMPANION
WITH INSIGHTS AND INTERPRETATIONS
FOR INSPIRATION AND RETELLING

Published by

Mesorah Publications, ltd

in conjunction with

Zeirei Agudath Israel of America

The Haggadah Treasury

Edited by
Rabbi Nosson Scherman

FIRST EDITION
Il Adar, 5738 / March, 1978

SECOND EDITION
Shevat, 5740 / January, 1980
Teves, 5742 / January, 1982

THE HAGGADAH TREASURY
© Copyright 1978
by ZEIREI AGUDATH ISRAEL OF AMERICA
New York City

© Copyright 1980
by MESORAH PUBLICATIONS, Ltd.
1969 Coney Island Avenue
Brooklyn, New York 11223
(212) 339-1700

ISBN:

0-89906-200-8
(hard cover)

0-89906-201-6
(paperback)

Printed by Moriah Offset

Table of Contents

6-7   Haskamos/Approbations

9   Preface

11   Foreword

14   Required Amounts of Ritual Foods

17-19   Pre-Seder Preparations

20   Symbols of the Seder

24   The Seder

RABBI MOSES FEINSTEIN

455 F. D. R. DRIVE

New York 2, N. Y.

ORegon 7-1222

משה פיינשטיין

ר"מ תפארת ירושלים

בנוא יארק

בע"ה

יום ג' לסדר צו תשל"ח לפ"ק

ברכות יחולו על ראשם של הני בני עליה בחורי

חמד עסקני צעירי אגודת ישראל באמעריקא שטרחו ואספו

ממעינות רבותינו הראשונים והאחרונים לחבר דבר נאה

ומהודר להגדה של פסח בשפה המדוברת במדינתנו לרוות

נפשם של אחב"י הצמאים לשמע את דבר ה' ולהרבות

לספר ביציאת מצרים. ובראותי תוקף עמלם ופעולותיהם

הכבירים בהרבצת תורה בין הנוער וחיזוק הדת ושאר

מפעלים לשם שמים אמרתי לברכם ולעודדם ולחזקם.

יה"ר שתשרה שכינה במעשה ידיכם וחפץ ה' בידכם יצליח.

[חתימה בכתב יד]

הסכמת מרן הגאון ר' גדלי' הלוי שארר שליט"א

RABBI GEDALIA SCHORR
417 E. 5TH STREET
BROOKLYN, N. Y. 11218

גדלי' הלוי שארר
ר"מ ומנהל במתיבתא תו"ד
ברוקלין, נ. י. יע"א

בס"ד

[כתב יד בכתב ידו של הרב]

לכבוד הנהלת צעירי אגודת ישראל הי"ו
ואחדשה"ט

כבר נודע בשערים לתהלה "הגדה של פסח" שיצא לאור אשתקד ע"י צעירי אגודת ישראל.
שמחתי מאד לשמוע כי מוכנים אתם להוציא לאור עוד הפעם בשנה זו דוגמתו עם הוספות וכל
המרבה הרי זה משובח.

כל המשתתפים והמתעסקים יזכו להוסיף אומץ להפיץ תורה ודעת ד' טהורה ויקוים
במהרה בימינו "הנה שולח לכם את אלי' הנביא והשיב לב אבות וכו' "

החותם בברכה לכל פעולתכם
גדלי' הלוי שארר
ר"ח אדר השני תשל"ח

Preface

Without a doubt, no sefer has had as many commentaries composed on it as the Haggadah. The majesty of the Seder night, the position of the Exodus as the genesis of Jewish nationhood, and the Haggadah's exhortation that 'the more one tells about Yetzias Mitzrayim, the more praiseworthy he is,' have all contributed to the Haggadah's position as a lodestone of thought and inspiration.

In its position in the life of the Jewish family, too, the Haggadah is unique. For it is at the Seder that families join and listen attentively to elucidations and embellishments of the Exodus narrative. If the greatest figures in the age of tannaim could spend the entire night delving into the events and laws of that fateful night, then surely we should attempt to follow their example in whatever humble way we can.

It is to assist the Torah public in so elevating its Seder night that this Haggadah Treasury was conceived. From a wide range of sources, the young men of Zeirei Agudath Israel have selected insights, parables, and interpretations on the Haggadah that are suitable for easy reading and retelling. The purpose of this collection is not to be a scholarly commentary on the Haggadah; rather it is to enable young and old — harried and exhausted after the endless preparations for Pesach — to find a wealth of material to study, to enjoy, and from which to choose countless gems that will enhance their Seder and, indeed, their appreciation of the entire festival. Layman and scholar will find much here that is new and provocative, and that is familiar and beloved. It captures the essence of the Seder itself — old and well-remembered, yet an eternal wellspring of stimulation and inspiration. Zeirei Agudath Israel has rendered a significant service to the community.

I am deeply grateful to HARAV DAVID FEINSTEIN שליט"א for taking the time to review the halachic instructions which are based primarily on his Kol Dodi, and for allowing the reproduction of his Required Amounts of Ritual Foods and Beverages for the Pesach Seder.

May I take this opportunity to thank the entire staff of ArtScroll Studios whose cooperation and skill have transformed this project from dream to reality: RABBI MEIR ZLOTOWITZ *whose own Torah publications have already indebted the Jewish public to him, has devoted much time and zeal to this project;* REB SHEA BRANDER *whose graphic skill already enhances thousands of libraries;* RABBI AVIE GOLD *who read proofs and made innumerable valuable suggestions;* SHIMON SHAMILZADEH *who provided graphic and technical back-up; and* MISS ROCHEL BRISMAN *and* MISS LAURIE MENDELOWITZ *who set type with skill and dedication.*

Finally, I am grateful to the gifted B'nai Torah of ZAI for allowing me the privilege of participating in their effort. May this become Volume I of a succession of Haggadah Treasuries *that will enhance countless* sedarim *with the glow of the* Yetzias Mitzrayim *narrative, and may* Hashem Yisborach *enable them to continue to expand their work for the sanctification of His Name.*

Rabbi Nosson Scherman

Ta'anis Esther 5738 / March, 1978

Foreword and Acknowledgements

Zeirei Agudath Israel is proud to participate in offering **The Haggadah Treasury** to the Jewish public in the hope that it will help add meaning and inspiration to many *sedorim*. We see this venture as an extension of *Zeirei's* continuous work for Torah life, and Zeirei proceeds from this volume will go directly into the financing of the activities carried out at the behest and under the guidance of the *Gedolei Yisrael* who lead *Zeirei* and our parent organization, *Agudath Israel of America*.

As defined by them, *Zeirei's* purpose is three-fold:

1 — To transmit and articulate the Torah outlook to Yeshiva students and Orthodox young people;

2 — To act as the collective voice of *B'nai Torah* ; and

3 — To provide opportunities for Torah youth · to give of themselves and their resources for projects essential to the spiritual and physical well-being of the Jewish people.

Among *Zeirei Agudath Israel's* many activities are:

Reshet Shiurei Torah which has organized Torah study sessions for many hundreds of adults; classes and large gatherings to hear presentations on *halachah* and *hashkafah*; and publication of the scholarly journal *Am HaTorah*; and many bulletins and lectures from *Gedolei Yisrael* presenting the Torah view on many topics.

JEP, the *Jewish Education Program*, mobilizes hundreds of volunteers to bring the word of Torah to many thousands of boys and girls whose Jewish heritage was alien to them.

TAP, the *Torah Action Program*, raises funds to dispatch packages — already in the tens of thousands of dollars — to our brethren behind the Iron Curtain. Additionally, TAP assists in absorption projects in Israel and has helped establish a yeshiva in B'nai Brak for Russian immigrants.

Among ZAI's chesed projects are the *Shmuel Wald Memorial Fund* which provides free loans and summer camp scholarships for the needy; and the *Yehoshua Eisen Krias Megillah* and *Tekias Shofar* campaigns which mobilize hundreds of B'nai Torah to visit hospitals, nursing homes, and private homes to bring *mitzvos* to those who could not otherwise observe them.

The above are far from the whole of *Zeirei*'s work, but they present a pattern of fulfillment, for ZAI exists in order to carry forward the program of Kattowitz, the program that great Torah leaders of earlier generations formulated to bring Torah ideals into every facet of Jewish community life. Indeed, before there was an Agudath Israel in America, there was a Zeirei Agudah on the Lower East Side in the 1920's. Those young men planted seeds that produced today's flourishing Agudath Israel of America which, in so many ways, is the vanguard of organized American Jewish life.

We are deeply grateful to the *Moetzes Gedolei Torah* of Agudah for their guidance and inspiration. The Agudah administraiton, led by Rabbi Moshe Sherer — to whom no praise can do justice — and Rabbi Boruch Borchardt, have firmly supported and guided the work of *Zeirei*. Rabbi Yaakov Bender, our National Director, is a driving force behind much of our work in all its facets. Especially, however, we express our heartfelt appreciation to the hundreds of selflessly dedicated *B'nai Torah* who *are* ZAI, and who are responsible for a brilliant past that is but an augury of a brighter future.

Finally, we wish to acknowledge the many people who made this *sefer* a reality. The original concept was envisioned last year by *Matis Blum* who was a principal force in last year's production of *Ki Lo Yoeh*, the *Torah Loda'as* on the *Haggadah*, which was the forerunner of this *Haggadah Treasury* and the source of much of its material.

Yossi Abramczyk devoted many hours to provide material from which the anthologized thoughts were selected. Others who contributed significantly to the store of material were *Mordechai Avigdor, Schachne Weinberger,* and *Avrohom Brickman*. Also on the research staff, were *Yaakov Zev Klein, Avi Katz,* and *Hirsh Michel Chinn*. The arduous task of researching sources was done by *Shmuel Gut;* and the preliminary writing was done by *Zvi Daniel Gross* with the assistance of *Berish Freund*. Technical organization of the project was facilitated in the main by *Shimshon Lonner,* with the assistance of *Yechiel Steinman* and *Moshe Friedman*.

Particularly noteworthy and gratifying is the fact that these *B'nai Torah* made all their contributions to this *sefer* in *addition* to — and not at the expense of — their own *sedorim* at *Mesivta Torah Vodaath*.

We are deeply grateful to *Harav Yisroel Belsky* שליט"א and *Harav Yitzchok Meir Schorr* שליט"א who reviewed the major por-

tion of *divrei Torah* which were submitted, and to *Rabbi Nisson Wolpin* שליט״א for his constant willingness to help.

We sincerely thank *Rabbi Meir Zlotowitz* of ArtScroll Studios without whose cooperation and advice this production would not have been possible. Our gratitude goes also to his entire staff who graciously accommodated themselves to inconvenience and time pressure.

Rabbi Zundel Berman, a synonym for *seforim* in the yeshivah world, earns our gratitude for his unique ability to bring the printed word of Torah to the largest possible audience.

Finally we express our sincere appreciation to *Rabbi Nosson Scherman* שליט״א whose editorial and writing skills have made this volume worthy of the Jewish public.

We thank *Hashem Yisborach* for helping ZAI utilize the *Haggadah Treasury* as one more way to heed the call of the Torah leader who have stated in our *Kol Korei:*

הִתְאַגְּדוּ וְהִתְאַסְּפוּ בְּצִלָּהּ שֶׁל צְעִירֵי אֲגוּדַת יִשְׂרָאֵל לְמַעַן רִבּוּי כְּבוֹד שְׁמוֹ יִתְבָּרַךְ בָּעוֹלָם וּכְבוֹד הַתּוֹרָה וְלוֹמְדֶיהָ.

Unite and gather under the banner of Zeirei Agudath Israel for the glory of His blessed Name in the world and for the glory of Torah and its scholars.

On behalf of ZAI,

Yosaif Aszknazy
President, National Council of ZAI

৳ Required Amounts of Ritual Foods and Beverages for the Seder

The following guide is reprinted courtesy of **Beth Medrosh L'Torah V'Horoah,** *145 East Broadway, New York, N.Y. 10002, which was founded and is led by* Maran Hagaon Rabbi Moshe Feinstein שליט״א.

The computations and measurements were made by Harav David Feinstein שליט״א. *The halachic background on which many of the conclusions are based may be found in his* Kol Dodi. *Requests for clarification, or questions may be addressed to him at the above address.*

**All minimum requirements listed below
apply to men and women alike.**

Minimum Size of Wine Cups (Kosos)

1. For the *Arbah Kosos* and for *Kiddush* (except on Friday night) and for *Havdalah* the cup must be at least **3.3 Fluid ounces** in size.

2. When the *Seder* is on Friday evening, the *Kiddush* cup should be at least **4.42 fluid ounces** in size. This also applies to the *Kiddush* Cup used **every Friday evening,** throughout the year.

NOTE: When the *Seder* occurs on Friday night, if one person recites the *Kiddush* on behalf of those assembled, then his cup must be at least **4.42 fluid ounces.** The Cups of the assembled (each of whom must drink to fulfill the *Mitzvah* of the first of the *Four Cups)* may be **3.3 fluid ounces** in size.

Minimum Strength of Wine

1. Full-strength wine (without dilution) is required for the *Arbah Kosos.*

2. Only if one's health does not permit him to drink wine may he dilute his wine with grape juice. However, he should use the *least* amount of grape juice possible.

3. If, for health reasons, one cannot use (even diluted) wine, he may use grape juice.

4. If one must dilute grape juice with water, the ratio should not exceed **2/3 cup of water to 1/3 cup of grape juice.**

5. If one does not have enough **wine** to perform the *mitzvah (Kiddush, Havdalah,* etc.) he may add water, but not in excess of **2/5 cup of wine to 3/5 cup of water.**

(NOTE: The *Brachah* for all these mixtures is *Borei P'ri Hagafen.)*

Minimum Amount of Matzah Sh'murah

Everyone must eat the minimum amount of *Matzah Sh'murah* each of the following **three** times: 1) After the *Brachah: Al Achilas Matzah* 2) for *Korech* 3) for the *Afikoman.*

1. After *Al Achilas Matzah* and for the *Afikoman* — the required amount of *matzah* is equivalent in size to **7 inches by 6 1/4 inches.**

2. For *Korech* — a piece equivalent in size to **7 inches by 4 inches.**

If for health reasons, one cannot eat *matzah,* then *Matzah Sh'murah* meal (upon which one is permitted to recite *Hamotzi)* may be substituted as follows:

1. After the *Brachah, Al Achilas Matzah* and *Afikoman* — an amount of meal that can be compacted into a vessel measuring **1.5 fluid ounces.**

2. For *Korech* — an amount of meal that can be compacted into a vessel holding **1.1 fluid ounces.**

Minimum Amount of Maror

Everyone must eat *Maror* twice during the *Seder.* Once after the *Brachah* of *Al Achilas Maror,* and once for *Korech.*

1. If using pure, grated **horseradish,** use the following minimum amounts:

    a. After *Al Achilas Maror* — an amount that can be compacted into a volume of **1.1 fluid ounces.**

    b. For *Korech* — an amount that can be compacted into a volume of **.7 fluid ounces.**

2. If using whole leaves of Romaine lettuce, enough leaves to cover an area of **8 by 10 inches** — both after reciting *Al Achilas Maror*, and for *Korech*.

3. If using only stalks of Romaine lettuce, use enough stalks to cover an area of **3 by 5 inches,** both after *Al Achilas Maror* and for *Korech*.

Special Note

It is suggested that one prepare before Pesach a paper or cardboard with the required dimensions for *matzah* and Romaine lettuce, and a pre-measured jigger for determining the required amounts of horseradish and *matzah* meal.

Metric Equivalents

One inch = 2.54 centimeters
One fluid ounce = 29.57 milliliters
The 1.5 fluid ounces requirement of *matzah* meal = 31 grams.

Required Measurements According to Chazon Ish

Cup for wine — 5.3 ounces
Olive-size
‎(לפי הצל״ח דחצי ביצה) — 1.6—1.8 ounces
‎(לפי שיטת הצל״ח דשליש ביצה) — 1.2 ounces

Bedikas Chametz/בדיקת חמץ

The search for *Chametz* begins upon nightfall of the fourteenth day of *Nissan*, the evening before Passover. The purpose of the commandment is the removal of all *chametz*, and it requires a thorough search of all areas where *chametz* may have been brought during the course of the year — despite the fact that a thorough cleaning has been done in the days and weeks before *Pesach*. The search should be made by candle-light, and one may not speak until the search is completed — unless he must give instructions or make inquiries *directly relating* to the search.

בָּרוּךְ אַתָּה יהוה אֱלֹהֵינוּ מֶלֶךְ הָעוֹלָם אֲשֶׁר
קִדְּשָׁנוּ בְּמִצְוֹתָיו וְצִוָּנוּ עַל בִּעוּר חָמֵץ:

Blessed are You, HASHEM, our God, King of the universe, Who has sanctified us by His commandments, and commanded us concerning the removal of Chametz.

Upon completion of *Bedikas Chametz*, the following declaration is made. The declaration must be understood in order to take effect; one who does not understand the Aramaic text may recite it in English, Yiddish or any other language. Any *chametz* that will be used for the next day's breakfast or for any other purpose prior to the final removal of *chametz* the next morning is not included in this declaration.

כָּל חֲמִירָא וַחֲמִיעָא דְּאִכָּא בִרְשׁוּתִי דְּלָא חֲמִתֵּה
וּדְלָא בְעַרְתֵּהּ וּדְלָא יָדַעְנָא לֵהּ לִבָּטֵל וְלֶהֱוֵי הֶפְקֵר
כְּעַפְרָא דְאַרְעָא:

Any Chametz which is in my possession which I did not see, and remove, nor know about shall be nullified and become ownerless, like the dust of the earth.

The following declaration includes *all* chametz without exception. It is to be said after the burning of left-over *chametz* and after the sale to a non-Jew has taken effect. It should be recited in a language which one understands.

כָּל חֲמִירָא וַחֲמִיעָא דְּאִכָּא בִרְשׁוּתִי דַּחֲזִתֵּהּ וּדְלָא
חֲזִתֵּהּ דַּחֲמִתֵּהּ וּדְלָא חֲמִתֵּהּ דְּבַעַרְתֵּהּ וּדְלָא בַעַרְתֵּהּ
לִבָּטֵל וְלֶהֱוֵי הֶפְקֵר כְּעַפְרָא דְאַרְעָא:

Any Chametz which is in my possession which I did or did not see, which I did or did not remove, shall be nullified and become ownerless, like the dust of the earth.

Eruv Tavshilin/עירוב תבשילין

It is forbidden to prepare on *Yom Tov* for the next day even if that day is Shabbos. If, however, Shabbos preparations were begun before *Yom Tov* began, they may be continued on *Yom Tov*. *Eruv Tavshillin* constitutes this preparation. A *matzah* and any cooked food (such as fish, meat, or an egg) are set aside on *Erev Yom Tov* to be used on Shabbos and the following is recited.

בָּרוּךְ אַתָּה יהוה אֱלֹהֵינוּ מֶלֶךְ הָעוֹלָם אֲשֶׁר
קִדְּשָׁנוּ בְּמִצְוֹתָיו וְצִוָּנוּ עַל־מִצְוַת עֵרוּב:

Blessed are You, HASHEM, our God, King of the universe, Who has sanctified us by His commandments, and commanded us concerning the commandment of Eruv.

בְּהָדֵין עֵרוּבָא יְהֵא שָׁרֵא לָנָא לַאֲפוּיֵי וּלְבַשׁוּלֵי
וּלְאַצְלוּיֵי וּלְאַטְמוּנֵי וּלְאַדְלוּקֵי שְׁרָגָא וּלְתַקָּנָא
וּלְמֶעְבַּד כָּל צָרְכָּנָא מִיּוֹמָא טָבָא לְשַׁבַּתָּא לָנוּ וּלְכָל
יִשְׂרָאֵל הַדָּרִים בָּעִיר הַזֹּאת:

Through this Eruv may we be permitted to bake, cook, fry, insulate, kindle flame, prepare for, and do anything necessary on the festival for the sake of the Sabbath — for ourselves and for all Jews who live in this city.

Candle Lighting/הדלקת הנרות

The *Seder* table should be set with the finest available linen, cutlery, and utensils. This is symbolic of the royal status Israel was granted on this night, and also in memory of the wealth with which Israel left Egypt.

The following blessings are recited when the candles are to be kindled.

[If Pesach falls on a Sabbath, add words in parentheses]

בָּרוּךְ אַתָּה יהוה אֱלֹהֵינוּ מֶלֶךְ הָעוֹלָם אֲשֶׁר
קִדְּשָׁנוּ בְּמִצְוֹתָיו וְצִוָּנוּ לְהַדְלִיק נֵר שֶׁל (שַׁבָּת וְשֶׁל)
יוֹם טוֹב:

[If Pesach falls on a Sabbath, add words in parentheses]

Blessed are You, HASHEM, our God, King of the universe, Who has sanctified us through His commandments, and commanded us to kindle the flame of (Sabbath and the) festival.

בָּרוּךְ אַתָּה יהוה אֱלֹהֵינוּ מֶלֶךְ הָעוֹלָם שֶׁהֶחֱיָנוּ
וְקִיְּמָנוּ וְהִגִּיעָנוּ לַזְּמַן הַזֶּה:

Blessed are You, HASHEM, our God, King of the universe, Who has kept us alive, sustained us, and brought us to this season.

19 **The Haggadah Treasury**

Symbols of the Seder/סמני הסדר

The name *Seder* [literally: *Order*] was chosen for the ritual of the evening because every detail of the evening represents an aspect of the Exodus and also prepares the way for the ultimate Redemption. Thus, each detail of the evening has a purpose — even those which may seem to be superfluous *(Maharal)*.

The brief poem which follows has become universally accepted as the summary of the Seder's fifteen observances. It was composed either by *Rashi* or *Rabbi Shmuel of Falaise*, one of the *Ba'alei Tosafos*. The very source of its authorship is sufficient to prove that it is far more than a convenient device used to remember the order of the evening's *mitzvos*. Although the poem is of great importance in order to enable people to recall the sequence of the evening's rituals — especially in view of *Maharal's* comment above — the poem has been given many deeper interpretations over the years. Many people pronounce the applicable word of the סִמָנֵי הַסֵּדֶר before performing the *mitzvah* to which it applies — קַדֵּשׁ before making *Kiddush*, וּרְחַץ before washing the hands, and so on.

קַדֵּשׁ — The recitation of *Kiddush*

(First cup)

וּרְחַץ — Washing the hands before *Karpas*.

כַּרְפַּס — Eating of a vegetable dipped in salt water.

יַחַץ — Breaking of the middle *matzah*, part of which becomes the לַחְמָא עַנְיָא, *bread of affliction*, over which the Yetzias Mitzrayim narrative is recited, and part of which becomes the *afikoman*.

מַגִּיד — Narrative of *Yetzias Mitzrayim* — the Exodus from Egypt.

(Second cup)

רָחְצָה — Washing the hands prior to the meal.

מוֹצִיא — The blessing over *matzah* as a food.

מַצָּה — The blessing over *matzah* as the special *mitzvah* of the *Seder*.

מָרוֹר — The blessing for the eating of *Maror*.

כּוֹרֵךְ — The 'sandwich' of *matzah* and *maror*.

שֻׁלְחָן עוֹרֵךְ — The 'table prepared' with the *Yom Tov* feast.

צָפוּן — The eating of the *afikoman* which had been צָפוּן, *hidden*, all during the *Seder*.

בָּרֵךְ — *Bircas Hamazon*, the blessings after the meal.

(Third cup)

הַלֵּל — *Hallel*, including additional praises aside from the *Hallel* that is recited on festivals all year round.

(Fourth cup)

נִרְצָה — The concluding prayer that Hashem accept our observance and speedily send Messiah.

סֵדֶר לֵיל פֶּסַח ‎🦢

The Seder

קַדֵּשׁ

Kiddush should be recited and the *Seder* begun as soon as possible — however, not before nightfall. Each participant's cup should be poured by someone else to symbolize the majesty of the evening; as though each participant had a servant. For the requirement of the cup, see Halacha section.

[On Friday night begin with וַיְהִי עֶרֶב *amd include the passages in parentheses. On other nights, omit those passages.]*

(וַיְהִי־עֶרֶב וַיְהִי־בֹקֶר)

יוֹם הַשִּׁשִּׁי: וַיְכֻלּוּ הַשָּׁמַיִם וְהָאָרֶץ וְכָל צְבָאָם: וַיְכַל אֱלֹהִים בַּיּוֹם הַשְּׁבִיעִי מְלַאכְתּוֹ אֲשֶׁר עָשָׂה וַיִּשְׁבֹּת בַּיּוֹם הַשְּׁבִיעִי מִכָּל מְלַאכְתּוֹ אֲשֶׁר עָשָׂה: וַיְבָרֶךְ אֱלֹהִים אֶת יוֹם הַשְּׁבִיעִי וַיְקַדֵּשׁ אֹתוֹ כִּי בוֹ שָׁבַת מִכָּל מְלַאכְתּוֹ אֲשֶׁר בָּרָא אֱלֹהִים לַעֲשׂוֹת:)

סַבְרִי מָרָנָן וְרַבָּנָן וְרַבּוֹתַי:

בָּרוּךְ אַתָּה יהוה אֱלֹהֵינוּ מֶלֶךְ הָעוֹלָם בּוֹרֵא פְּרִי הַגָּפֶן:

בָּרוּךְ אַתָּה יהוה אֱלֹהֵינוּ מֶלֶךְ הָעוֹלָם אֲשֶׁר בָּחַר בָּנוּ מִכָּל־עָם וְרוֹמְמָנוּ מִכָּל־לָשׁוֹן וְקִדְּשָׁנוּ בְּמִצְוֹתָיו. וַתִּתֶּן לָנוּ יהוה אֱלֹהֵינוּ בְּאַהֲבָה (שַׁבָּתוֹת לִמְנוּחָה וּ)מוֹעֲדִים לְשִׂמְחָה חַגִּים וּזְמַנִּים לְשָׂשׂוֹן אֶת יוֹם (הַשַּׁבָּת הַזֶּה, וְאֶת־יוֹם) חַג הַמַּצוֹת הַזֶּה זְמַן חֵרוּתֵינוּ (בְּאַהֲבָה) מִקְרָא קֹדֶשׁ זֵכֶר לִיצִיאַת מִצְרָיִם. כִּי בָנוּ בָחַרְתָּ וְאוֹתָנוּ קִדַּשְׁתָּ מִכָּל־הָעַמִּים (וְשַׁבָּת) וּמוֹעֲדֵי קָדְשֶׁךָ (בְּאַהֲבָה וּבְרָצוֹן) בְּשִׂמְחָה וּבְשָׂשׂוֹן הִנְחַלְתָּנוּ. בָּרוּךְ אַתָּה יהוה מְקַדֵּשׁ (הַשַּׁבָּת וְ) יִשְׂרָאֵל וְהַזְּמַנִּים:

Kaddesh

Kiddush should be recited and the *Seder* begun as soon as possible — however, not before nightfall. Each participant's cup should be poured by someone else to symbolize the majesty of the evening; as though each participant had a servant. For the requirement of the cup, see Halacha section.

[*On Friday night begin with* וַיְהִי עֶרֶב *amd include the passages in parentheses. On other nights, omit those passages.*]

(And there was evening and there was morning)

The sixth day. Thus the heaven and the earth were finished, and all their array. On the seventh day God completed His work which He had done, and He abstained on the seventh day from all His work which He had done. God blessed the seventh day and hallowed it, because on it God abstained from all His work which God created to make.)

By your leave, my masters and teachers:

Blessed are You, HASHEM, our God, King of the universe, Who creates the fruit of the vine.

Blessed are You, HASHEM, our God, King of the universe, Who has chosen us from all nations and exalted us above all tongues and sanctified us by His commandments. And You, HASHEM, our God, have lovingly given us (Sabbaths for rest), appointed times for gladness, feasts and seasons for joy, (this Sabbath and) this Feast of Matzos, the season of our freedom (in love,) a holy convocation in memoriam of the Exodus from Egypt. For You have chosen and sanctified us above all peoples, (and the Sabbath) and Your holy festivals (in love and favor), in gladness and joy have You granted us as a heritage. Blessed are You, HASHEM, Who sanctifies (the Sabbath,) Israel, and the festive seasons.

[בָּרוּךְ אַתָּה יהוה אֱלֹהֵינוּ מֶלֶךְ הָעוֹלָם בּוֹרֵא מְאוֹרֵי הָאֵשׁ:

בָּרוּךְ אַתָּה יהוה אֱלֹהֵינוּ מֶלֶךְ הָעוֹלָם הַמַּבְדִּיל בֵּין קֹדֶשׁ
לְחוֹל בֵּין אוֹר לְחֹשֶׁךְ בֵּין יִשְׂרָאֵל לָעַמִּים בֵּין יוֹם הַשְּׁבִיעִי
לְשֵׁשֶׁת יְמֵי הַמַּעֲשֶׂה. בֵּין קְדֻשַּׁת שַׁבָּת לִקְדֻשַּׁת יוֹם טוֹב
הִבְדַּלְתָּ וְאֶת יוֹם הַשְּׁבִיעִי מִשֵּׁשֶׁת יְמֵי הַמַּעֲשֶׂה קִדַּשְׁתָּ.
הִבְדַּלְתָּ וְקִדַּשְׁתָּ אֶת עַמְּךָ יִשְׂרָאֵל בִּקְדֻשָּׁתֶךָ. בָּרוּךְ אַתָּה
יהוה הַמַּבְדִּיל בֵּין קֹדֶשׁ לְקֹדֶשׁ:]

בָּרוּךְ אַתָּה יהוה אֱלֹהֵינוּ מֶלֶךְ הָעוֹלָם שֶׁהֶחֱיָנוּ
וְקִיְּמָנוּ וְהִגִּיעָנוּ לַזְּמַן הַזֶּה:

8

The wine should be drunk leaning on one's left side, and without delay. It is preferable to drink the entire cup, but at the very least, most of the cup should be drunk.

ורחץ

The head of the household — according to many opinions, all participants in the Seder — washes his hands as if to eat bread, but without a blessing.

כרפס

All participants take a vegetable other than *maror* and dip it into salt-water. A piece smaller than an olive should be used. The following *brachah* is recited with

[On Saturday night, add the bracketed paragraphs]

[Blessed are You, HASHEM, our God, King of the universe, Who creates the illumination of the fire.

Blessed are You, HASHEM, our God, King of the universe, Who distinguishes between the sacred and the secular, between light and darkness, between Israel and the nations, between the seventh day and the six days of activity. You have distinguished between the holiness of the Sabbath and the holiness of a Festival, and have sanctified the seventh day above the six days of activity. You distinguished and sanctified Your nation, Israel, with Your holiness. Blessed are You, HASHEM, Who distinguishes between holiness and holiness.]

Blessed are You, HASHEM, our God, King of the universe, Who has kept us alive, sustained us, and brought us to this season.

The wine should be drunk leaning on one's left side, and without delay. It is preferable to drink the entire cup, but at the very least, most of the cup should be drunk.

U'rechatz

The head of the household — according to many opinions, all participants in the *Seder* — washes his hands as if to eat bread, but without a blessing.

Karpas

All participants take a vegetable other than *maror* and dip it into salt-water. A piece smaller than an olive should be used. The following *brachah* is recited with

the intention that it also applies to the *maror* which will be eaten during the meal. There are conflicting opinions concerning the requirement of הֲסֵבָּה, *reclining*, during the eating of *Karpas*.

בָּרוּךְ אַתָּה יהוה אֱלֹהֵינוּ מֶלֶךְ הָעוֹלָם בּוֹרֵא פְּרִי הָאֲדָמָה:

יחץ

The head of the household breaks the middle *matzah* in two. He puts the smaller part back between the two whole *matzos*, and wraps up the larger part for later use as the *Afikoman*. Some briefly place the *Afikoman* portion on their shoulders in memory of the Biblical verse recounting that Israel left Egypt carrying their *matzos* on their shoulders. They then set it aside.

כַּרְפַּס — The eating of a vegetable dipped in salt-water.

Symbolism of Word
◄§ The word כַּרְפַּס contains the letters: ס,=*sixty*, and פֶּרֶךְ, *hard labor*. Thus the word symbolizes the *sixty* myriads of Jews [600,000 male adults who were redeemed from Egypt (*Bamidbar* 1:46)] who were enslaved at back-breaking labor. Because the name כַּרְפַּס alludes to an aspect of the Egyptian exile, it was chosen as the title of this Rabbinic enactment.

Symbolism of Mitzvah
◄§ A person should never be satisfied with the level of spiritual growth he has attained, nor should he despair of his ability to attain greater heights. These concepts are both symbolized by the vegetable used for the *Karpas*. Though it originates under the earth, it grows until it appears on the holy *Seder* table of a Jewish family. Thus it is a lesson to everyone that G-d in His mercy can raise us from the depths to the promised redemption (*Yismach Yisrael*).

the intention that it also applies to the *maror* which will be eaten during the meal. There are conflicting opinions concerning the requirement of הֲסָבָּה, *reclining*, during the eating of *Karpas*.

Blessed are You, HASHEM, our God, King of the universe, Who creates the fruit of the earth.

Yachatz

The head of the household breaks the middle *matzah* in two. He puts the smaller part back between the two whole *matzos*, and wraps up the larger part for later use as the *Afikoman*. Some briefly place the *Afikoman* portion on their shoulders in memory of the Biblical verse recounting that Israel left Egypt carrying their *matzos* on their shoulders. They then set it aside.

יַחַץ — The middle matzah is broken.

Why a matzah is broken ◆§ This is another reminder of the slavery and suffering of Egypt. Unlike benevolent slave-owners whose own self-interest requires that they be concerned with the health and nutrition of their slaves, the Egyptians sought to deplete the Jews through malnutrition, overwork, and murder of the male infants. Therefore, a slave would never eat a complete matzah; he would always hoard part of it for a later meal when he might have no food at all. Therefore, too, the *larger* part of the *Yachatz* matzah is set aside for the *Afikoman*: a hungry slave would seek to conserve as much food as he could (*Rav Hai Gaon*).

מַגִּיד

The broken *matzah* is lifted up as the head of the household proclaims
הָא לַחְמָא עַנְיָא. The *Haggadah*, should be translated if necessary, and the story of
the Exodus should be amplified upon.

מַגִּיד — The narrative of the Exodus

Question and Answer

◦§ Since the Torah commands that the story of the redemption from Egypt be recalled every day, *(Devarim* 16:3) what is unique about this commandment on the *Seder* night?

The *Minchas Chinuch* replies that the Torah places special emphasis on the question/answer aspect of this night's recitation. The Torah specifies that one's child will inquire about the events of the Exodus and their significance, and that the parents should explain to him (see later on *The Four Sons*). To comply with those verses, the Haggadah was composed in the form of answers to the questions posed in the *Mah Nishtanah*. In this respect, the narrative of the *Seder* night is unique.

Another unique feature

◦§ In other ways, too, the *Seder* night is different.

— On other nights, the requirement is simply that the Exodus be *mentioned*, while on this night the *entire narrative* must be *recited* and *discussed*.

— At the *Seder* there is the extraordinary provision that כָּל הַמַּרְבֶּה לְסַפֵּר בִּיצִיאַת מִצְרַיִם הֲרֵי זֶה מְשֻׁבָּח, *the more one tells about the Exodus from Egypt, the more praiseworthy he is (Haggadah).*

Why no blessing?

◦§ As we know, the Sages formulated blessings to be recited prior to the performance of all commandments. Since we are commanded to tell the story of the Exodus, *(Sh'mos* 13:3; 13:8; *Devarim* 16:3) why is there no בְּרָכָה, *blessing,* to be recited before the narration?

— The *Haggadah* opens with the blessing of Kiddush, *Sanctification* over wine. The Kiddush declares that the festival was given by G-d זֵכֶר לִיצִיאַת מִצְרָיִם, *as a*

Maggid

The broken *matzah* is lifted up as the head of the household proclaims הָא לַחְמָא עַנְיָא. The *Haggadah*, should be translated if necessary, and the story of the Exodus should be amplified upon.

remembrance of the Exodus from Egypt. This *does* constitute, in effect, a blessing over the elucidation of the narrative *(R' Yerucham).*

Alternate blessing

— Before drinking the Second Cup of the *Seder*, we recite the blessing אֲשֶׁר גְּאָלָנוּ, *Who has redeemed us.* This blessing of God for having liberated us from Egypt constitutes a blessing over the narration of the Exodus tale *(Rav Amram Gaon).*

Self-understood mitzvah

—The text of blessings recited prior to the performance of commandments implies that without a Divine commandment, the deed would not be performed: אֲשֶׁר קִדְּשָׁנוּ בְּמִצְוֹתָיו וְצִוָּנוּ, *Who has sanctified us with His commandments, and has commanded us* ... The inference is that we perform the *mitzvah* because it was commanded, otherwise we would *not* perform it. Therefore, no blessings are recited for the performance of commandments that are ordained by simple logic and respect for decency. For example, one does not pronounce a blessing for honoring his parents, because logic and decency demand that one honor those who gave him life and cared for him selflessly. So, too with the narrative of the Exodus. G-d took a powerless, helpless nation from the most degraded condition imaginable and raised it to enormous spiritual and material heights. Simple justice would decree that they express their gratitude even if they had not been commanded to do so *(S'fas Emes).*

Why a blessing at conclusion?

[However, *Chasam Sofer* notes that the solution of *Rav Amram Gaon* raises a new difficulty. There is a general rule that blessings must be pronounced prior to the performance of a commandment *(Pesachim 7a).* If so, how can we say that אֲשֶׁר גְּאָלָנוּ is the blessing over the *Haggadah* — if it were, then it should be recited at

Raising the matzos, the leader declares:

הָא לַחְמָא עַנְיָא דִי אֲכָלוּ אַבְהָתָנָא בְּאַרְעָא

the very beginning of the Haggadah, not after the narration of the Exodus has been completed.

Like a Ger   *Chasam Sofer* replies that, as we sit around the *Seder* table, we imagine ourselves still to be enslaved to Egypt and, as the narrative progresses, we move vicariously through the Jewish historical experience until we *ourselves* are freed. So we say in the Haggadah: חַיָּב אָדָם לִרְאוֹת אֶת עַצְמוֹ כְּאִלּוּ הוּא יָצָא מִמִּצְרַיִם, *a person is required to see himself as if he had gone out of Egypt (Pesachim* 116b). Among these re-lived experiences is מִתְּחִלָּה עוֹבְדֵי עֲבוֹדָה זָרָה הָיוּ אֲבוֹתֵינוּ, *at the beginning* [of our history] *our ancestors were idol worshipers.* Thus, at the outset of the *Haggadah,* we are symbolically equivalent to non-Jewish idolators. This being the case, we *cannot* pronounce a blessing which would contain the words אֲשֶׁר קִדְּשָׁנוּ בְּמִצְוֹתָיו, *Who has sanctified us with His commandments* — as 'non-Jews' we are not subject to the commandments directed toward Jews! Therefore, the blessing of אֲשֶׁר גְּאָלָנוּ is reserved for the conclusion of the narrative when we have left the status of idolators and been redeemed by G-d to become His people.

[Another *halachah* is based on the same reasoning. A non-Jew who converts to Judaism does not recite a blessing prior to his ritual immersion. It is only *after* his immersion that the conversion takes effect and he is obligated to fulfill all commandments. Only then, therefore, can he recite a blessing.]

Only for prescribed limits   ◆§ Blessings are recited only over commandments which have definite requirements and limits. Because such commandments as giving charity, prayer, and honoring parents have no defined limits, no blessings are possible. The narrative of the Exodus falls under the same general heading since, as we say in the *Haggadah,* כָּל הַמַּרְבֶּה לְסַפֵּר בִּיצִיאַת מִצְרַיִם הֲרֵי זֶה מְשֻׁבָּח, *the more one tells about the Exodus the more he is*

Raising the matzos, the leader declares:

This is the bread of affliction that our fathers ate in the land

praiseworthy. Therefore, no blessing is possible over the telling of the *Haggadah (Rashba).*

הָא לַחְמָא עַנְיָא — This is the bread of affliction.

Joyous though exiled   ◦§ The present exile has been far longer and, in many ways, far more bitter than the Egyptian exile. What reason have we, therefore, to rejoice in the Exodus? *Chasam Sofer* responds that there is a basic difference between the present exile and the period of Egyptian servitude. Then, the exile had been decreed for a pre-ordained length: וַעֲבָדוּם וְעִנּוּ אֹתָם אַרְבַּע מֵאוֹת שָׁנָה, *and they* [the Israelites] *will serve them* [the Egyptians] *and they* [the Egyptians] *will oppress them* [the Israelites] *for four hundred years (Bereishis* 15:13). The Jews were powerless to speed the redemption; all they could do was maintain their uniqueness in order to be worthy of redemption. During our present exile, however, the time of redemption is in our hands. As the Sages have taught זָכוּ אֲחִישֶׁנָּה, *if they are worthy, I will hasten it (Sanhedrin* 98a) [I.e. although there is an assigned time beyond which the exile will not endure, Israel, by its merits, can hasten the redemption.] Therefore we are grateful for the Exodus — as a result of it, our destiny lies in our own hands.

Temporary pauperdom   ◦§ The *Dubner Maggid* illustrated this concept with a parable:

A pauper became immensely wealthy. Not wanting to take his new-found affluence for granted, he adapted the practice of concluding each meal with a piece of hard bread dipped in water as a reminder of his lot during the years when stale bread and water were all he could expect after a day's hard labor. After the passage of many years, he lost his fortune and became a pauper once again. But his custom of dipping bread in water continued.

33 **The Haggadah Treasury**

"Why do you continue this practice?" someone asked him. "You no longer need this reminder for now you are truly poor."

The erstwhile magnate replied, "The answer is simple. When I was wealthy, I made someone a long-term loan of ten thousand gold coins. Now I have no money because the loan is not yet due, but I am not truly poor for I know that the loan will be repaid. Whatever my present difficulties, I am still rich, and my habits of poverty are no more than reminders."

The *Maggid* concluded: Israel is like that rich-poor man. In Egypt we ate *matzah*, the poor bread of affliction and our lives were a reflection of מָרוֹר, *bitter herbs*. But after the redemption, our eating of *matzah* and *maror* became reminders of the exile that once was. Why, though, do we require reminders now when we are truly in exile?

The Haggadah gives the answer: הָשַׁתָּא הָכָא לְשָׁנָה הַבָּאָה בְּאַרְעָא דְיִשְׂרָאֵל, הָשַׁתָּא עַבְדֵי לְשָׁנָה הַבָּאָה בְּנֵי חוֹרִין, *Now, we are here, next year may we be in the Land of Israel! Now, we are slaves, next year may we be free men!* Our poverty is but temporary because it is in our power — through repentance and good deeds — to speed the redemption.

Slave diet ⋖§ This declaration implies that *matzah*, 'the bread of affliction,' was the diet of the Jewish slaves in Egypt. What evidence have we that such was the case?

Ibn Ezra related that once, during his prolific travels, he came to be imprisoned for a time in India. There, the jailers would feed *matzah* to the prisoners because it was difficult to digest and remained in their systems longer, with the result that the men had to be fed less often. Thus, we may surmise that the Egyptian slave-masters followed a similar practice. Why feed the Israelites bread if hard-to-digest *matzah* would prevent them from becoming hungry for a longer period of time? Therefore, *matzah* is the symbol of the slave diet in Egypt (*Avudraham*).

⋖§ There is another version of the text: ... כְּהָא, 'like this was ...' Why the different versions?

The real thing The *Dubner Maggid* explains that the texts had their origins in different periods of Jewish history; each version was relevant to its own time. During periods of actual exile, poverty, and suffering, the text was הָא, *'this' is the bread of affliction.* During such periods, the humble *matzah* of the Seder plate was not merely a reminder of times past; it was also an accurate symbol of the downtrodden state of Jewish life. But when the Temple stood and Jews were free, stalwart people on their own land amid holiness and security — then the *matzah* was but a reminder of the Egyptian servitude. During those happy years, the text was כְּהָא, *'like'* this was the bread of affliction which our ancestors ate in ancient Egypt.

As long as the Temple Mount remains denuded of the *Bais HaMikdash,* and the coming of *Mashiach* is still awaited, we cannot think of the *matzah* as a reminder of past suffering and nothing more. On the contrary, it is a symbol of the still-existing state of exile. Therefore we say הָא, *'This'* is the bread of [our present] affliction.

Funds for freedom ◢§ Prior to Passover, funds for the festival are distributed to the poor, and as part of the *Seder,* an open invitation is extended to the needy and the hungry. What is unique about Passover that requires far more attention to the poor than do other festivals?

It is true that each of the three Festivals — *Pesach, Shavuos,* and *Succos* — commemorates freedom from Egyptian slavery (*Devarim* 16:1,12; *Vayikra* 23:43), but there is a basic difference. The primary observance of *Shavuos* is to commemorate the Giving of the Torah; *Succos* to commemorate the protection which God gave Israel as He led the nation through the wilderness. If one were to overlook the Exodus during his observance of *Shavuos* and *Succos,* his observances would still be heavily laden with meaning. But Passover's very essence is that it is זְמַן חֵרוּתֵנוּ, *the time of our freedom* — let one forget that, and he has deprived his Passover of its basic meaning. Because that is the particular message of the festival, it is observed particularly by concern for and assistance to the poor — those who must be 'freed' from need *(Harav Zalman Sorotzkin).*

דְּמִצְרָיִם. כָּל דִּכְפִין יֵיתֵי וְיֵכוֹל כָּל־דִּצְרִיךְ יֵיתֵי
וְיִפְסַח. הָשַׁתָּא הָכָא לְשָׁנָה הַבָּאָה בְּאַרְעָא דְיִשְׂרָאֵל.
הָשַׁתָּא עַבְדֵי לְשָׁנָה הַבָּאָה בְּנֵי חוֹרִין:

**The needy
and the
hungry**

§ כָּל דִּכְפִין ... כָּל דִּצְרִיךְ — *Whoever is hungry ...
whoever is needy.*

We invite the hungry (דִּכְפִין) *to come and eat* (יֵיתֵי
וְיֵכוֹל), but we invite those *in need* (דִּצְרִיךְ) *to come and
celebrate Passover* (יֵיתֵי וְיִפְסַח). Why is our invitation to
the meal extended only to the *hungry*, while our invitation to celebrate Passover is extended only to the *needy*
and not to the *hungry*?

Harav Yitzchok Ze'ev Soloveitchick of Brisk explained that the two calls refer to different aspects of
the *Seder*. It is assumed that those seated at the *Seder*
table are hungry since any eating of *matzah*, and all
other excessive eating were forbidden for most of the
day in order that the *Seder* participants approach the
evening with good appetites. To these 'hungry' guests
at his table, the host extends an invitation to eat. The
Afikoman (concluding morsels of the evening)
however, is in memory of the Passover offering which
was eaten when the *Beis HaMikdash* stood. The meat of
the offering was to be eaten only at the end of the meal,
but never while the eater was still hungry (*Rambam,
Hilchos Chametz u'Matzah* 6:9). Therefore, the invitation to partake of the *Afikoman* which is symbolic of
the Passover offering, is given only to those who *need*
it, but not to the hungry.

**Hunger
and
affliction**

§ כָּל דִּכְפִין יֵיתֵי וְיֵכוֹל — *Whoever is hungry, let him
come and eat.*

What is the connection between this generous invitation and the somber description of *matzah* as the 'bread
of affliction'?

Midrash Eichah gives two reasons for the exile of
Israel: גָּלְתָה יְהוּדָה מֵעֹנִי, Judah has gone into exile
because of עֹנִי [lit. *suffering*] (*Eichah* 1:3): because it
has neglected two commandments that are called עֹנִי —

of Egypt. Whoever is hungry — let him come and eat! Whoever is needy — let him come and celebrate Passover! Now, we are here; next year may we be in the Land of Israel! Now, we are slaves; next year may we be free men!

they neglected to eat *matzah* which is called 'the bread of עוני, *affliction*; and they neglected to help the poor [עָנִי = עָנִי, *a pauper*]. At the *Seder* which is designed not only to commemorate the past redemption, but to sow the seeds of the future one, we attempt to remedy both flaws of the past. Hence, this paragraph combines mention of the two sins of antiquity — and demonstrates our resolve not to be trapped by them again: we display the *matzah* and invite the poor (*Chidah* in *Simchas HaRegel*).

The desirable abstinence ◆§ לְשָׁנָה הַבָּאָה בְּאַרְעָא דְיִשְׂרָאֵל — *Next year may we be in the Land of Israel.*

What is the connection between the reference to *matzah* and poverty, and the prayer for next year in Eretz Yisrael?

Chovos HaLevavos explains in *Sha'ar HaPerishus* that there are three forms of abstinence, only one of which is desirable. 1 — A *pauper* abstains because he cannot afford luxury; 2 — A *miser* hoards his money in preference to enjoying it; 3 — A *righteous* person *can* afford to indulge himself, but chooses not to, lest he succumb to temptation and desire, thereby going astray from the path of God's service.

At the *Seder*, one is required by the Halachah to use his most precious utensils and display his finery. Nevertheless, the meal consists primarily of humble bread and bitter herbs. The abstinence of the night is not caused by *lack* of means — the elegance of the setting proves that. It is not caused by *miserliness* — the open invitation to needy strangers proves that. The abstinence is caused by a sincere desire *to serve God better.*

This is in obedience to the Torah's admonition that overindulgence in the abundance of Eretz Yisrael would

The second cup of wine is poured, and the youngest present asks *Mah Nishtanah*:

מַה נִּשְׁתַּנָּה הַלַּיְלָה הַזֶּה מִכָּל־הַלֵּילוֹת. שֶׁבְּכָל

cause Israel to forget God and stray from His service (*Devarim* 8:12-14; 32:15). Therefore, it becomes plain that the ability not to be dominated by wealth, but to control it for the good, is the prerequisite for eternal possession of the Land. That is why this introduction to the *Seder*, — demonstrating as it does the resolve to abstain from indulgence — is the prerequisite for a free, new life in Eretz Yisrael (*K'sav Sofer*).

מַה נִּשְׁתַּנָּה — The Four Questions

Quadruple thanksgiving   ⋅§ The Four Questions call to mind that much of the *Seder* revolves around multiples of four: the Four Cups, the Four Questions, and the Four Sons. The *Vilna Gaon* explains that this use of 'four' alludes to the injunction that one who has been saved from danger must bring a קָרְבַּן תּוֹדָה, *Offering* of *Thanksgiving*, to the Temple as an expression of gratitude. There are four general categories of such people (*Tehillim* ch. 107): *those who cross a wilderness, (vs. 4-9), those who have been imprisoned, (vs. 10-16) those who have been dangerously ill (vs. 17-21), and those who have crossed a sea (vs. 23-31)*. All these people were in situations that could have cost them their lives, but were spared thanks to God's mercy. The Jews who left Egypt fell into all four categories: they crossed the sea which split for them; they traveled across the desert wilderness; they had spent many years in the prison that was Egypt; and they were ill as a result of the merciless persecution, until God healed them all at Mount Sinai. In gratitude to God for these four expressions of mercy, we stress the number four in the rituals of the *Seder*.

How different!   ⋅§ מַה נִּשְׁתַּנָּה הַלַּיְלָה הַזֶּה — *Why is this night different ... ?*
Aruch HaShulchan differs from the conventional translation cited above. He maintains that if מַה were to mean *why*, then the proper word would have been לָמָּה.

The second cup of wine is poured, and the youngest present asks *Mah Nishtanah*:

Why is this night different from all other nights?

Prominence of children

Instead, he interprets מַה as an exclamation: *How different is this night from other nights!*

◆§ *Mah Nishtanah* is symbolic of the prominent role given to children in the customs and observances of the Seder. They play a particular part in the celebration of the Exodus because they were singled out for persecution by Pharaoh:

1 — The king ordered the Jewish midwives to slaughter male babies (*Sh'mos* 1:16);

2 — All male babies were to be thrown to their deaths in the river (*ibid. v.* 22);

3 — When Pharaoh became a leper, he ordered the slaughter of Jewish children so that he could bathe in their blood (*Midrash*);

4 — Many children were burned in Egyptian furnaces (*ibid.*);

5 — If the Jewish slaves failed to fill their quota of bricks, children were cemented into the walls in place of bricks (*ibid.*);

6 — Family life was disrupted to prevent the birth of children (*ibid.*);

7 — Even when Pharaoh announced his willingness to let the Jews leave Egypt for three days to worship God, he refused to allow the children to accompany their parents (*Sh'mos* 10:10).

A teaching principle

◆§ The Talmud (*Pesachim* 114b) says that the reason why we do so many things differently at the seder is so that the children should ask and be answered, as the Torah states (*Sh'mos* 13:14) וְהָיָה כִּי יִשְׁאָלְךָ בִנְךָ, *and it will be when your son 'inquires' of you.* However, why did the Torah specify that the Exodus narrative be told in question and answer form?

Chasan Sofer notes the pedagogical principle that learning is best understood and longest remembered if it engages the interest and curiosity of the student. He who is driven to inquire after solutions to problems will

succeed best. On the night of Passover, we strive to inculcate in ourselves, and especially in our impressionable children, a firm belief in Hashem Who brought about the Exodus and demonstrated thereby that only He is the Master of the Universe. In order to instill this lesson and leave a lasting impression, we seek to excite the children so that they will seek answers and reasons. We assure that they will retain the lesson of the night. By engaging their curiosity and interest, we hope to ensure that the lessons of the evening will have a lasting effect on them.

Better to ask ⋙ One of the great masters of Mussar [i.e., ethical teaching] explained succinctly, 'It is better to urge the children to ask questions *while they are at home* and their parents and teachers can respond, than to wait until *outsiders* incite them to doubt and question.' When that happens, it is often too late because questions can become the tools of the skeptic who neither seeks nor accepts valid answers. By that time, it may חלילה be too late to steer them back onto the right path.

Built-in contradiction ⋙ Although, simply understood, the Four Questions represent logical inquiries concerning obvious unusual characteristics of the *Seder* night, commentators explain that the questions are not randomly chosen. Two comprehensive interpretations will be cited:

Abarbanel notes that the underlying theme of the evening is that Israel was catapulted from slavery to majesty in the blink of an eye. They began the night's observance as chattels of Pharaoh but, at the stroke of midnight, they were transformed into free men about to journey to Mount Sinai to receive the Torah. This is expressed in the apparently contradictory rituals of the evening:

We eat *matzah*, 'the bread of affliction', and *maror*, the bitter herbs — both reminiscent of the grinding suffering of enslavement and servitude. On the other hand, we dip our food in sauces and recline on pillows, both customs symbolic of wealth and luxury. The inquiring child is thus responding to the inconsistency he sees about him. The answer will be that there is no inconsistency — on this night we recall the two conditions

in which our ancestors found themselves on the first Passover in history: they began the night as slaves and ended it as free men.

Abarbanel's commentary also explains the order of the questions. They are grouped in pairs, the first alluding to slavery and the second to freedom. Otherwise, we would have expected the questions concerning dipping and reclining to have come first since those acts are done in the *Seder* ritual before the eating of *matzah* and *maror*.

This tragic exile ◅§ The author of *Kli Yakar* interprets the *Mah Nishtanah* homiletically in a novel manner:

Why is this 'night' — an allegorical term meaning the dark night of exile — different from all the other nights? Why is the current exile so long and seemingly unending while the early periods of exile and/or subjugation were of limited duration? To this question, four answers are offered:

1 — In earlier times, while there may have been a certain degree of discord and rivalry among Jews, there was also a considerable degree of harmony and internal peace. In the current exile, the harmony has been submerged in constant strife. Until we are at peace with one another, we cannot expect Hashem to ease our plight among the nations. The word חָמֵץ, *leavening,* alludes to strife, for yeast causes dough to ferment and become agitated which, in turn, makes it rise. On the other hand מַצָּה, simple flour and water remaining in their humble, pristine state, represents peace and harmony. In olden days, we sadly proclaim, our life contained both harmony and strife — and so, even suffering was not unrelieved. But now, we are entirely filled with strife! [The words כֻּלּוֹ מַצָּה, *full of matzah,* is used as a euphemistic reference to strife, in the sense that a blind man is called a סַגִּי נָהוֹר, *one with abundant 'lights';* and in the sense that curses that befall Israel are described as having come upon שׂוֹנְאֵיהֶם שֶׁל יִשְׂרָאֵל, *the 'enemies' of Israel.* It should be noted, however, that the word מַצָּה can be interpreted literally to refer to strife, as in וְכִי יִנָּצוּ אֲנָשִׁים (*Sh'mos* 21:22).]

2 — In other exiles, we were not in such assiduous, single-minded pursuit of material wealth and luxury.

הַלֵּילוֹת אָנוּ אוֹכְלִין חָמֵץ וּמַצָּה הַלַּיְלָה הַזֶּה כֻּלּוֹ
מַצָּה. שֶׁבְּכָל הַלֵּילוֹת אָנוּ אוֹכְלִין שְׁאָר יְרָקוֹת
הַלַּיְלָה הַזֶּה מָרוֹר. שֶׁבְּכָל הַלֵּילוֹת אֵין אָנוּ מַטְבִּילִין
אֲפִילוּ פַּעַם אֶחָת הַלַּיְלָה הַזֶּה שְׁתֵּי פְעָמִים. שֶׁבְּכָל

We sought שְׁאָר יְרָקוֹת, *any vegetables*, i.e. simple, un-
pretentious living. But in the current exile we have
descended to an excessive craving for מָרוֹר, a *bitter*,
misery-causing passion for excess and luxury.

3 — In other exiles, we did not provoke gluttonous
cravings by dipping our foods into exotic sauces, i.e. we
did not seek ways to excite our senses. But in this exile,
we allow ourselves a double portion of 'dipping', i.e. we
ravenously pursue physical pleasures.

4 — In times past, we were sometimes מְסֻבִּין, *arrogant*, as symbolized by haughty reclining in a position of comfortable disregard, but we were sometimes
יוֹשְׁבִין, *sitting*, in simple humility. In this exile,
however, we have grown arrogant, constantly *reclining*,
consumed by the feeling that our *own* wealth, wisdom,
and strength are responsible for whatever successes we
have attained *(Olelos Ephraim)*.

Significance of challenge ◆§ כֻּלּוֹ מַצָּה §◆ — *Only matzah.*

The *halachah* is that the obligation to eat *matzah*
can be discharged only by using flour that *can*, if left
unattended, become leavened. Other sorts of flour —
potato meal, for example — are unacceptable ingredients for *matzah*. The question arises, wouldn't it
be even better to bake *matzos* from ingredients which
could not possibly become stringently-forbidden *chametz*?

Chasam Sofer derived an ethical lesson from this law.
To keep potato meal from becoming *chametz* is an
achievement with no meaning. Only by zealously
supervising the preparation of flour and water to prevent its leavening does a Jew manifest his loyalty to the

1. On all other nights we may eat chametz and matzah, but on this night — only matzah.

2. On all other nights we eat any vegetables, but on this night — we eat maror.

3. On all other nights we do not dip even once, but on this night — twice.

Torah. Similarly, God put the destiny of the universe into the hands of imperfect man with all his inclinations and potential for evil. The achievement for which God longs is that man conquer his deficiencies and elevate himself.

This concept was also found in the story of the dispute between Moses and the angels (Shabbos 88b): The heavenly hosts argued that mortal man was unworthy of receiving the Torah. Moses' triumphant reply was that angels without jealousy, temptation, or evil inclination have no need for a Torah which was plainly meant for man with his constant internal battle between good and evil.

Double dipping ⇢§ הַלַּיְלָה הַזֶּה שְׁתֵּי פְעָמִים — *But on this night [we dip] two times.*

Commentators note that the two dippings allude to two historical events which are connected with the Egyptian experience. The first was the act of Joseph's brothers who, after selling him into slavery, dipped his shirt into blood in order to help them convince Jacob that Joseph had been devoured by a wild beast (Bereishis 37:31). That deed precipitated the Egyptian exile because Joseph became viceroy of Egypt and the provider of food to whom Jacob's family had to turn. The second dipping was the prelude to freedom, for the Jews were commanded to dip a bunch of hyssop grass into the blood of the Pesach offering and touch the blood to their lintels and doorposts as a sign that the Jews inside the house should be unharmed while the firstborn Egyptians were being killed (Shemos 12:22, 23).

הַלֵּילוֹת אָנוּ אוֹכְלִין בֵּין יוֹשְׁבִין וּבֵין מְסֻבִּין הַלַּיְלָה
הַזֶּה כֻּלָּנוּ מְסֻבִּין:

The *matzos* are kept uncovered as the *Haggadah* is recited.

עֲבָדִים הָיִינוּ לְפַרְעֹה בְּמִצְרָיִם. וַיּוֹצִיאֵנוּ יהוה
אֱלֹהֵינוּ מִשָּׁם בְּיָד חֲזָקָה וּבִזְרוֹעַ נְטוּיָה. וְאִלּוּ לֹא
הוֹצִיא הַקָּדוֹשׁ בָּרוּךְ הוּא אֶת אֲבוֹתֵינוּ מִמִּצְרַיִם הֲרֵי
אָנוּ וּבָנֵינוּ וּבְנֵי בָנֵינוּ מְשֻׁעְבָּדִים הָיִינוּ לְפַרְעֹה

Everpresent hope ◆§ כֻּלָּנוּ מְסֻבִּין — *We all recline.*
The *Mishnah* declares that even a Jewish pauper should recline at the *Seder* (*Pesachim* 99b). Why this stress on a pauper when the obligation extends to all Jews?

Wealthy or even middle class people can recline contentedly, for their lives are reasonably comfortable and insulated from the problems of grinding poverty. But a poor person might well wonder whether life as a slave might not be preferable to insecurity and hunger. Therefore the *Midrash* directs itself to the poor as if to say: 'Your ancestors were slaves who suffered bitter oppression. Yet, when the proper time arrived, G-d not only redeemed them, He punished their subjugators, split the sea, and supplied their every need for forty years in the wilderness. History dictates, therefore, that however miserable your present circumstances, you should recline happily and securely, for G-d hovers over you, and your lot can be improved as dramatically as was that of your forefathers.' (*K'sav Sofer*).

עֲבָדִים הָיִינוּ — We were slaves

All alike ◆§ Some commentators explain that the slavery in Egypt was precipitated by the arrogant behavior of the six sons of Leah. They treated the sons of Bilhah and Zilpah as if they were inferior and regarded them as

4. On all other nights we eat either sitting or reclining, but on this night — we all recline.

The *matzos* are kept uncovered as the *Haggadah* is recited in unison:

We were slaves to Pharaoh in Egypt, but HASHEM our God took us out from there with a mighty hand and an outstretched arm. Had not the Holy One Blessed be He taken our fathers out from Egypt, then we, our children, and our children's children would have remained enslaved to Pharaoh in Egypt.

בְּנֵי הַשְׁפָחוֹת, *the children of maidservants.* In order to remove this taint from the brotherhood of Israel and put all Jews on equal footing, G-d caused them to be enslaved in Egypt. Now all Jews alike can say עֲבָדִים הָיִינוּ, *We were slaves.*

Indebted to only One
◆§ מְשֻׁעְבָּדִים הָיִינוּ — *We would have remained enslaved.* Why does the Hagaddah not remain consistent by saying *we would have been* [עֲבָדִים] *slaves,* the same expression used at the outset of the paragraph? Why the change to the פֻּעַל, *reflexive,* expression: *been enslaved?*

Additionally, we might ask why it was necessary for God to allow Pharaoh to oppose our freedom. Since לֵב מְלָכִים וְשָׂרִים בְּיַד ה', *the hearts of kings and ministers are in the hand of G-d,* why did He not simply influence Pharaoh to free us?

Rabbi Shlomo Kluger (Imrei Shefer) replied by pointing out that the word מְשֻׁעְבָּדִים has another meaning: *indebted.* Had Pharaoh generously freed us, the Exodus would have been a simpler affair, but we would have remained morally indebted to Pharaoh as our emancipator and savior. This G-d did not want. His intention was to make clear to Jew and gentile alike that only He rules the world and that we are beholden to no one but Him. This is a deeper dimension of freedom: that the Jew has no master or benefactor other than G-d.

בְּמִצְרָיִם. וַאֲפִילוּ כֻּלָּנוּ חֲכָמִים. כֻּלָּנוּ נְבוֹנִים. כֻּלָּנוּ
זְקֵנִים. כֻּלָּנוּ יוֹדְעִים אֶת הַתּוֹרָה. מִצְוָה עָלֵינוּ לְסַפֵּר
בִּיצִיאַת מִצְרָיִם. וְכָל הַמַּרְבֶּה לְסַפֵּר בִּיצִיאַת מִצְרָיִם
הֲרֵי זֶה מְשֻׁבָּח:

Permanent   ⁌ כָּל הַמַּרְבֶּה לְסַפֵּר בִּיצִיאַת מִצְרָיִם — *The more one tells*
wealth   *about the Exodus.*

Why should Israel continue to celebrate the Exodus
and expansively recount its miracles even after nineteen
centuries of exile?

The explanation can be found in the parable of a
poor man who won a lottery and became enormously
wealthy overnight. He had always wanted to become a
scholar; now he used his newfound wealth to hire accomplished scholars to tutor him. On the anniversary
of his good fortune, he would hold an annual feast to
commemorate the event that changed his life. As time
went by, however, he lost his money and became poor
again. Nevertheless, he continued his custom of
celebrating the day he won the lottery.

'Why do you celebrate', his friends asked him, 'when
your money is gone?'

He replied, 'True, my *money* is gone, but the wisdom
I acquired thanks to my money can never be taken from
me. My main joy is in the knowledge I gained — and for
that I will always celebrate.'

The same is true of Israel. Our Land, *Bais
HaMikdash*, and freedom could be taken from us, but
our greatest treasure, the Torah, remains a legacy of the
Exodus *(Divrei Shaul).*

Everyday   ⁌ *K'sav Sofer* comments that it is improper to lavish
miracles   constant praise on God for the extraordinary events
of the Exodus, because preoccupation with miracles can
make one lose sight of the daily events that are no less
miraculous even though we take them for granted. That
we walk, talk, breathe; that the sun shines and rain
falls, are also acts of God, as we say in *Shmoneh Esrai*

Even if we were all men of wisdom, understanding, experience, and knowledge of the Torah, it would still be an obligation upon us to tell about *Yetzias Mitrayim*. The more one tells about the Exodus, the more he is praiseworthy.

when we thank God for נִסֶּיךָ שֶׁבְּכָל יוֹם עִמָּנוּ, *Your daily miracles with us.* Therefore, when *Pesach* arrives, we seize upon the opportunity to expound upon the miracles of the Exodus in a manner that would be inappropriate at other times of the year.

[We find also that the Sages frown upon one who recites the הַלֵּל הַגָּדוֹל, *the Great Hallel*, every day, for, by so doing, he implies that God is to be praised only for the great miracles that defy the laws of nature in an extraordinary manner. Thus the Sages refer to the person who emphasized only such miracles as a blasphemer *(Shabbos* 118b). However, one who recites *Psalm* 145 every day is assured of a share in the World to Come *(Berachos* 4b), for that psalm praises God for the 'everyday' miracles thus acknowledging His mastery and mercy in every event *(Meshech Chochmah).*]

The eyes of the beholder ◆§ *Harav Avraham Pam* notes in this connection that every person's concept of a miracle depends on his daily experience. The Jews who were raised in the Wilderness for forty years had no need to plow, plant, or search for water because God supplied them with daily manna and an abundant well that followed them wherever they went. When they entered Canaan and saw seeds put in freshly plowed earth take root, and produce crops they must have praised God for the 'miracle' of vegetation. The Canaanite farmers, on the other hand, would have been amazed to have seen manna. By the same token, we account the Splitting of the Sea as a great miracle — only because it is beyond the realm of our normal experience. The breath of life, however, is no less a miracle; we are unawed by it simply because we are accustomed to it.

מַעֲשֶׂה בְּרַבִּי אֱלִיעֶזֶר וְרַבִּי יְהוֹשֻׁעַ וְרַבִּי אֶלְעָזָר בֶּן־
עֲזַרְיָה וְרַבִּי עֲקִיבָא וְרַבִּי טַרְפוֹן שֶׁהָיוּ מְסֻבִּין בִּבְנֵי־
בְרַק וְהָיוּ מְסַפְּרִים בִּיצִיאַת מִצְרַיִם כָּל־אוֹתוֹ הַלַּיְלָה
עַד שֶׁבָּאוּ תַלְמִידֵיהֶם וְאָמְרוּ לָהֶם. רַבּוֹתֵינוּ הִגִּיעַ זְמַן
קְרִיאַת שְׁמַע שֶׁל שַׁחֲרִית:

אָמַר רַבִּי אֶלְעָזָר בֶּן־עֲזַרְיָה. הֲרֵי אֲנִי כְּבֶן שִׁבְעִים
שָׁנָה. וְלֹא זָכִיתִי שֶׁתֵּאָמֵר יְצִיאַת מִצְרַיִם בַּלֵּילוֹת. עַד

מַעֲשֶׂה בְּרַבִּי אֱלִיעֶזֶר ... — It happened that Rabbi Eliezer ...

No exceptions ◄§ The obvious reason for the parenthetical insertion of this story, which breaks the train of the narrative previously begun by the *Haggadah*, is to illustrate the point just made. We have just been told that even the wisest and most profound people should consider themselves obligated to discuss the events of the Exodus. This is proven by the all-night *Seder* of five of the greatest sages of the Mishnaitic era.

Even Rabbi Akiva ◄§ The question is asked, however, why the *Haggadah* chose these particular sages to support the point, when there were surely countless others who did the same.

— The full extent of the miracle of the Exodus is that the Jews had descended to מ״ט שַׁעֲרֵי טוּמְאָה, *the forty-ninth level of impurity*. Had they not been redeemed at the very moment they were, the descent to the fiftieth and lowest level of impurity would have ensued and redemption would have been impossible. Moses, however, was at מ״ט שַׁעֲרֵי קְדוּשָׁה, *the forty-ninth level of holiness*. His forty-nine degrees of exaltation succeeded in counteracting the forty-nine levels of degradation with the result that Israel was rescued. Of Rabbi Akiva, however, the Sages say that he attained the *fiftieth* level of holiness. That being so, he may not have been impressed by the Exodus for he could have

It happened that Rabbi Eliezer, Rabbi Yehoshua, Rabbi Elazar ben Azaryah, Rabbi Akiva, and Rabbi Tarfon were reclining (at the *seder*) in Bnei Brak. They discussed the Exodus all that night until their students came and said to them: 'Our teachers, it is time for the reading of the morning *Shema*.'

Rabbi Elazar ben Azaryah said: I am like a seventy year old man, but I could not succeed in having the Exodus from Egypt

brought about even a greater miracle; therefore, Rabbi Akiva might not have considered himself obligated to recount the miracles. The *Haggadah* informs us that even Rabbi Akiva was no exception to the rule (*Tzemach David*).

Part of the nation ⋖§ Each of these five sages could have excused himself from participation in the limitless discussion of the Exodus because each could have considered himself uninvolved in the miracles. Rabbi Akiva was a descendant of proselytes; his ancestors were never in Egypt. Rabbi Elazar ben Azaryah, Rabbi Eliezer, and Rabbi Tarfon were kohanim and Rabbi Yehoshua was a Levite; all of them were thus members of the tribe of Levi which was not enslaved in Egypt, and therefore they might have felt that *Yetzias Mitzrayim* did not have the same significance for them as it did for the rest of the nation. Nevertheless, they considered themselves equally obligated with all other Jews (*Simchas HaRegel*).

אָמַר רַבִּי אֶלְעָזָר בֶּן עֲזַרְיָה ... — Rabbi Elazar ben Azaryah said

A great forebear ⋖§ הֲרֵי אֲנִי כְּבֶן שִׁבְעִים שָׁנָה — *I am like a seventy year old man.*

Rabbi Elazar ben Azariah was only eighteen years old, but he was appointed *Nassi*, leader of Israel. Because of his extremely youthful appearance, there was a danger that the masses would not respect him. In order to overcome this obstacle, a miracle occurred and his beard turned white (*Berachos* 28a).

שֶׁדְּרָשָׁה בֶּן זוֹמָא. שֶׁנֶּאֱמַר לְמַעַן תִּזְכֹּר אֶת יוֹם
צֵאתְךָ מֵאֶרֶץ מִצְרַיִם כֹּל יְמֵי חַיֶּיךָ. יְמֵי חַיֶּיךָ הַיָּמִים.
כֹּל יְמֵי חַיֶּיךָ הַלֵּילוֹת. וַחֲכָמִים אוֹמְרִים. יְמֵי חַיֶּיךָ
הָעוֹלָם הַזֶּה. כֹּל יְמֵי חַיֶּיךָ לְהָבִיא לִימוֹת הַמָּשִׁיחַ:

Kabbalists wrote that Rabbi Elazar had the soul of
the prophet Samuel who died when he was fifty-two
years old. Rabbi Elazar alluded to this when he compared himself to a seventy year old: his own eighteen
years plus the fifty-two years during which his soul
resided in Samuel's body come to a total of seventy
years (S'fas HaYam).

Which miracle is greater? ◂§ What bearing has Rabbi Elazar's appearance on the
fact that he had been unable to prove his contention
that the Exodus must be mentioned during evenings as
well as mornings?

Rabbi Shlomo Kluger cites a Talmudic dispute concerning the nature of miracles. Rav Yosaif maintains
that a supernatural miracle indicates the great stature of
its beneficiary. Abaye disagrees, holding that if the
person were even greater, he would not have required a
distortion of God's natural laws (*Shabbos* 53b). The
miracles of the first day of Passover in Egypt contained
miracles of both kinds: At night, the Egyptian first-
born were killed and their idols were melted, both being
miracles of the supernatural sort. Israel's march to
freedom in the morning was a miracle which did not
upset the natural order of the world because the Egyptians had reached the point where they were anxious to
rid themselves of the Jews.

According to Ben Zoma who attempts to prove that
the Exodus should be mentioned at night, an unnatural
miracle is of greater status and should be recalled.
Hence, mention of the Exodus is more desirable during
the evening for it would tend to recall the *unnatural*
miracles of that fateful event. The Sages, on the other
hand, disagree. Because they hold that *natural* miracles

mentioned at night, until Ben Zoma expounded it [*Devarim 16:3*]: *In order that you may remember the day you left Egypt all the days of your life.* The phrase *the days of your life* would have indicated *only* the days; the addition of the word *all*, includes the nights as well. But the Sages declare that *the days of your life* would mean only the present world; the addition of *all* includes the era of the Messiah.

are of a higher order, they hold that the Exodus should be recalled only by day.

Rabbi Elazar who benefited from the unnatural miracle of his premature aging, would have hoped that his very appearance would not serve as an embarrassing testimony of a miracle of a lower order. He was therefore desirous — *because he looked like a seventy year old* — that the principle be accepted that the miracles of *Pesach* night be accorded a status of honor.

Comparing miracles ◆§ כָּל יְמֵי חַיֶּיךָ לְהָבִיא לִימוֹת הַמָּשִׁיחַ — *'All the days of your life' includes* [lit. *to bring*] *the era of the Messiah.*

Why do the Sages use the seemingly superfluous word לְהָבִיא, *to include*? [In typical Talmudical discourse, the word לְהָבִיא in this sort of context is understood and, therefore, omitted.]

In their discussion, *Ben Zoma* cited to the Sages a passage in Jeremiah (23:7-8) that supported his view. There the prophet said that days will come [i.e., the days of Messiah] when people will not speak about the miracles of the Exodus, but about the miracles of the final redemption. Ben Zoma argued that this was a clear indication that the Exodus would no longer be recalled in the time of Messiah; hence the superfluous כָּל, which is meant to broaden the duty to recall the Exodus, must come to include *nights* in the obligation to remember *Yetzias Mitzrayim*. The Sages replied that Jeremiah merely meant to say that the miracles of Egypt will pale beside those of the future, and seem insignificant by comparison. However, though the primary

בָּרוּךְ הַמָּקוֹם. בָּרוּךְ הוּא. בָּרוּךְ שֶׁנָּתַן תּוֹרָה לְעַמּוֹ

focus of those glorious days will be on the miracles of the final redemption, nevertheless, the word כָּל should be interpreted לְהָבִיא, to include, i.e., to imply that the Exodus will not be forgotten, but will be *included secondarily* in reciting the catalog of miracles (*Rabbi Akiva Eiger*).

Way of living ⋦ *Tiferes Shlomo* interprets the phrase homiletically as as injunction to every single person: 'All of your life should be devoted to living and acting in such a way that you will bring closer the days of Mashiach.'

בָּרוּךְ הַמָּקוֹם בָּרוּךְ הוּא — Blessed be the Omnipresent, blessed be He.

A manner of blessing ⋦ After having established the point that it is obligatory on all Jews to discuss *Yetzias Mitzrayim* at the *Seder*, the Haggadah turns to verses from the Torah which indicate that the method of doing so is not identical for everyone. Just as there are Four Sons, there are *four general categories of people*, each of which requires a different approach. Naturally, each individual human being will have his unique needs which will indicate how he may best learn and develop.

Although, as explained above, there is no requirement to recite a blessing before the recitation of the *Haggadah*, nor is a blessing recited before each time the study of the Torah is commenced during the day, the composers of the Haggadah considered it fitting that the first introduction of passages from the Torah be preceded by the semblance of a blessing. Because we are about to quote the four passages from the Torah referring specifically to the Four Sons and in a broader sense to the lessons needed by the four categories of people, we bless Hashem by saying בָּרוּךְ, *blessed*, four times — one for each of the four passages.

⋦ Two aspects of Hashem's manifestations are

Blessed be the Omnipresent; blessed be He.
Blessed be the One Who has given the Torah to His people

All embracing Torah specified. He is מָקוֹם, the Omnipresent [lit. *The Place*] Who is everywhere. As the Sages put it: 'He is the place of the universe, and the universe is not His place.' He is also the Giver of the Torah. Thus, He is the G-d of all situations — as indicated by His name מָקוֹם, Place — and His Torah contains the lessons needed to deal with all situations. Just as G-d's presence is everywhere, all necessary wisdom can be found in His Torah. Therefore, before the *Haggadah* goes to the different types of people as exemplified by the Four Sons, it gives this preface to establish that G-d's Torah contains the guidance needed to deal with every type of person *(Elias Haggadah).*

Role mode is for all ◂§ In a view similar to this concept that the Torah enables everyone to deal with his own particular situation, the previous Rebbe of Belz commented on a Talmudic passage in *Yoma* 35b: After death, when a person is asked to give account for his deeds on earth, he is asked לָמָּה לֹא עָסַקְתָּ בַּתּוֹרָה, *Why did you not engage in Torah study?* If he replies that poverty prevented him from doing so, he is told, 'Were you poorer than Hillel who did not allow poverty to deter him from the pursuit of Torah knowledge?' If he claims that the responsibilities and distractions of wealth stood in his way, he is told, 'Were you wealthier than Rebbe Eliezer ben Charsum?' If he contends that his lustful nature prevented proper concentration, he is told, 'Was your nature more lustful than that of Joseph [son of the Patriarch, Jacob]? Thus, the Torah contains role models who are adequate to provide guidance for every predicament. The *Belzer Rebbe* found this alluded to in the verse רַבּוֹת מַחֲשָׁבוֹת בְּלֶב אִישׁ וַעֲצַת ה' הִיא תָקוּם, *Many are the thoughts in the heart of man, but the counsel of HASHEM — it [הִיא] shall prevail (Mishle 19:21)* The word הִיא *it*, i.e. Hashem's counsel, is formed of the initials of Hillel, Joseph, and Eliezer ben Charsum.

יִשְׂרָאֵל. בָּרוּךְ הוּא. כְּנֶגֶד אַרְבָּעָה בָנִים דִּבְּרָה תוֹרָה. אֶחָד חָכָם. וְאֶחָד רָשָׁע. וְאֶחָד תָּם. וְאֶחָד שֶׁאֵינוֹ יוֹדֵעַ לִשְׁאוֹל:

חָכָם מָה הוּא אוֹמֵר. מָה הָעֵדֹת וְהַחֻקִּים וְהַמִּשְׁפָּטִים אֲשֶׁר צִוָּה יהוה אֱלֹהֵינוּ אֶתְכֶם. וְאַף אַתָּה אֱמָר־לוֹ כְּהִלְכוֹת הַפֶּסַח. אֵין מַפְטִירִין אַחַר הַפֶּסַח אֲפִיקוֹמָן:

Four sons — four merits

৯§ כְּנֶגֶד אַרְבָּעָה בָנִים דִּבְּרָה תוֹרָה — *Concerning four sons did the Torah speak.*

The 'four' sons represent four types of people who were saved from Egypt because of four different types of merit. The forms of merit were: 1 — זְכוּת אָבוֹת, *The merit of the Patriarchs* [אֱלֹקֵי אֲבוֹתֵיכֶם שְׁלָחַנִי אֲלֵיכֶם, *the G-d of your forefathers sent me to you (Sh'mos 3:13)*].

2 — בְּרִית אָבוֹת, The Covenant of the Patriarchs [וַיִּזְכֹּר אֱלֹקִים אֶת בְּרִיתוֹ, *and G-d remembered His covenant (ibid 2:24).*]

3 — זְכוּת קַבָּלַת הַתּוֹרָה, The merit of Israel which was prepared to accept the Torah [בְּהוֹצִיאֲךָ אֶת הָעָם מִמִּצְרַיִם תַּעַבְדוּן אֶת הָאֱלֹקִים עַל הָהָר הַזֶּה, *When you remove the nation from Egypt, you will serve G-d on this mountain (ibid 3:12)*]

4 — זְכוּת הַמִּצְוֹת, The merit of the performance of commandments [וְרָאִיתִי אֶת הַדָּם וּפָסַחְתִּי עֲלֵכֶם, *and I shall see the blood* (i.e. of the Passover sacrifice) *and I will pass over you (ibid 12:13).*]

The חָכָם, inquires about the commandments because he is utterly devoted to their performance. That type of Jew was saved from Egypt because of זְכוּת הַמִּצְוֹת, *the merit of the commandments.*

The תָּם, *simple son* represents the person of limited attainment who was nevertheless saved because of זְכוּת קַבָּלַת הַתּוֹרָה, his *willingness to accept the Torah.*

The אֵינוֹ יוֹדֵעַ לִשְׁאוֹל, *son who is unable to ask,* is far

Israel; blessed be He.

Concerning four sons did the Torah speak: a wise one, a wicked one, a simple one, and one who is unable to ask.

The wise son — what does he say? [Devarim 6:20] 'What are the testimonies, decrees, and ordinances which HASHEM, our God, has commanded you?' Therefore explain to him the laws of the Pesach: that one may not eat after the final taste of the Pesach Afikoman.

removed from his heritage, but such people were saved because of זְכוּת אָבוֹת, the *merit of the Patriarchs.*

The רָשָׁע, *wicked son*, has no redeeming virture, but even such people were saved thanks to בְּרִית אָבוֹת, because a covenant, by definition, must be honored even if its beneficiaries possess no independent merit.

... חָכָם — The Wise Son ...

Listen for ∾§ מָה הוּא אוֹמֵר — *What does he say?*

your
answer The *Haggadah* gives us a clue concerning how to deal with the various types of people. Listen to what he says. By the *way* a person asks a question or makes a statement we can gain an insight into his character and formulate our response accordingly. The חָכָם, *wise son*, asks probing questions concerning the observance of commandments. He should not be answered with parables or homiletics, but with specific and detailed information. The תָּם, *simple son*, is obviously ill-equipped for halachic discussion; he must be inspired by the narrative of God's special relationship with Israel. The אֵינוֹ יוֹדֵעַ לִשְׁאוֹל who is not perceptive enough even to inquire must be drawn into the observance through affection and inspiration. The רָשָׁע, *wicked son*, in his arrogance refuses even to consider himself part of the group. The first step is to shatter his haughtiness. Then, perhaps he can be influenced to re-join Israel in its service of G-d *(Harav Yisrael Belsky).*

רָשָׁע מָה הוּא אוֹמֵר. מָה הָעֲבוֹדָה הַזֹּאת לָכֶם.

A pleasant aftertaste

§ — כְּהִלְכוֹת הַפֶּסַח אֵין מַפְטִירִין אַחַר הַפֶּסַח אֲפִיקוֹמָן

[Like] *the laws of the Pesach; that one may not eat after the final taste of the Pesach afikoman.*

The *Haggadah* instructs us to inform the wise son כְּהִלְכוֹת, literally *'like'* the laws. Why is the prefix כ, *like*, used?

The *Haggadah* suggests a major pedagogical principle. A teacher should not content himself merely with imparting information. He should attempt to make his teaching as tempting and enjoyable as delicious food; the student should leave his lesson with a pleasant 'taste' which will help him retain his learning. Therefore, the *Afikoman* is used as the illustration. Nothing may be eaten after the *Afikoman* in order that its taste should linger in the mouth long after the meal is over. Teaching should be like that law — pleasant and therefore enduring (*Rabbi Yissachar Dov of Belz*).

רָשָׁע ... — The Wicked Son ...

Without respect

§ — מָה הָעֲבוֹדָה הַזֹּאת ... בַּעֲבוּר זֶה — *Of what purpose is this work ... because of this.*

Even the worst sinner can yet repent as long as he retains a modicum of respect for his parents and elders. If, however, he descends to the level of ridicule, then there is little hope for him, for cynical ridicule can destroy the efficacy of even the most sincere attempts to bring home the truth. This son betrays the extent of his wickedness by defying and audaciously challenging his elders with: *'Of what purpose is this work?'* To that sort of declaration — more a statement than a question — a reasoned reply is pointless. Instead the answer is simply, בַּעֲבוּר זֶה, *because of this* — because of our attitudes of respect and acceptance of the authority of our elders were we redeemed from Egypt. We listened to Moshe. Otherwise, we would have perished there along with the arrogant sinners like you (*K'sav Sofer*).

The wicked son — what does he say? [ibid 12:26] 'Of what

When Hashem is present

❧ מָה הָעֲבוֹדָה הַזֹּאת לָכֶם — *Of what purpose is this work to you?*

How can we see from the questions that one son is wise and the other wicked? Both use second person words — the wise one says אֶתְכֶם, *you,* and the wicked one says לָכֶם, *to you,* why do we interpret the words of the second one as meaning to exclude himself in a haughty and disbelieving manner?

The difference between them is not indicated by the second person pronoun, but by the fact that the first son said ה' אֱלֹקֵינוּ, *HASHEM, 'our' G-d.* He clearly accepts Hashem's sovereignty over himself: *'our* G-d'. The wicked son leaves G-d out of his calculations.

This interpretation is based on a comment of the *Vilna Gaon* to *Koheles* (2:13): יִתְרוֹן לַחָכְמָה מִן הַסִּכְלוּת כִּיתְרוֹן הָאוֹר מִן הַחֹשֶׁךְ, *wisdom excels folly as light excels darkness.* The *Gaon* homiletically refers the mention of *light* and *darkness* to the account of the creation of those two states. Concerning the creation of light, Scripture states וַיִּקְרָא אֱלֹקִים לָאוֹר יוֹם וְלַחֹשֶׁךְ קָרָא לָיְלָה *G-d called to the light: Day; and to the darkness He called: Night (Bereishis 1:5).* The *Midrash* notes that G-d's Name is specified only in connection with the day, thus indicating that G-d's Name is associated only with good, but not with evil. Hence, *Koheles* tells us that the excellence of wisdom [i.e. good] over folly [i.e. evil] is similar to the excellence of light over darkness. That excellence is indicated by the presence of G-d's Name.

Thus the failure of a son to associate himself with the Name is sufficient indication of his evil nature.

A time to ask

❧ *Chasam Sofer* notes another difference between the two sons — a basic conflict in their attitude toward the commandments. That one does not understand a commandment should not prevent him from performing it. Fundamental to Jewish belief is that all commandments derive from G-d and must be done even

57 **The Haggadah Treasury**

לָכֶם וְלֹא לוֹ. וּלְפִי שֶׁהוֹצִיא אֶת־עַצְמוֹ מִן הַכְּלָל כָּפַר
בְּעִקָּר. וְאַף אַתָּה הַקְהֵה אֶת־שִׁנָּיו וֶאֱמֹר לוֹ בַּעֲבוּר
זֶה עָשָׂה יהוה לִי בְּצֵאתִי מִמִּצְרָיִם. לִי וְלֹא לוֹ. אִלּוּ
הָיָה שָׁם לֹא הָיָה נִגְאָל:

though they are beyond human comprehension. One has the right to raise questions in an attempt to know more and understand better, but not to negate the obligation to obey the Torah. The wise son asks in order to learn what he is obligated to do. But the wicked son questions the very obligation. He speaks of הָעֲבוֹדָה הַזֹּאת, 'this' work; the demonstrative pronoun indicates plainly that the service about which he asks is ready to be done. Yet, instead of doing it, he asks why it should be done. This proves that he does not believe in the duty to perform the commandment unless it suits his fancy.

Questions and Statements ◄§ *Meshech Chochmah* comments that the language of the Scriptural verses themselves makes plain the difference between the wise and the wicked sons. In introducing the words of the former, the Torah says כִּי יִשְׁאָלְךָ בִנְךָ, *when your son 'asks' you (Devarim 6:20)*; he asks a question and deserves an answer. But in the case of the wicked son, the Torah says כִּי יֹאמְרוּ אֲלֵיכֶם, *when they 'say' to you (Sh'mos 12:26)*. He does not seek answers, for he asks no questions — he *'says'*. He makes an abusive statement to the effect that the service of G-d is pointless.

Not for servants ◄§ The wicked son asks of his parents, Why must *you* do הָעֲבוֹדָה, *the labor* — the difficult menial tasks necessary to prepare for commandments? Why don't you assign that sort of work to servants?

The answer is that we make the preparations ourselves because Hashem, too, acted Himself when removing us from Egypt. He did not assign angels to perform the task *(K'sav Sofer)*.

purpose is this work to you? He says, 'To *you*', thereby excluding *himself*. By excluding himself from the community (of believers), he denies the basic principle of Judaism. Therefore, blunt his teeth and tell him [*ibid* 13:8]: *It is because of this that HASHEM did so for me when I went out of Egypt.* 'For me,' but not for *him* — had *he* been there, he would not have been redeemed.

Always a   ◈§ *Harav Zalman Sorotzkin* comments that to the
burden   wicked, any inconvenience encountered in the service of G-d is a cumbersome burden.

Useless   ◈§ הַקְהֵה אֶת שִׁנָּיו — *Blunt his teeth*
teeth   Wicked people think that G-d can be served only through wailing, fasting, and praying. They refuse to recognize that even eating and drinking should be a divine service, for it is done in order that a person may have the health to serve G-d, and as a vehicle to bless Him. We tell such a person that his teeth should be blunted, for he uses them only to satisfy his lust for food, but not to serve G-d (*Maggid of Kozhnitz*).

No use   ◈§ לִי וְלֹא לוֹ — *For me, but not for him.*
answering   The *Vilna Gaon* notes that the *Haggadah* should have said לִי וְלֹא לְךָ, *for me, but not for 'you'*, in second person since the wicked son is being addressed.

He explains that the author of the *Haggadah* based himself on the language of the Torah. In the case of the other sons, the Torah says וְהִגַּדְתָּ לְבִנְךָ, *tell your son* (*Sh'mos* 13:8), or וְאָמַרְתָּ אֵלָיו, *say to him* (ibid 13:14). In the case of the wicked son, however, the verse reads וַאֲמַרְתֶּם זֶבַח פֶּסַח, *you are to say it is a Passover sacrifice* (*ibid.* 12:27). The implication is that the wicked son is not to be addressed directly. The surliness of his statement is such that it is pointless to answer him. Rather, the statement given in response to his challenge is to be directed at the rest of the household.

תָּם מָה הוּא אוֹמֵר. מַה זֹּאת. וְאָמַרְתָּ אֵלָיו
בְּחֹזֶק יָד הוֹצִיאָנוּ יהוה מִמִּצְרַיִם מִבֵּית־עֲבָדִים:

וְשֶׁאֵינוֹ יוֹדֵעַ לִשְׁאוֹל אַתְּ פְּתַח לוֹ. שֶׁנֶּאֱמַר וְהִגַּדְתָּ
לְבִנְךָ בַּיּוֹם הַהוּא לֵאמֹר בַּעֲבוּר זֶה עָשָׂה יהוה לִי
בְּצֵאתִי מִמִּצְרַיִם:

יָכוֹל מֵרֹאשׁ חֹדֶשׁ. תַּלְמוּד לוֹמַר בַּיּוֹם הַהוּא. אִי
בַּיּוֹם הַהוּא יָכוֹל מִבְּעוֹד יוֹם. תַּלְמוּד לוֹמַר בַּעֲבוּר

תָּם — The Simple Son ...

Wholes-ome — when? ◄§ Here, the term תָּם for the simple son is slightly derogatory. However, the Patriarch Jacob is described as אִישׁ תָּם, *a simple*, or *wholesome, person* (*Bereishis* 25:27). The *Chafetz Chaim* explained that wholesomeness *is*, indeed a virute if it is used discriminatingly. A Jew is commanded to be wholesome and simple in his relations to G-d, [תָּמִים תִּהְיֶה עִם ה' אֱלֹקֶיךָ (*Devarim* 18:13)] by trusting that whatever Hashem does is for the good. However, in dealing with people, one must keep his wits about him, remaining aware that some people are honest and others are not. Jacob was an אִישׁ תָּם, *simple person;* but the word אִישׁ also means *master* as in אִישׁ נָעֳמִי, the *husband* or *master* of Naomi (*Ruth* 1:3). He was in full control of his wholesome nature; when he dealt with the dishonest Laban, he was fully capable of exercising guile. The simple son of the *Haggadah* lacks the judgment to distinguish between those who deserve his trust and those who don't.

Never hopeless ◄§ בְּחֹזֶק יָד הוֹצִיאָנוּ ה' מִמִּצְרַיִם — *With a strong hand did HASHEM take us out of Egypt.*
This fact is told to the simple son because, throughout Jewish history, there have been countless periods when suffering and persecution were so much the rule of the day, that ordinary people could hardly be blamed for losing hope. Therefore we reiterate that G-d withdrew us from Egypt with a strong hand. The

The simple son — what does he say? [*ibid* 13:14]: '*What is this?*' Tell him [*ibid*]: *With a strong hand did HASHEM take us out of Egypt, from the house of bondage.*'

As for the son who is unable to ask, you must initiate the subject for him, as it is stated [*ibid*. 13:8]: '*You shall tell your son on that day: It is because of this that HASHEM did so for me when I went out of Egypt.*'

One might think that the obligation to discuss the Exodus commences with the first day of the month of Nissan, but the Torah says [*ibid*. 13:8]: *'(You shall tell your son) on that day.*' But the expression '*on that day*' could be understood to mean only during the daytime; therefore the Torah adds: *It is*

Jewish people were never in a more pathetic state than they were then. If Hashem saved us then, there is no reason ever to lose hope. *(Rabbi Marcus Lehmann).*

וְשֶׁאֵינוֹ יוֹדֵעַ לִשְׁאוֹל ... — As for the son who is unable to ask

Blameless but not worthy

◄§ בַּעֲבוּר זֶה עָשָׂה ה' לִי — *Because of this, HASHEM did for me ...*

It seems strange that this pathetic son is taught the same verse as that which is hurled into the teeth of the wicked son. Surely the ignorance of this last son cannot be compared to the wickedness of the other! However, there is a lesson to be learned from this similarity. Great rewards must be earned. Had Israel in Egypt or during any other period been a nation merely of ignorant people who could not even inquire into their uniqueness, or how to elevate themselves, then it could never have deserved to receive the Torah and be given *Eretz Yisrael*. The ignorant person may be blameless for his inadequacies, but he cannot be rewarded for them, either.

יָכוֹל ... — One might think

Twelve deeds

◄§ בַּעֲבוּר זֶה — *Because of this.*

Avudraham and *Kol Bo* point out that the word

זֶה. בַּעֲבוּר זֶה לֹא אָמַרְתִּי אֶלָּא בְּשָׁעָה שֶׁיֵּשׁ מַצָּה
וּמָרוֹר מֻנָּחִים לְפָנֶיךָ:

מִתְּחִלָּה עוֹבְדֵי עֲבוֹדָה זָרָה הָיוּ אֲבוֹתֵינוּ. וְעַכְשָׁיו
קֵרְבָנוּ הַמָּקוֹם לַעֲבוֹדָתוֹ. שֶׁנֶּאֱמַר וַיֹּאמֶר יְהוֹשֻׁעַ אֶל
כָּל הָעָם כֹּה אָמַר יהוה אֱלֹהֵי יִשְׂרָאֵל בְּעֵבֶר הַנָּהָר
יָשְׁבוּ אֲבוֹתֵיכֶם מֵעוֹלָם תֶּרַח אֲבִי אַבְרָהָם וַאֲבִי נָחוֹר

זֶה has the numerical value of twelve [ז=7; ה=5]. This
alludes to the twelve specific *mitzvos* that are performed during the *Seder*. They are: Drinking of four
cups, *karpas*, the washing of the hands, eating the
matzah of *motzi*, the second *matzah*, *maror*, *charoses*,
korech, and *afikoman*. [Telling about the Exodus,
however, has no limit and is therefore not included
among the specific *mitzvos*.]

מִתְּחִלָּה עוֹבְדֵי עֲבוֹדָה זָרָה הָיוּ אֲבוֹתֵינוּ — Originally our
ancestors were idol worshipers.

From
sinful
beginnings
•§ People often claim that they have sinned too much
even to think of repenting. To counter this attitude,
the *Haggadah* notes that Israel's history began amid the
idol worship of Charan where Abraham's father,
Terach, bowed to idols. Nevertheless, Israel grew from
that beginning. And according to the *Midrash*, even
Terach repented *(Avodas Yisrael)*.

Who is
modern?
•§ A *Maskil* [i.e. so-called enlightened Jew who was a
non-believer] challenged the *Malbim*, asking how
the great rabbi could persist in following 'outmoded,
antiquated teachings that were no longer relevant to the
times.' *Malbim* replied that our passage of the *Haggadah* shows that from a historical perspective, the
maskil's argument was totally mistaken. 'Far back in
the days of antiquity our ancestors were already
worshipers of idols devised by their own imaginations,

because of this [that HASHEM did so for me when I went out of Egypt]. That expression implies because of something tangible, it applies only when matzah and maror lie before you — at the Seder.

Originally our ancestors were idol worshipers, but now the Omnipresent has brought us near to His service, as it is written [*Joshua 24:2-4*]: *Joshua said to all the people, 'So says HASHEM, God of Israel: Your fathers always lived beyond the Eurphrates River, Terach the father of Abraham and Nachor,*

just as the current *maskilim* create their own sets of values and rituals. It was only much later that G-d drew us close to His service. So, in reality, we who are loyal to the Torah, are quite modern — it is *you*, who worship your pseudo-idols, who are old-fashioned!'

Beneficial suffering

⋖§ The idol worship of our ancestors was a factor in the Egyptian exile. All the nations wallowed in impurity, and even the offspring of Abraham were affected by the prevailing sinfulness of the times. In order for Israel to be worthy to receive the Torah, it had to be purified and perfected. The means which Hashem in His infinite wisdom chose for this was the exile of Egypt during which the suffering and anguish cleansed Israel. As the Sages say יִסּוּרִין מְמָרְקִין עֲוֹנוֹתָיו שֶׁל אָדָם, *suffering removes the sins of a person (Berachos 5a).* As a result of the exile Hashem was able to *draw us close to His service.* Therefore, we thank G-d for having inflicted the exile. Were it not beneficial, it would be ludicrous to thank Him for it, just as one does not thank a jailer for releasing a victim who was unlawfully imprisoned in the first place. We are grateful for the exile, because it was the means for cleansing us from the legacy of our idolatrous ancestors *(Lail Shimurim).*

And still He loves

⋖§ Why should we speak of the degradation of our ancestors? However, this opening statement is meant to emphasize Hashem's love for us. It is easy for a father to love a perfect child, but a father who loves a wayward child shows a much more meaningful affec-

וַיַּעַבְדוּ אֱלֹהִים אֲחֵרִים: וָאֶקַּח אֶת־אֲבִיכֶם אֶת־
אַבְרָהָם מֵעֵבֶר הַנָּהָר וָאוֹלֵךְ אוֹתוֹ בְּכָל־אֶרֶץ כְּנָעַן
וָאַרְבֶּה אֶת זַרְעוֹ וָאֶתֶּן לוֹ אֶת־יִצְחָק: וָאֶתֵּן לְיִצְחָק
אֶת־יַעֲקֹב וְאֶת עֵשָׂו וָאֶתֵּן לְעֵשָׂו אֶת־הַר שֵׂעִיר
לָרֶשֶׁת אוֹתוֹ וְיַעֲקֹב וּבָנָיו יָרְדוּ מִצְרָיִם:

בָּרוּךְ שׁוֹמֵר הַבְטָחָתוֹ לְיִשְׂרָאֵל. בָּרוּךְ הוּא.
שֶׁהַקָּדוֹשׁ בָּרוּךְ הוּא חִשֵּׁב אֶת הַקֵּץ לַעֲשׂוֹת כְּמָה

tion. Thus we say that even though our forefathers in Egypt descended to the forty-ninth level of impurity — to the point where they too were idol worshipers — G-d still loved them and rescued them (K'sav Sofer).

The price of the Land ⋙ וָאֶתֵּן לְעֵשָׂו אֶת הַר שֵׂעִיר — And to Esau I gave the mountain of Seir.

The Haggadah mentions Esau's inheritance for a purpose which is very germane to the narrative of the Exodus. At the בְּרִית בֵּין הַבְּתָרִים, Covenant between the Parts, when Hashem promised Eretz Yisrael to Abraham, He said that prior to their conquest of the Land, Abraham's descendants would spend four hundred years in exile and slavery. Thus the inheritance of the Land is dependent on servitude in a strange land. The only member of Abraham's family to submit to this ordeal was Jacob. Esau, on the other hand was immediately awarded his inheritance of Mount Seir. Not having undergone the exile, he can have no claim to Eretz Yisrael (Brisker Rav).

בָּרוּךְ שׁוֹמֵר הַבְטָחָתוֹ לְיִשְׂרָאֵל — Blessed be He Who keeps His pledge to Israel.

A promise in the balance ⋙ At first glance it seems strange that G-d is praised merely for keeping a promise, something which everyone is expected to do as a matter of course. The import of the blessing, however, is that He chose Israel

and they served other gods. Then I took your father Abraham from beyond the river and led him through all the land of Canaan. I multiplied his offspring and gave him Isaac. To Isaac I gave Jacob and Esau; to Esau I gave Mount Seir to inherit, but Jacob and his children went down to Egypt.

Blessed be He Who keeps His pledge to Israel; blessed be He!

For the Holy One, Blessed be He, calculated the end of the bondage in order to do as He said to our father Abraham at

rather than Esau for the fulfillment of a promise that could have referred to either of the brothers. The pledge was originally to Abraham that בְּיִצְחָק יִקָּרֵא לְךָ זָרַע *through Isaac offspring will be considered yours* (*Bereishis* 21:12). Upon this, the Sages expound בְּיִצְחָק וְלֹא כָּל יִצְחָק, *part of* Isaac's [offspring] *but not all* of Isaac's [offspring] will be heir to the covenant of Abraham. Thus, both Jacob and Esau were equally eligible and, in fact, Isaac was prepared to confer the blessings upon *Esau*, rather than Jacob. Therefore, we express our gratitude to G-d for having chosen Israel [i.e. Jacob] as the nation upon whom the blessings would be conferred (*Yad HaChazakah*).

Resolving the dates חִשַּׁב אֶת הַקֵּץ — *Calculated the end*

Three seemingly contradictory time spans are found in connection with the Jewish exile in Egypt:

1 — At the Covenant between the Parts (*Bereishis* 15:13), Abraham was told that the exile would last 400 years;

2 — The Egyptian exile actually endured for 210 years;

3 — The Torah says that Israel lived in Egypt for 430 years (*Shemos* 12:40) [Tradition dates this from the Covenant between the Parts which took place thirty years before the birth of Isaac. See Rashi.]

According to the interpretation of the *Midrash*, there should have been 400 years of actual slavery to comply with the prophecy given to Abraham. However, that

שֶׁאָמַר לְאַבְרָהָם אָבִינוּ בִּבְרִית בֵּין הַבְּתָרִים. שֶׁנֶּאֱמַר

would have been more than Israel could endure without becoming totally assimilated into the Egyptian nation. Had the exile been that long, they would have descended to the fiftieth level of impurity and lost all hope for redemption. Therefore, G-d caused the Egyptians to impose a servitude so harsh that its intensity made it equivalent to the 400 years originally contemplated.

The word קֵץ, means a deadline beyond which a condition cannot go on. Thus, the coming of Messiah to conclude the current exile can be hastened if Israel proves worthy, but in any case, it cannot last beyond a specific predetermined קֵץ, *a deadline* known only to G-d. The 430 mentioned in connection with the Egyptian exile was the קֵץ, the deadline beyond which the exile could not continue.

Now, the contradictions between the three numbers are resolved. There was a קֵץ of 430 years. During that duration there would be exile and slavery lasting 400 years each. The exile was reckoned from the birth of Isaac. The slavery, however, could not be allowed to last any longer than it did or it would have stretched beyond the קֵץ. Therefore G-d חִשַּׁב אֶת הַקֵּץ, *'calculated' the end*, i.e. he reckoned all the components of the historic event so that all three — the deadline, the period of exile, and the intensity of servitude — would coincide, ending at precisely the instant when the Exodus took place (*Brisker Rav*).

Anguished thoughts ◆§ Knowing of the prophecy that their offspring would be persecuted in Egypt, the Patriarchs suffered grievously. Hashem, in His mercy counted 190 of those years of anguish to complement the 210 years of actual exile to arrive at the total of 400 years. This is alluded to by the expression חִשַּׁב, *reckoned*. The word חִשַּׁב is related to מַחְשָׁבָה, *thought*. Thus Hashem considered the agonizing *'thoughts'* of the Patriarchs which they harbored for 190 years [קֵץ has the numerical value of 190] (*Kedushas Levi*).

the Covenant between the Parts, as it states: [*Bereishis* 15:13-

A time to awaken ◄§ The *Dubner Maggid* gives a different interpretation of the word קֵץ. He asks why the *Haggadah* uses the word קֵץ instead of סוֹף since both words mean *end;* what is the particular implication of קֵץ? Also, many great people down through the ages predicted that Messiah would come at specific times, yet he still has not come. How can so many great people have been wrong? The *Maggid* explained with a parable. A merchant hired a wagon and driver to take him to a distant city. Night fell as they were far from any town. They pulled over to the side of the road and lay down to sleep. Unaccustomed to the hard ground, the merchant was unable to sleep. Finally, he drank some whiskey — and then a little more and a little more — to warm himself and induce slumber. When he finally fell asleep he slept through the day, not waking up until the middle of the next night. Thinking it was still the same night, he drank more whiskey — and fell asleep again until the middle of the *next* night. Again he drank and fell asleep. After a few nights of this, he woke up his driver and angrily asked, 'What sort of place is this? The night never ends here! '

'Foolish man,' the driver replied. 'There have been many days, but you slept through them all.'

So, too, is the story of Jewish history. There have been many 'days' which could have illuminated the dark night of exile, but we were not awake to see their light and bring Messiah. The word קֵץ is related to הֵקִיץ, *to awaken.* The coming of Messiah is called קֵץ because it cannot happen unless we are *awake* to receive him as was Israel in Egypt.

Unalterable covenant ◄§ בִּבְרִית בֵּין הַבְּתָרִים — *At the Covenant between the Parts.*

The unique feature of a covenant, as opposed to a promise, is that a covenant cannot be revoked even though the one with whom it was made is no longer deserving. A Divine promise, however, can be revoked if its beneficiary becomes a sinner or if he lacks suf-

 67   **The Haggadah Treasury**

וַיֹּאמֶר לְאַבְרָם יָדֹעַ תֵּדַע כִּי־גֵר יִהְיֶה זַרְעֲךָ בְּאֶרֶץ לֹא לָהֶם וַעֲבָדוּם וְעִנּוּ אֹתָם אַרְבַּע מֵאוֹת שָׁנָה: וְגַם אֶת־הַגּוֹי אֲשֶׁר יַעֲבֹדוּ דָּן אָנֹכִי וְאַחֲרֵי כֵן יֵצְאוּ בִּרְכֻשׁ גָּדוֹל:

ficient merit. Thus we find that the Patriarchs often feared that they were no longer deserving of the fulfillment of a Divine pledge. G-d's Covenant between the Parts gave the pledge of the Land a permanent, irrevocable nature independent of the virtue of Israel. As the Talmud says, even though זְכוּת אָבוֹת, *the merit of the Patriarchs* may someday be exhausted, בְּרִית אָבוֹת, the *Covenant of the Patriarchs* is eternal (*Shabbos* 55a). Therefore, the *Haggadah* thanks Hashem for the Covenant and then goes on to say וְהִיא שֶׁעָמְדָה לַאֲבוֹתֵינוּ וְלָנוּ, *And it is this* [i.e. the Covenant] *that has stood for our fathers and for us.* During all periods, even when we lacked all forms of merit, the Covenant remained our stronghold (*Brisker Rav*).

According to the effort ⊰ וַעֲבָדוּם ⊱ — *And they will serve them.*

The Talmud teaches that the merit which enabled Pharaoh to enslave Israel was that he escorted Abraham when the latter left Egypt: בִּזְכוּת ד' אַמּוֹת שֶׁלִּוָּה פַּרְעֹה אֶת אַבְרָהָם נִגְזַר עֲלֵיהֶם שֶׁיִּשְׁתַּעְבְּדוּ עִם בָּנָיו רד"ו שָׁנָה, *In the merit of the four cubits which Pharoah escorted Abraham, it was decreed upon the children of Israel that he enslave them for 210 years* (*Sotah* 46b). But Nevuchadnezzar, who took four steps in honor of Hashem was rewarded with only *seventy* years of domination of Israel (*Sanhedrin* 96a). Why was Pharoah's reward so much greater?

The Talmud gives the height of the average man as three cubits; the average footstep, which is one-third of a person's height, would thus be one cubit. Pharaoh was a midget who was only one cubit tall (*Moed Katan* 18a). Therefore, in order to walk four cubits he had to take three times as many steps as Nevuchadnezzar. Therefore his reward was three times greater (*Rabbi Yonasan Eybescheutz*).

14]: *He said to Abram, 'Know with certainty that your offspring will be aliens in a land not their own, they will serve them and they will oppress them four hundred years; but also upon the nation which they shall serve will I execute judgment, and afterwards they shall leave with great possessions.'*

Levels of exile ⊷§ גֵּר יִהְיֶה זַרְעֲךָ בְּאֶרֶץ לֹא לָהֶם וַעֲבָדוּם וְעִנּוּ אֹתָם § — *Your offspring will be aliens in a land not their own, they will serve them and they will oppress them.*

The verse contains three aspects of the Egyptian experience: exile, enslavement, and affliction. This refers to three different levels of the Egyptian ordeal, at least one of which was experienced by every Jew. The tribe of Levi was never enslaved, but they were *aliens.* The Jewish taskmasters were forced to execute the enslavement of their brethren, thereby becoming the agents who ensured that Israel would serve Egypt. The bulk of the nation endured the backbreaking affliction of hard labor *(Nachalas Yaakov).*

A plea to borrow ⊷§ וְאַחֲרֵי כֵן יֵצְאוּ בִּרְכֻשׁ גָּדוֹל § — *And afterwards they shall leave with great possessions.*

G-d asked Moses to plead with the Jews to borrow valuable utensils and clothing from the Egyptians in order that the promise to Abraham would be fulfilled. Otherwise, Abraham would complain to Hashem, 'You fulfilled Your prophecy that my children would work and suffer in Egypt, but You did not fulfill Your pledge that they would leave *with great possessions' (Brachos* 9a; *Rashi* to *Shemos* 11:2). This *Midrashic* interpretation is exceedingly difficult. Can it be that there was no other reason for G-d to keep His word than to avoid the recriminations of Abraham?

The *Dubner Maggid* explained the *Midrash* with a parable. Once, a father apprenticed his son to a printer to be taught the trade. The agreement was that after a certain number of years during which the child would work, the master printer would pay him. At the end of the apprenticeship, the printer gave the boy a generous check, but the youngster ran home to his father in tears

The *matzos* are covered and the cups lifted as the following paragraph is proclaimed joyously. Upon its conclusion, the cups are put down and the *matzos* again uncovered.

וְהִיא שֶׁעָמְדָה לַאֲבוֹתֵינוּ וְלָנוּ. שֶׁלֹּא אֶחָד בִּלְבָד
עָמַד עָלֵינוּ לְכַלּוֹתֵנוּ. אֶלָּא שֶׁבְּכָל דּוֹר וָדוֹר עוֹמְדִים
עָלֵינוּ לְכַלּוֹתֵנוּ. וְהַקָּדוֹשׁ בָּרוּךְ הוּא מַצִּילֵנוּ מִיָּדָם:

complaining that for all his labor, he had been rewarded with nothing 'but a piece of paper!'

The father went to the printer and said, 'You and I know that the check is very valuable, but my son does not understand. Please give him cash so that he, too, will appreciate your generosity.'

So, too, it was when the Jews left Egypt. Both Hashem and Abraham realized that the slavery of Egypt would result in the most priceless of all possessions — the Torah. But Abraham would have legitimate grounds for complaint. The slavery and suffering were in a form that even the simplest Jew could comprehend — lashes, hunger, and oppression. Is it fair that the promise of *great possessions* be fulfilled only symbolically, in a form that could be understood only spiritually? Therefore, G-d asked Moses to arrange for its fulfillment in a tangible, monetary form that everyone would understand.

Borrow as an investment

‌ In addition to the question of why the request that the Jews enrich themselves at the expense of the Egyptians was only to forestall the recriminations of Abraham, *Chasam Sofer* raises another difficulty: The *Midrash (Shir HaShirim Rabbah* to 1:11) states that the treasures amassed by Israel after the Splitting of the Sea were even greater than those it took out of Egypt. That being so, it was hardly necessary for them to borrow from the Egyptians in order to fulfill the Divine pledge to Abraham.

Chasam Sofer replies that the Jews feared that if they were to leave Egypt, Pharaoh and his legions would swiftly reconsider having allowed so huge a source of

The *matzos* are covered and the cups lifted as the following paragraph is proclaimed joyously. Upon its conclusion, the cups are put down and the *matzos* again uncovered.

It is this that has stood by our fathers and us. For not only one has risen against us to annihilate us, but in every generation they rise against us to annihilate us. But the Holy One, Blessed be He, rescues us from their hand.

free labor to leave the country. The result would be an armed pursuit that would force the Jews back into slavery. However, they rationalized away this fear by claiming that Egypt would see no absolute necessity for the presence of a large slave nation — after all, had its neighbors not prospered without slaves? But if the Jews were to 'borrow' extremely valuable possessions from their erstwhile masters, wouldn't the Egyptians be outraged at the flight of the Jews and pursue them to retrieve their possessions? That being so, the Jews would be reluctant to borrow from the Egyptians. Hence the need to plead with them to borrow, because that would create the pretext for the Egyptians to pursue them wearing the finery that would fall into Jewish hands after the drowning of their pursuers.

וְהִיא שֶׁעָמְדָה — **It is this that has stood.**

Hashem's guarantee ◄§ What is this הִיא, *it*, which has protected us? [See above that it refers to the Covenant between the Parts.]

It refers to the שְׁכִינָה, *Hashem's Presence*, as in the following parable: A king exiled his son to a distant land for a specific period of time. The queen pleaded with her husband that he assure her that when the time of exile would elapse, he would remember to bring their son back home. The king said, 'You go with him. Since I can never forget you, I will be sure to think of him as well. Similarly, the *Shechinah* accompanies Israel into exile as the Psalmist said עִמוֹ אָנֹכִי בְצָרָה, *I [Hashem] am with him [Israel] in distress (Psalms 91:15)*. Since G-d's

צֵא וּלְמַד. מַה בִּקֵּשׁ לָבָן הָאֲרַמִּי לַעֲשׂוֹת לְיַעֲקֹב אָבִינוּ. שֶׁפַּרְעֹה לֹא גָזַר אֶלָּא עַל הַזְּכָרִים וְלָבָן בִּקֵּשׁ לַעֲקוֹר אֶת הַכֹּל. שֶׁנֶּאֱמַר. . .

Presence must always be safe from Its enemies, Israel, too, is protected (Haggadah Yetzias Mitzrayim).

Ingredients of survival

◦§ Abarbanel sees in the word וְהִיא an acronym that embodies the ingredients of Jewish survival:
וּ — Vav = 6: the Six Orders of the Mishnah;
ה — He = 5: the Five Books of Moses;
י — Yod = 10: the Ten Commandments;
א — Aleph = 1: the One G-d.

The unfriendly reminder

◦§ Rabbi Marcus Lehmann comments that this very persecution is the guarantor of Jewish eternity. Often in our history, the cordiality of a host has tempted us to assimilate and let go of our sense of apartness. Then, antisemitic hatred has shown us that we are indeed unique; we may forget it temporarily, but our enemies will always remind us that we are Jews. Thus, *this has stood* to protect us — what is this secret of our survival? The underlying enmity of our enemies.

The One Who matters

◦§ שֶׁלֹּא אֶחָד בִּלְבָד עָמַד עָלֵינוּ לְכַלּוֹתֵנוּ — *For not only one has arisen against us to destroy us.*
This expression of praise has been homiletically interpreted as an expression of confidence that no enemy, no matter how powerful, can defeat us because Hashem has not turned against us. Thus: We rejoice because אֶחָד בִּלְבָד, *The One and Only* [i.e., Hashem] has not arisen against us (Rabbi Baruch of Mezhibozh).

צֵא וּלְמַד — Go and learn

Search for the truth

◦§ Although the following paragraphs of the Haggadah elucidate the entire series of verses which are quoted from Devarim, no proof is cited for the first phrase which states that Laban attempted to destroy the family of Jacob. As a matter of fact, the Scriptural narrative of Laban and Jacob could be understood as rather

Go and learn what Laban the Aramean attempted to do to our father Jacob! For Pharaoh decreed only against the males, Laban attempted to uproot everything, as it is said: *(Devarim*

sympathetic to Laban. Only if one delves deeply into the inner motives behind Laban's surface gentility, and analyzes the eventual outcome of his supercilious conniving can one understand his true hostility to the destiny of Israel. To provide this sort of background would be too lengthy for it to be included in the *Haggadah.* Therefore, the author tells us וּלְמַד צֵא, *go and learn* — only through intensive study can we comprehend the truth of the statement about Laban *(Lail Shimurim).*

Do not be deceived

◄§ The *Haggadah* stresses the evil designs of Laban to accentuate a lesson that has relevance to all of Jewish history. It was only hundreds of years after Jacob's experience with Laban — when the Torah with this interpretation was given — that the extent of Laban's perfidy became known. For, as the *Midrash* states, when Laban pursued Jacob, he pretended wounded innocence at being denied the opportunity of kissing his daughters and grandchildren good-bye, his true intention was to murder Jacob. Often in our history we have been lulled into feelings of security in countries where our neighbors smiled upon us. More than one 'golden era' has ended in bloody disaster. Therefore, the *Haggadah* teaches us that after acknowledging that בְּכָל דּוֹר וָדוֹר, *in every generation,* there are enemies who rise up against us, we should go *out and learn* from the early affair of Laban that G-d shields us even when we are unaware of the danger — even when centuries go by before we become aware of the fangs lurking behind the smile *(Vilna Gaon).*

The extent of His mercy

◄§ שֶׁפַּרְעֹה לֹא גָזַר אֶלָּא עַל הַזְּכָרִים — *For Pharaoh decreed only against the males.*
It seems strange that on this night which is devoted to recounting the miracles of *Yetzias Mitzrayim,* we should make this statement which diminishes the extent

73   The Haggadah Treasury

אֲרַמִּי אֹבֵד אָבִי וַיֵּרֶד מִצְרַיְמָה וַיָּגָר שָׁם בִּמְתֵי
מְעָט וַיְהִי שָׁם לְגוֹי גָּדוֹל עָצוּם וָרָב:

of Pharaoh's evil. The intent, however, is to magnify
our perception of G-d's graciousness. The Torah
promises that Hashem will never allow Israel to be completely destroyed (Vayikra 26:44). This being so we
could understand that G-d was compelled to rescue
Jacob from the designs of Laban, but there would have
been no obligation under His pledge for G-d to combat
Pharaoh whose plan was to eliminate only a portion of
the nation. Nevertheless, G-d's love for Israel would
not permit even a *partial* destruction of His people
(*Ateres Zekeinim*).

Utilizing
halacha
to
destroy

וְלָבָן בִּקֵּשׁ לַעֲקוֹר אֶת כֹּל 🖎 — *Laban attempted to uproot*
everything.

Laban sought to destroy Israel's future by making it
impossible for Jacob to be born. The Torah relates that
Abraham dispatched Eliezer to find a suitable bride for
Isaac. The *Midrash* states that Laban attempted to
poison Eliezer. Had he succeeded, Isaac would have
been forbidden ever to marry because of the assump-
tion that an agent can be relied upon to have carried out
his mission. The *halachah* states that if an agent com-
pletes the act of קִדּוּשִׁין, *consecration*, by giving a con-
tract or money [the 'ring' of a marriage ceremony
creates a binding consecration because of its monetary
value] to a woman, and then the agent dies before in-
forming the groom of his bride's identity, the man is
forbidden ever to marry. The reason is that, lacking
conclusive proof as to who his bride is, whatever other
woman he may choose to marry may be a forbidden
relative of his unknown bride (*Gittin* 64a). Thus,
Laban's design against Eliezer would have had a result
even more far-reaching than Pharaoh's because the
Jewish nation would never have come into being
(*Chida*).

🖎 *Targum Yonason* to *Balak* states that Laban and
Bilam were one and the same. According to the

26:5) *An Aramean attempted to destroy my father. Then he descended to Egypt and sojourned there, with few people; and there he became a nation — great, mighty, and numerous.*

Laban's continuation

Midrash, Bilam was the one who advised Pharaoh to drown the Jewish infants. And as we know from the Torah's account in *Numbers (Ch.* 22-24), Bilam attempted to curse Israel in the desert. The *Midrash* relates that it was the same Bilam who caused a devastating plague against Israel by instigating the Midianites to send their women to seduce the Israelites. Thus, Laban's design to uproot Israel was one that he consistently pursued both against Jacob and, later, as Bilam, against the entire nation *(Sh'loh).*

The chain of events

אֲרַמִּי אֹבֵד אָבִי וַיֵּרֶד מִצְרַיְמָה — *An Aramean attempted to destroy my father. Then he descended to Egypt.*

The connection between these two unrelated events — Laban's duplicity and Jacob's descent to Egypt — requires explanation. Joseph, although the eleventh-born of Jacob's sons, was intended to be his first-born, both physically and spiritually because Jacob had intended to marry Rachel, Joseph's mother, before any of his other wives. As it was, Joseph was spiritually superior to his brothers, a fact that is apparent from Jacob's favored treatment of him, the award of *shevet* [i.e. separate tribe] status to each of Joseph's sons, Ephraim and Menashe, and Moses' reference to Joseph as בְּכוֹר, *first-born (Devarim* 33:17). The reason Joseph was not *born* first was because Laban tricked Jacob into marrying Leah instead of Rachel. Since Joseph was not the oldest, his brothers resented the special attention Jacob showed him with the tragic result that they sold Joseph into slavery, the precipitating factor in the eventual Egyptian exile *(Shabbos* 10b). Thus the connection of the two events — because of Laban's trickery which resulted in Joseph's enslavement, Jacob was forced to descend to Egypt. *(Alshich).*

וַיֵּרֶד מִצְרַיְמָה. אָנוּס עַל פִּי הַדִּבּוּר:

וַיָּגָר שָׁם. מְלַמֵּד שֶׁלֹּא יָרַד יַעֲקֹב אָבִינוּ לְהִשְׁתַּקֵּעַ
בְּמִצְרַיִם אֶלָּא לָגוּר שָׁם. שֶׁנֶּאֱמַר וַיֹּאמְרוּ אֶל פַּרְעֹה
לָגוּר בָּאָרֶץ בָּאנוּ כִּי אֵין מִרְעֶה לַצֹּאן אֲשֶׁר לַעֲבָדֶיךָ
כִּי־כָבֵד הָרָעָב בְּאֶרֶץ כְּנָעַן וְעַתָּה יֵשְׁבוּ נָא עֲבָדֶיךָ
בְּאֶרֶץ גֹּשֶׁן:

בִּמְתֵי מְעָט. כְּמָה שֶׁנֶּאֱמַר בְּשִׁבְעִים נֶפֶשׁ יָרְדוּ
אֲבֹתֶיךָ מִצְרָיְמָה וְעַתָּה שָׂמְךָ יהוה אֱלֹהֶיךָ כְּכוֹכְבֵי
הַשָּׁמַיִם לָרֹב:

Purging impurity ◆§ The *Midrash* relates that not only Rachel and Leah were daughters of Laban, but Bilhah and Zilpah, Jacob's other wives, were also daughters of Laban by his concubine. Thus all of Jacob's children were grandsons of the impure and immoral Laban. This impurity had to be purged from Israel before it could receive the Torah and Eretz Yisrael. The vehicle for this purging of impurity was the bitter exile of Egypt. Therefore, Egypt is called בּוּר הַבַּרְזֶל, *our iron smelting pot.* The word בַּרְזֶל (BaRZeL) is formed of the initials of Bilhah, Rachel, Zilpah, and Leah. This explains the connection between Laban and the exile (*Chasam Sofer*).

Softened exile ◆§ אָנוּס עַל פִּי הַדִּבּוּר — *Compelled by Divine deree.*
    This is an apparent contradiction in terms — if G-d commanded him to go then he cannot be considered to have been *coerced*!
    Vilna Gaon explains the discrepancy by citing the Talmud (*Shabbos* 89b): Jacob would have been dragged to Egypt in chains, if necessary, but because of his great merit, G-d caused him to go into exile as an honored guest of Pharaoh and Joseph who enabled him to live out his years serenely and prestigiously. Thus he

Then he descended to Egypt — compelled by Divine decree.

He sojourned there — this teaches that our father Jacob did not descend to Egypt to *settle*, but only to *sojourn temporarily*, as it says: *(Bereishis 47:4) They* (the sons of Jacob) *said to Pharaoh: 'We have come to sojourn in this land because there is no pasture for the flocks of your servants, because the famine is severe in the land of Canaan. And now, please let your servants dwell in the land of Goshen.'*

With few people — as it is written: *(Devarim 10:22) With seventy persons, your forefathers descended to Egypt, and now HASHEM, your God, has made you as numerous as the stars of heaven.*

was אָנוּס, *coerced,* in the sense that there was no way he could have avoided the exile which he feared so much, but it was softened for him עַל פִּי הַדִּבּוּר, *by the word of HASHEM,* who assured him that the outcome of his descent to Egypt would be that his children would flourish and become a great nation.

Power of unity ⧉§ בְּשִׁבְעִים נֶפֶשׁ — *With seventy persons.*

There is an apparent inconsistency in the phrase since the word שִׁבְעִים is plural, while the word נֶפֶשׁ [lit. *person* or *soul*] is singular.

However, the use of the singular alludes to an essential characteristic of Jewish life — unity. Any individual, no matter how great, cannot rise to the level of many people acting in concert. Thus we find that אֵין דָּבָר שֶׁבִּקְדוּשָׁה פָּחוֹת מֵעֲשָׂרָה, *no prayer of great holiness* [i.e. *Kedushah, Kaddish,* or *Borchu*] *may be uttered in the presence of less than ten people (Berachos 21b).* Ten teen-agers who pray together may recite passages which are forbidden to a great sage who prays alone. Therefore, too, we have the dictum that כָּל יִשְׂרָאֵל עֲרֵבִים זֶה לָזֶה, *all Jews are responsible for one another (Shavous 39a);* just as each limb of the body af-

וַיְהִי שָׁם לְגוֹי. מְלַמֵּד שֶׁהָיוּ יִשְׂרָאֵל מְצֻיָּנִים שָׁם:

גָּדוֹל עָצוּם. כְּמָה שֶׁנֶּאֱמַר וּבְנֵי יִשְׂרָאֵל פָּרוּ
וַיִּשְׁרְצוּ וַיִּרְבּוּ וַיַּעַצְמוּ בִּמְאֹד מְאֹד וַתִּמָּלֵא הָאָרֶץ
אֹתָם:

וָרָב. כְּמָה שֶׁנֶּאֱמַר רְבָבָה כְּצֶמַח הַשָּׂדֶה נְתַתִּיךְ
וַתִּרְבִּי וַתִּגְדְּלִי וַתָּבֹאִי בַּעֲדִי עֲדָיִים שָׁדַיִם נָכֹנוּ
וּשְׂעָרֵךְ צִמֵּחַ וְאַתְּ עֵרֹם וְעֶרְיָה:

fects the well-being of the others, so each Jew is important to the nation. Hence, when the Jewish *nation* began
to take shape, it was called נֶפֶשׁ, as if it were a *single
person.* The six members of Esau's family, however, are
called נְפָשׁוֹת, *persons (Bereishis 36:6)* — in the plural —
because they did not possess this unity *(Divrei Shaul).*

A nation ⋖§ וַיְהִי שָׁם לְגוֹי מְלַמֵּד שֶׁהָיוּ ... מְצֻיָּנִים — *There it became
a nation this teaches that Israel was distinctive.*

How can we tell from the Scriptual text that they
remained distinctive?

The key word is גּוֹי, a nation. Experience shows that
immigrant groups tend to adopt the customs and
culture of their host country until, with the passage of a
few generations, they assimilate and become in-
distinguishable as a separate entity. The fact that the
Torah refers to Israel as גּוֹי, *a* [recognizable] *nation,*
proves that they remained distinctive *(Yetzias
Mitzrayim).*

**Nevertheless
mighty** ⋖§ וַיִּרְבּוּ וַיַּעַצְמוּ — *They multiplied and became mighty.*

In the case of multiple births such as twins or
triplets, it is common that the infants will be less sturdy
than a baby born in a single birth. In Egypt, since
Jewish mothers gave birth to six babies in a single litter
(see *Rashi* to *Shemos* 1:7), we would have expected the
infants to be particularly frail. Therefore, the verse

There he became a nation — this teaches that Israel were distinctive there.

Great, mighty — as it says: *(Sh'mos 1:7) And the Children of Israel were fruitful, increased greatly, multiplied, and became very, very mighty; and the land was filled with them.*

Numerous — as it says: *(Yechezkel 16:7) I made you as numerous as the plants of the field; you grew and developed, and became charming, beautiful of figure; your hair grown long; but, you were naked and bare. (Yechezkel 16:6) And I passed over you and saw you downtrodden in your blood and*

emphasizes that, to the contrary, they not only *multiplied*, but were *mighty (Divrei Shaul).*

Strength in numbers ⋄ כְּצֶמַח הַשָּׂדֶה — *Like the plants of the field.* What is the analogy of *plants?*—
Individual blades of grass have no value; it is only the combination of countless blades which are significant. So, too, Israel — the greatness of Israel is its unity as a nation; no individual can equal the greatness of the group working together *(Lail Shimurim).*

Affliction strengthens ⋄ — It is a characteristic of grass that the more it is cut the more it grows. Israel is the same. The more Egypt afflicted the Jews, the more they flourished, as the Torah testifies וְכַאֲשֶׁר יְעַנּוּ אֹתוֹ כֵּן יִרְבֶּה וְכֵן יִפְרֹץ, *as they afflicted it* [i.e. the Jewish nation] *so it increased and so it spread (Sh'mos 1:12).* As *Ramban* explains, this is why the tribe of Levi was much smaller than the other tribes. The Levites were not enslaved and afflicted, therefore they did not receive G-d's blessing of increase in the face of Egyptian persecution *(Bamidbar 3:14).*
The presence of an egg on the *Seder* plate alludes to this characteristic of Israel. Generally, foods become softer as they are cooked longer and longer; eggs, however, become harder. Israel, too, becomes firmer in its loyalty to G-d in the face of persecution.

79   The Haggadah Treasury

וָאֶעֱבוֹר עָלַיִךְ וָאֶרְאֵךְ מִתְבּוֹסֶסֶת בְּדָמָיִךְ וָאֹמַר לָךְ
בְּדָמַיִךְ חֲיִי וָאֹמַר לָךְ בְּדָמַיִךְ חֲיִי:

וַיָּרֵעוּ אֹתָנוּ הַמִּצְרִים וַיְעַנּוּנוּ וַיִּתְּנוּ עָלֵינוּ עֲבֹדָה
קָשָׁה:

וַיָּרֵעוּ אֹתָנוּ הַמִּצְרִים. כְּמָה שֶׁנֶּאֱמַר הָבָה נִתְחַכְּמָה
לוֹ פֶּן יִרְבֶּה וְהָיָה כִּי תִקְרֶאנָה מִלְחָמָה וְנוֹסַף גַּם הוּא
עַל שֹׂנְאֵינוּ וְנִלְחַם בָּנוּ וְעָלָה מִן הָאָרֶץ:

Willingness to be apart

◈§ וָאֹמַר לָךְ בְּדָמַיִךְ חֲיִי, וָאֹמַר לָךְ בְּדָמַיִךְ חֲיִי — *And I said to you, 'Through your blood shall you live!' And I said to you, 'Through your blood shall you live!'*

In Yechezkel's parable the Jewish people are described as 'naked' in the sense that they had no commandments to make them deserving of G-d's intervention. But the time for redemption had come, as symbolized by the phrase בָּעֲדִי עֲדָיִים, *you came to be of great charm*, which, *Alshich* notes, has the numerical equivalent of 210, the number of years which Israel had been in Egypt. [*Alshich's gematria* apparently omits the last *yod* which could conceivably be considered superfluous.] In order to provide them with sufficient merit to make them worthy of redemption, G-d gave them two commandments: circumcision — which, although commanded to Abraham, had come to be neglected in Egypt — and the sacrifice of the Passover lamb. Both commandments involved blood, a fact which is alluded to by the repetition of *'Through your blood shall you live'*, one refers to the blood of circumcision and the other to the blood of the sacrifice (*Mechilta*).

These commandments indicated a willingness to separate themselves from the world of Egypt: circumcision by carrying on one's body the distinctive mark of the *Milah* covenant, and the Passover offering which

I said to you: 'Through your blood shall you live!' And I said to you: 'Through your blood shall you live!'

The Egyptians did evil to us and afflicted us; and imposed hard labor upon us *(Devarim 26:6):*

The Egyptians did evil to us — as it says: *(Sh'mos 1:10) Let us deal with them wisely lest they multiply and, if we happen to be at war, they may join our enemies and fight against us and then leave the country.*

meant the sacrifice of the animal which the Egyptians considered to be a god. Both of these commandments involved danger: the circumcision from the serious nature of the operation, and the sacrifice from the potential retaliation by the Egyptians. Thus, by their willingness to die for the sake of G-d's command, the Jews proved they deserved to ennoble life as G-d's people *(Elias Haggadah).*

וַיָּרֵעוּ אֹתָנוּ הַמִּצְרִים — And the Egyptians did evil to us

Accusing us of evil ⧫§ The phrase is grammatically difficult. According to the accepted translation which we have followed [i.e. that the Egyptians inflicted evil upon Israel] the word לָנוּ, *to us*, would be the proper object of the verb. The use of אֹתָנוּ, *us*, however, indicates that *they made us become evil.*

Alschich comments that the Egyptians carried their evil even further than the physical oppression. They justified their cruelty by accusing the Jews of ingratitude for the 'generous' hospitality of Egypt. Thus their propaganda made *us* appear to be the evil ones. *Chasam Sofer* elaborates on that concept by noting that the destruction of a reputation is a great evil in itself. That the Egyptians impugned a nation noted for its feelings of appreciation to its benefactors adds another dimension to their evil-doing.

וַיְעַנּוּנוּ. כְּמָה שֶׁנֶּאֱמַר וַיָּשִׂימוּ עָלָיו שָׂרֵי מִסִּים
לְמַעַן עַנֹּתוֹ בְּסִבְלֹתָם וַיִּבֶן עָרֵי מִסְכְּנוֹת לְפַרְעֹה אֶת
פִּתֹם וְאֶת רַעַמְסֵס:

וַיִּתְּנוּ עָלֵינוּ עֲבֹדָה קָשָׁה. כְּמָה שֶׁנֶּאֱמַר וַיַּעֲבִדוּ
מִצְרַיִם אֶת בְּנֵי יִשְׂרָאֵל בְּפָרֶךְ:

Parasites ◆§ In a similar view *Abarbanel* comments that it has
been a standard procedure for the enemies of Israel
to lay the foundation for acceptance of their vicious
decrees by slandering us. Thus we are depicted as dis-
loyal parasites who exploit the host country for our
own ends, but who are in reality its enemies and a
danger to its citizens. That done, the persecution to follow has been justified. To this, the *Haggadah* alludes:
וַיָּרֵעוּ אֹתָנוּ, they made *us* the bad ones.

The   ◆§ וַיִּבֶן עָרֵי מִסְכְּנוֹת — *And it* [i.e. the nation of Israel]
ultimate   *built treasure cities.*
cruelty   The *Midrash* states that Pisom and Raamses were so
vulnerable to earthquakes and other natural disasters,
that the buildings put up by the Jews were constantly
demolished. This being so, why didn't the Egyptians
have their cities built in a more practical part of the
country?
    Harav Avraham Pam explained the motives of
Pharaoh by citing a tragic incident that occurred in a
Siberian prison camp. A prisoner sentenced to twenty-
five years at hard labor was chained to a heavy stone
wheel which he was forced to turn day after day. Once
he asked a guard what the wheel was attached to. The
guard told him that it was connected to a flour mill. The
prisoner was gratified — at least his back-breaking
labor was productive. Thanks to him, flour was
produced which would feed hungry people. Upon being released at the end of his sentence, he asked to see
the mill which he had operated for all of those years.
The prison official looked at him incredulously.

And Afflicted us — as it says: *(Sh'mos 1:11) They set taskmasters over them in order to oppress them with their burdens; and they built Pithom and Raamses as treasure cities for Pharaoh.*

They imposed hard labor upon us — as it says: *(ibid. 1:13) The Egyptians subjugated the children of Israel with hard labor.*

'What mill?' he asked. 'Your wheel was attached to nothing.'

Hearing this, the prisoner was horrified. For twenty-five years, he had suffered inhumanly — to no purpose! He fell into a state of depression from which he never recovered.

This was Pharaoh's intention. Not content to break Israel's body, he wanted to break its spirit as well by subjecting it to the purposeless task of constructing doomed buildings.

When a friend betrays
◆§ בְּפָרֶךְ — *With hard labor*

Noting that פֶּרֶךְ, *hard labor*, contains the word רַךְ, *soft*, the Sages comment that at first, the service was 'soft' and easy, for the Egyptians spoke in terms of voluntary service to the state. Only later did it become hard and back-breaking.

The *K'sav Sofer* explains that the 'soft' treatment referred to Jacob's years in Egypt when his hosts smothered his family in kindness and friendship. The Jews became convinced that the Egyptians were truly their friends. Then, their subsequent betrayal became much harder to bear; the treachery of an ally hurts much more than the barbs of an enemy. The Torah purposely alludes to the early friendship in order to emphasize how much deeper was the later hurt.

Disrupted lives
◆§ The hard work which the Jews were forced to do was בְּחֹמֶר וּבִלְבֵנִים וּבְכָל עֲבֹדָה בַּשָּׂדֶה, *with mortar, with bricks, and with all the work of the field (Sh'mos 1:14)*. In mentioning the varieties of work, the Torah indicates why it was so difficult. People can adjust to

וַנִּצְעַק אֶל יְהוָה אֱלֹהֵי אֲבֹתֵינוּ וַיִּשְׁמַע יְהוָה אֶת
קֹלֵנוּ וַיַּרְא אֶת־עָנְיֵנוּ וְאֶת־עֲמָלֵנוּ וְאֶת־לַחֲצֵנוּ:

וַנִּצְעַק אֶל־יְהוָה אֱלֹהֵי אֲבֹתֵינוּ. כְּמָה שֶּׁנֶּאֱמַר וַיְהִי
בַיָּמִים הָרַבִּים הָהֵם וַיָּמָת מֶלֶךְ מִצְרַיִם וַיֵּאָנְחוּ בְנֵי־

hardship and even backbreaking labor as long as it is constant, for then they can develop resistance and learn to cope with it. But if people are constantly re-assigned from one task to another, they cannot cope with the uncertainty and the impossibility of forming patterns in their lives. The Egyptians devised a variety of tasks and constantly shifted the slaves from one to another, never giving them a chance to accustom themselves to any one task (K'sav Sofer).

וַנִּצְעַק אֶל ה' אֱלֹקֵי אֲבֹתֵנוּ וַיִּשְׁמַע ה' אֶת קֹלֵנוּ — And we cried out to HASHEM, the God of our fathers, and HASHEM heard our cry.

Greatness in humility ⋅≈ When the Jews cried to Hashem, they thought themselves undeserving of His help. Therefore, they prayed to Him as the G-d of their *forefathers*, hoping to be rescued in their merit. But G-d heard קֹלֵנוּ, 'our' voice. As the Sages say (*Berachos* 10b), one who modestly seeks assistance only in the merit of others, is considered to be deserving on his own account (*Pidyon Shevuyim*).

The proper outcry ⋅≈ There are two types of enslavement: the physical one which subjugates the body, and the spiritual one which stifles the soul. The very cruel physical affliction had caused Israel to cry out in anguish for many years, but G-d ignored that outcry because it was not directed against the true danger. However, when they cried out אֶל ה' אֱלֹקֵי אֲבֹתֵנוּ, *to HASHEM the G-d of our forefathers*, indicating that it was a spiritual outcry seeking salvation from the cancer that was eating away at their souls — now וַיִּשְׁמַע ה' אֶת קֹלֵנוּ, *HASHEM heard our outcry* (*Harav Yonasan Steif*).

We cried out to HASHEM, the God of our fathers; and HASHEM heard our cry and saw our affliction, our burden, and our oppression. (Devarim 26:7).

We cried out to HASHEM, the God of our fathers — as it says: *(Sh'mos 2:23) It happened in the course of those many days that the king of Egypt died; and the children of Israel*

Sovereignty in life

⋖§ וַיָּמָת מֶלֶךְ מִצְרַיִם — *The king of Egypt died.*

The Sages comment that Pharaoh died not literally, but figuratively: he became a מְצוֹרָע, *leper*, who is considered as if dead. How do the Sages know that the narrative is not to be taken literally?

Vilna Gaon explains that the word מֶלֶךְ, *king*, implies sovereignty. Because a dead king no longer reigns he should not be referred to by his royal title, but by his given name only. For example, in relating the death of King David, Scripture says וַיִּשְׁכַּב דָּוִד עִם אֲבֹתָיו, *and David lay with his forefathers (I Melachim 2:10)*. He is called only *David*, not *King* David.

According to this rule, had Pharaoh truly died he should not have been described as the *king* of Egypt. Therefore the Sages infer that he was still alive, and that his 'death' was figurative.

Proof of corruption

⋖§ וַיָּמָת מֶלֶךְ מִצְרַיִם וַיֵּאָנְחוּ בְנֵי יִשְׂרָאֵל — *The king of Egypt died and the Children of Israel groaned.*

It was when one Pharaoh died and his successor continued the cruel decrees against the Jews that Israel groaned and cried out to Hashem. For, as long as injustice is not passed on from one reign to the next, there is hope that a country will modify its laws for the better. But when injustice and cruelty become a tradition, then it is no longer possible to eradicate them. Therefore, it was when the Jews saw that a change of rulers brought no change in policy that they cried out in anguish *(Hirsch).*

A double horror

⋖§ According to *Rashi*, the king had become a leper and began the wholesale slaughter of Jewish children so that he could bathe in their blood. This

יִשְׂרָאֵל מִן־הָעֲבֹדָה וַיִּזְעָקוּ וַתַּעַל שַׁוְעָתָם אֶל־
הָאֱלֹהִים מִן־הָעֲבֹדָה:

וַיִּשְׁמַע יהוה אֶת־קֹלֵנוּ. כְּמָה שֶׁנֶּאֱמַר וַיִּשְׁמַע
אֱלֹהִים אֶת־נַאֲקָתָם וַיִּזְכֹּר אֱלֹהִים אֶת־בְּרִיתוֹ אֶת־
אַבְרָהָם אֶת־יִצְחָק וְאֶת־יַעֲקֹב:

וַיַּרְא אֶת־עָנְיֵנוּ. זוֹ פְּרִישׁוּת דֶּרֶךְ אֶרֶץ. כְּמָה
שֶׁנֶּאֱמַר וַיַּרְא אֱלֹהִים אֶת־בְּנֵי יִשְׂרָאֵל וַיֵּדַע אֱלֹהִים:

created a new horror for Israel, quite apart from the
atrocity visited upon their children. Until then, Israel
had known that there were two ways by which it could
leave Egypt before the 400 years were up: by becoming
so populous than an equivalent amount of work would
be done in a briefer period of time; or by being sub-
jected to so intense a servitude that fewer years of hard
labor would be equivalent to the full 400 years of normal work. Now that their population was being
reduced by the murder of their children, the Jews
realized that only by a severe intensification of the
slavery could they succeed in being redeemed sooner.
Thus the extent of their anguish at the loss of the infants was made even more by the realization of what
the effects would be on the living.

For G-d's ⇛ וַתַּעַל שַׁוְעָתָם אֶל הָאֱלֹקִים מִן הָעֲבֹדָה — *And their*
suffering *cry because of their servitude rose up to G-d.*
Rabbi Levi Yitzchok of Berditchev, the great lover
and protagonist of Israel, interprets thus: The Jews had
two reasons to cry out. They could endure the painful
affliction no longer, and they realized that G-d, too,
suffers when Israel is afflicted. This verse says in their
praise that their outcry *to G-d* [i.e. their anguish for His
suffering] was far more pronounced than the groaning
because of the work.

groaned because of the servitude and cried; their cry because of the servitude rose up to God.'

HASHEM heard our cry — as it says: *(Sh'mos 2:24) God heard their groaning, and God recalled His covenant with Abraham, with Isaac, and with Jacob.*

And saw our affliction — that is the disruption of family life, as it says: *(ibid. v. 25) God saw the children of Israel and God took note.*

Three causes for redemption

וַיַּרְא אֶת עָנְיֵנוּ זוֹ פְּרִישׁוּת דֶּרֶךְ אֶרֶץ ... וְאֶת עֲמָלֵנוּ אֵלוּ הַבָּנִים ... וְאֶת לַחֲצֵנוּ זוֹ הַדְּחַק — *And He saw our affliction [this refers to the disruption of family life] ... and our burden [this refers to the children] ... and our oppression [this refers to the pressure].*

These three aspects of the suffering were instrumental in hastening the redemption. The Sages deal with the question of why Israel was redeemed after only 210 years instead of the 400 years prophesied to Abraham. Three explanations are offered:

1— The Egyptians forced the Jews to work at night as well as by day, thus hastening the completion of the work that would normally require 400 years.

2— Israel became so populous that the increased labor force completed the Divinely intended work in less time.

3— The severity of the oppression was so intense that the reduced time was equivalent to 400 years.

All three explanations are implied in this verse: The Jewish family life was disrupted because husbands were forced to work at night [אֶת עָנְיֵנוּ זוֹ פְּרִישׁוּת דֶּרֶךְ אֶרֶץ, *our affliction — this alludes to the disruption of family life*];

The large number of children enabled more work to be done [וְאֶת עֲמָלֵנוּ אֵלוּ הַבָּנִים, *and our burden — this alludes to the children*];

The intensity of the enslavement compensated for the diminished years of subjugation. [וְאֶת לַחֲצֵנוּ זוֹ הַדְּחַק

וְאֶת עֲמָלֵנוּ. אֵלוּ הַבָּנִים. כְּמָה שֶׁנֶּאֱמַר כָּל־הַבֵּן
הַיִּלּוֹד הַיְאֹרָה תַּשְׁלִיכֻהוּ וְכָל־הַבַּת תְּחַיּוּן:

וְאֶת לַחֲצֵנוּ. זֶה הַדְּחַק. כְּמָה שֶׁנֶּאֱמַר וְגַם־רָאִיתִי
אֶת־הַלַּחַץ אֲשֶׁר מִצְרַיִם לֹחֲצִים אֹתָם:

וַיּוֹצִאֵנוּ יְהֹוָה מִמִּצְרַיִם בְּיָד חֲזָקָה וּבִזְרֹעַ נְטוּיָה
וּבְמֹרָא גָּדֹל וּבְאֹתוֹת וּבְמֹפְתִים:

וַיּוֹצִאֵנוּ יְהֹוָה מִמִּצְרַיִם. לֹא עַל־יְדֵי מַלְאָךְ וְלֹא
עַל־יְדֵי שָׂרָף וְלֹא עַל־יְדֵי שָׁלִיחַ. אֶלָּא הַקָּדוֹשׁ בָּרוּךְ
הוּא בִּכְבוֹדוֹ וּבְעַצְמוֹ. שֶׁנֶּאֱמַר וְעָבַרְתִּי בְאֶרֶץ־
מִצְרַיִם בַּלַּיְלָה הַזֶּה וְהִכֵּיתִי כָל־בְּכוֹר בְּאֶרֶץ מִצְרַיִם
מֵאָדָם וְעַד בְּהֵמָה וּבְכָל אֱלֹהֵי מִצְרַיִם אֶעֱשֶׂה
שְׁפָטִים אֲנִי יְהֹוָה:

וְעָבַרְתִּי בְאֶרֶץ־מִצְרַיִם בַּלַּיְלָה הַזֶּה. אֲנִי וְלֹא
מַלְאָךְ. וְהִכֵּיתִי כָל־בְּכוֹר בְּאֶרֶץ־מִצְרַיִם. אֲנִי וְלֹא
שָׂרָף. וּבְכָל־אֱלֹהֵי מִצְרַיִם אֶעֱשֶׂה שְׁפָטִים. אֲנִי וְלֹא
הַשָּׁלִיחַ. אֲנִי יְהֹוָה. אֲנִי הוּא וְלֹא אַחֵר:

and our oppression — this alludes to the pressure].
(Chanukas HaTorah).

Vain ⋅§ עֲמָלֵנוּ אֵלוּ הַבָּנִים — Our burden — this refers to the
exertion children.

Divrei Shaul explains how the Sages knew that עָמָל,
burden, refers to children. The word is often used with
particular reference to vain exertions as in וְהָרָה עָמָל וְיָלַד
שָׁקֶר, he [i.e. a wicked person] is pregnant with evil
schemes and brings forth falsehood (Tehillim 7:15).
The tragic plight of Jewish parents was that they would

Our burden — refers to the children as it says: *(Sh'mos 1:2-2) Every son that is born you shall cast into the river, but every daughter you shall let live.*

Our oppression — refers to the pressure expressed in the words: *(ibid. 3:9) I have also seen how the Egyptians are oppressing them.*

HASHEM brought us out of Egypt with a mighty hand and with an outstretched arm, with great awe, with signs and with wonders (Devarim 26:8).

HASHEM brought us out of Egypt — not through an angel, not through a seraph, not through a messenger, but the Holy One, blessed be He, in His glory, Himself, as it says: *(Sh'mos 12:12) I will pass through the land of Egypt on that night; I will slay all the firstborn in the land of Egypt from man to beast; and upon all the gods of Egypt will I execute judgments; I, HASHEM.*

'I will pass through the land of Egypt on that night' — I and no angel;
'I will slay all the firstborn in the land of Egypt' — I and no seraph;
'And upon all the gods of Egypt will I execute judgments' — I and no messenger;
'I, HASHEM' — it is I and no other.

give birth in vain — because the Egyptians hurled the newborn infants into the river to drown.

וַיּוֹצִאֵנוּ ה' מִמִּצְרַיִם — HASHEM brought us out of Egypt

No natural deaths ⇛ וְהִכֵּיתִי כָל בְּכוֹר בְּאֶרֶץ מִצְרַיִם — אֲנִי וְלֹא שָׂרָף ⇦ — *And I will execute every first-born — I and not a seraph.* The *Haggadah* cites the *Midrash* which states that

בְּיָד חֲזָקָה. זוֹ הַדֶּבֶר. כְּמָה שֶׁנֶּאֱמַר הִנֵּה יַד יהוה
הוֹיָה בְּמִקְנְךָ אֲשֶׁר בַּשָּׂדֶה בַּסּוּסִים בַּחֲמֹרִים בַּגְּמַלִּים
בַּבָּקָר וּבַצֹּאן דֶּבֶר כָּבֵד מְאֹד:

וּבִזְרֹעַ נְטוּיָה. זוֹ הַחֶרֶב. כְּמָה שֶׁנֶּאֱמַר וְחַרְבּוֹ
שְׁלוּפָה בְּיָדוֹ נְטוּיָה עַל-יְרוּשָׁלָיִם:

וּבְמֹרָא גָּדֹל. זוֹ גִלּוּי שְׁכִינָה. כְּמָה שֶׁנֶּאֱמַר אוֹ
הֲנִסָּה אֱלֹהִים לָבוֹא לָקַחַת לוֹ גוֹי מִקֶּרֶב גוֹי בְּמַסֹּת
בְּאֹתֹת וּבְמוֹפְתִים וּבְמִלְחָמָה וּבְיָד חֲזָקָה וּבִזְרוֹעַ
נְטוּיָה וּבְמוֹרָאִים גְּדֹלִים כְּכֹל אֲשֶׁר-עָשָׂה לָכֶם יהוה
אֱלֹהֵיכֶם בְּמִצְרַיִם לְעֵינֶיךָ:

G-d Himself carried out the execution of the first-born,
but this seems to contradict the verse in which Moses
announced that (Sh'mos 12:23): Israel need not fear
that any of its number would suffer during the final
plague when the Egyptian first-born were killed: וְלֹא
יִתֵּן הַמַּשְׁחִית לָבֹא אֶל בָּתֵּיכֶם לִנְגֹּף, and He will not permit
the destroyer [i.e. the Angel of Death] to enter your
homes to kill. This verse implies that the plague was
carried out by a מַשְׁחִית, destroyer, not by Hashem!

The Vilna Gaon answers that there would have
otherwise been two forms of death that night: the
plague upon the first-born which was indeed carried
out exclusively by G-d without the intervention of the
Angel of Death, and the normal process of dying in the
course of which the Angel of Death would inflict
natural deaths upon people who had lived out their
years. Among Israel with its total of approximately
three million people, there were surely people who
would have died that night. Had they done so, however,
the Egyptians could have pointed to them and said that
they were victims of the plague. The Torah tells us that
to avoid that eventuality, G-d did not permit the

With a mighty hand — refers to the pestilence, as it says: *(Sh'mos 9:3) Behold, the* hand *of HASHEM shall strike your cattle which are in the field, the horses, the donkeys, the camels, the herds, and the flocks — a very severe pestilence.*

With an outstretched arm — refers to the sword, as it says; *(I Divrei Hayamim 21:16) His drawn sword in his hand, out-stretched over Jerusalem.*

With great awe — alludes to the revelation of the Shechinah, as it says: *(Devarim 4:34) Has God ever attempted to take unto Himself a nation from the midst of another nation by trials, miraculous signs, and wonders, by war and with a mighty hand and outstretched arm and by awesome revelations, as all that HASHEM your God did for you in Egypt, before your eyes?*

Two-fold plague
destroyer to go about even his normal rounds that night.

— *Bais Halevi* answers that a two-fold plague struck Egypt that night: the first-born were killed by the hand of G-d, after which G-d dispatched an angel to spread a pestilence caused by the multitude of dead bodies. It was that secondary plague of pestilence which G-d ordered the *destroyer* not to bring into the Jewish homes.

Demonstrating Hashem's might
◆§בְּיָד חֲזָקָה זוּ הַדֶּבֶר§◆ — *With a mighty hand — this refers to the pestilence.*

Why should דֶּבֶר, *pestilence*, be singled out from among all the plagues as symbolic of G-d's *mighty hand?*

Throughout history, people and nations have deified natural forces or phenomena, people or animals. Whenever these creatures are proven to be no less under Hashem's jurisdiction than any other aspect of the universe, His Name has been sanctified. Egypt worshiped its livestock, particularly its sheep. Thus, when the plague of *pestilence* struck at the animals, it

וּבְאֹתוֹת זֶה הַמַּטֶּה. כְּמָה שֶׁנֶּאֱמַר וְאֶת־הַמַּטֶּה הַזֶּה תִּקַּח בְּיָדֶךָ אֲשֶׁר תַּעֲשֶׂה בּוֹ אֶת־הָאֹתֹת:

וּבְמֹפְתִים זֶה הַדָּם. כְּמָה שֶׁנֶּאֱמַר וְנָתַתִּי מוֹפְתִים בַּשָּׁמַיִם וּבָאָרֶץ

As each of the words דָם, אֵשׁ, and עָשָׁן is said, a bit of wine is removed from the cup. Some do it with the finger and others by pouring. The same procedure is followed later upon mention of the Ten Plagues and again when saying דְּצַ"ךְ עַדַ"שׁ, בְּאַחַ"ב. The wine removed from the cup is not used.

דָם וָאֵשׁ וְתִמְרוֹת עָשָׁן:

became known that not they, but Hashem, is the true G-d. Thus, this plague was a clear demonstration of G-d's power — *a mighty hand!* (*Harav Yisrael Belsky*).

Inscribed on the staff
◆§ וּבְאֹתוֹת זֶה הַמַּטֶּה — *And with signs — this refers to [the miracles performed with] the staff.*
The staff of Moses was intimately involved with the plagues that were the *signs* of G-d's mastery. The word אֹתוֹת, *signs,* is interpreted as if it were spelled אֹתִיוֹת, *letters* — indicating that on the staff were inscribed the initials of the plagues [דְּצַ"ךְ עַדַ"שׁ בְּאַחַ"ב] because Moses was to use the staff to bring on the plagues (*Kol Bo*).

דָם וָאֵשׁ וְתִמְרוֹת עָשָׁן — **Blood, and fire, and columns of smoke**

Cup not full
◆§ It is customary to remove some wine from our cups when saying these words, and again later when the plagues are mentioned. There are two customary ways to remove the wine: some pour a bit from their cups while others remove it with their finger. *Harav Joseph Elias* in his *Haggadah* explains the derivation of the two customs.
Avudraham explains that wine is removed because '*you should not rejoice when your enemy falls (Mishlei*

With signs — refers to the miracles performed with the staff as it says: *(Sh'mos* 4:17) *Take this staff in your hand, that you may perform the miraculous signs with it.*

With wonders — alludes to the blood, as it says: *(Yoel* 3:3) *I will show wonders in the heavens and on the earth:*

As each of the words דָם, אֵש, and עָשָן is said, a bit of wine is removed from the cup. Some do it with the finger and others by pouring. The same procedure is followed later upon mention of the Ten Plagues and again when saying דְּצַ״ךְ עֲדַ״ש, בְּאַחַ״ב. The wine removed from the cup is not used.

Blood, fire, and columns of smoke.

24:17). Accordingly, wine would be *poured out* from the cup of happiness to indicate our sorrow at the suffering of other human beings.

Darkei Mosheh, however, cites the removal of the wine as a reminder that the plagues were *the finger* [i.e. a manifestation] *of G-d (Sh'mos* 8:15). Accordingly the symbolism indicates that the finger be used to remove the wine.

No joy in death ◄§ In accordance with the principle that one should not celebrate the downfall of his enemies, the Torah speaks of *Pesach* as the season of our liberation rather than as the time when the Egyptians were decimated. For the same reason, the festival status of the Seventh Day of *Pesach* was proclaimed to the Jews while they were still in Egypt, even though the observance of that day was not to commence until the following year. If the announcement of the Seventh Day festival had been delayed until the following year, it would have seemed as though it were celebrated only to commemorate the drowning of the Egyptians at the sea. That, however, was not the case — indeed, a festival would not have been proclaimed for that purpose. Therefore, the future celebration of the day was made known before the Splitting of the Sea took place *(Meshech Chochmah).*

דָּבָר אַחֵר בְּיָד חֲזָקָה שְׁתַּיִם. וּבִזְרֹעַ נְטוּיָה שְׁתַּיִם.
וּבְמֹרָא גָּדֹל שְׁתַּיִם. וּבְאֹתוֹת שְׁתַּיִם. וּבְמֹפְתִים
שְׁתַּיִם: אֵלּוּ עֶשֶׂר מַכּוֹת שֶׁהֵבִיא הַקָּדוֹשׁ בָּרוּךְ הוּא
עַל־הַמִּצְרִים בְּמִצְרַיִם וְאֵלּוּ הֵן:

דָּם. צְפַרְדֵּעַ. כִּנִּים. עָרוֹב. דֶּבֶר. שְׁחִין. בָּרָד. אַרְבֶּה.
חֹשֶׁךְ. מַכַּת בְּכוֹרוֹת:

Drop
in a
cup
◦§ Another reason for the pouring out of the wine is given by *Zevach L'Pesach*. The *Yerushalmi* comments that the Four Cups of the *Seder* represent the 'four cups of retribution and punishment' which G-d will bring upon the nations which persecute Israel. Therefore, upon the mention of each plague, we remove a *drop* of wine from our cup to suggest that the plagues brought upon the Egyptians were like 'a drop in the bucket' compared to what will occur during the time of the final redemption.

The angel
is
defeated
◦§ שֶׁהֵבִיא הקב״ה עַל הַמִּצְרִים בְּמִצְרַיִם — *Which the Holy One, Blessed be He, brought upon the Egyptians in Egypt.*
The word בְּמִצְרַיִם, *in Egypt*, seems to be redundant. *Simchas HaRegel* explains that Hashem appoints an angel to oversee the interests and needs of each nation. Among his responsibilities as G-d's agent, this heavenly being intercedes whenever his charges are threatened by punishment. For the Egyptians to be punished, their angel, the שַׂר שֶׁל מִצְרַיִם, *minister of Egypt*, had to be defeated first, in the sense that his arguments in defense of the Egyptians had to be refuted. Thus the phrase is rendered: These are the ten plagues which Hashem brought upon the Egyptians בְּמִצְרַיִם, *through* [having defeated] *Mitzrayim*, i.e. the heavenly angel of Egypt.

But not
the sea
◦§ Another reason that the Torah specifies 'in Egypt' is because, as the *Haggadah* will later cite, the Sages expound that the Egyptians were afflicted five-fold at the sea *(Reb Avrahan Yitzchak Gold).*

Another explanation of the preceding verse: [Each phrase represents two plagues], hence: *mighty hand* — two; *outstretched arm* — two; *great awe* — two; *signs* — two; *wonders* — two. These are the ten plagues which the Holy One, blessed be He, brought upon the Egyptians in Egypt, namely:

1.Blood   2. Frogs   3. Vermin   4. Wild Beasts
5. Pestilence   6. Boils   7. Hail   8. Locusts
9. Darkness   10. Plague of the First-born

אֵלּוּ עֶשֶׂר מַכּוֹת — These are the ten plagues.

Measure for measure   ᴇᔆ The *Midrash* states that the ten plagues were מִדָּה כְּנֶגֶד מִדָּה, *measure for measure;* each plague was in punishment for an injustice of a similar sort that the Egyptians inflicted upon the Jews:

דָּם, **Blood** — Because the Egyptians did not permit טְבִילָה, *ritual bathing,* in their waters, the waters of Egypt were changed to *blood,* making them unusable to the Egyptians themselves;

צְפַרְדֵּעַ, **Frogs** — Because the Egyptians forced Jews to carry various types of insects and rodents, *frogs* descended upon them, making it impossible for them to walk in peace;

כִּנִּים, **Vermin** — Because the Egyptians degraded the Jews by forcing them to sweep the dusty streets, the dust was transformed into *vermin;*

עָרוֹב, **Wild Beasts** — Because the Egyptians forced the Jews to endanger themselves by bringing wild animals for public entertainment, they were victimized by a plague of *wilds beasts;*

דֶּבֶר, **Pestilence** — Because the Egyptians disrupted Jewish family life by dispatching Jews to mountains and deserts as shepherds, their herds were decimated by *pestilence;*

שְׁחִין, **Boils** — Because the Jews were forced to heat water to prepare baths for the Egyptians, their bodies

רַבִּי יְהוּדָה הָיָה נוֹתֵן בָּהֶם סִמָּנִים:

דְּצַ"ךְ עַדַ"שׁ בְּאַחַ"ב:

were afflicted by *boils* that were too painful to touch, much less bathe;

בָּרָד, **Hail** — Because the Jews were forced to plant crops and orchards for the Egyptians, the produce was battered by *hail*;

אַרְבֶּה, **Locusts** — Because the Jews were forced to plant wheat and spelt for the Egyptians, *locusts* were dispatched to consume the crops;

חשֶׁךְ, **Darkness** — Because the Egyptians darkened the life of the Jews in a relentless exile, their own lives were blackened by *darkness*;

מַכַּת בְּכוֹרוֹת, **The Plague of the First-Born** — Because the Egyptians had the audacity to enslave Israel whom Hashem calls בְּנִי בְכֹרִי, *My Own first-born (Sh'mos 4:22)*, He punished them by taking away their *firstborn*.

Contaminating Goshen ◦§ כִּנִּים — *Lice.*

Ramban to *Avos* 5 comments that, unlike the other plagues, the land of Goshen was also smitten by lice although the Jews did not suffer from the plague.

Rabbi Zalman Sorotzkin explained why G-d brought the lice to Goshen at all. According to the *Midrash*, the Jews were freed from making bricks after the plague of lice because an after-effect of the plague was that the sand remained unfit for the manufacture of bricks. Had the sand of Goshen remained uncontaminated, the Jews would have been forced to continue their labors using sand from Goshen. In order to thwart that eventuality, G-d rendered the Goshenite sand as unfit as that of the rest of the country.

Civil war ◦§ מַכַּת בְּכוֹרוֹת — *The Plague of the First-Born.*

The *Midrash* relates that, upon hearing that they would be the victims of the last plague, the בְּכוֹרִים, *first-born*, insisted that Israel be released immediately. When the other Egyptians refused to accede to their

Rabbi Judah abbreviated them by their Hebrew initials:

D'TZACH, ADASH, B'ACHAB

pleas, the first-born became violent and a civil war ensued as the first-born attacked their fellow Egyptians.
Thus, the tenth plague was a double blow to Egypt —
not only were the first-born killed by Hashem, but
many other Egyptians had been killed by the angry
first-born. Therefore, only the last plague is called מַכַּת,
the plague of, i.e. מַכַּת בְּכוֹרוֹת, the *Plague of the First-
Born* [but we do not say, for example, מַכַּת דָּם, *the
plague of blood*]: the entire nation was plagued by the
violent anger of the first-born *(Baruch She'amar).*

דְּצַ"ךְ עַדַ"שׁ בְּאַחַ"ב

**Reasons
for the
acronym** ◈ What was the purpose of these acronyms? Several
reaons are offered by *Machzor Vitry:*
— It was simply a mnemonic device to make it easier
to remember the plagues and their order, and it was in
accordance with the Talmudic dictum לְעוֹלָם יִשְׁנֶה
אָדָם לְתַלְמִידוֹ דֶּרֶךְ קְצָרָה, *a person should teach his students succinctly (Pesachim* 3b).
— Rabbi Yehudah divided the plagues into these
three categories based on the narrative of the Torah.
We find that before the first two plagues of each group,
Moses warned Pharaoh of the impending punishment.
The last plague, however, was brought without prior
warning. Thus, the sequence of events suggests that
they are separate categories.
— The first three plagues — דְּצַ"ךְ — were brought by
Aaron using his staff. The second group — עַדַ"שׁ — was
brought by Moses without use of his staff. The third
group — בְּאַחַ"ב — was brought by Moses using his
staff.

**Three
levels** ◈ *Malbim* derives from the text of the *Chumash* that
the purpose of the entire series of ten plagues was
to inculcate three successively higher levels of faith:
1 — To prove that there is a Creator;

97 **The Haggadah Treasury**

רַבִּי יוֹסֵי הַגְּלִילִי אוֹמֵר. מִנַּיִן אַתָּה אוֹמֵר שֶׁלָּקוּ
הַמִּצְרִים בְּמִצְרַיִם עֶשֶׂר מַכּוֹת וְעַל הַיָּם לָקוּ חֲמִשִּׁים
מַכּוֹת. בְּמִצְרַיִם מָה הוּא אוֹמֵר. וַיֹּאמְרוּ הַחַרְטֻמִּם
אֶל־פַּרְעֹה אֶצְבַּע אֱלֹהִים הוּא. וְעַל־הַיָּם מָה הוּא
אוֹמֵר. וַיַּרְא יִשְׂרָאֵל אֶת־הַיָּד הַגְּדֹלָה אֲשֶׁר עָשָׂה

2 — To establish the concept of הַשְׁגָּחָה פְּרָטִית, that
Hashem watches over every aspect of creation;

3 — To prove that there is none like Him.

Each group of plagues, as divided by Rabbi
Yehudah's acronym was designed to prove one of these
principles of faith. In introducing the plague of blood,
the first in the series of דְּצַ״ךְ, Hashem said בְּזֹאת תֵּדַע כִּי
אֲנִי ה׳, by this shall you know that I am HASHEM
(Sh'mos 7:17). The implication is that this was a
foreign concept in Egypt, and it was about to be established beyond question. Before עָרוֹב, the mixture of
wild animals which began the series of עַד״שׁ, Hashem
introduced a new concept saying: לְמַעַן תֵּדַע כִּי אֲנִי ה׳
בְּקֶרֶב הָאָרֶץ, so that you will realize that I, HASHEM, am
in the midst of the earth (ibid. 8:18). Although G-d's
existence had been acknowledged, there was still doubt
that He either could or would deign to regulate even the
most minute aspect of activity on earth. Hashem
proved the untruth of this heresy by clearly limiting the
activity of each plague to the Egyptians, and denying it
entry into Jewish homes or the land of Goshen. The
third and last group — בְּאַחַ״ב — was introduced בַּעֲבוּר
תֵּדַע כִּי אֵין כָּמֹנִי בְּכָל הָאָרֶץ, so that you may realize that
there is none like Me in all the earth (ibid 9:14). Prior to
that group, there were those who acknowledged that
Hashem was also a god, but they still clung to the belief
that there were others.

By his division of the plagues into groups, Rabbi
Yehudah alludes to the different and ascending pur-
poses to be achieved by each set.

Rabbi Yose the Galilean said: How does one derive that the Egyptians were struck with ten plagues in Egypt, but with fifty plagues at the Sea? — Concerning the plagues in Egypt the Torah states that *(Sh'mos 8:15) The magicians said to Pharaoh, it is the* finger *of God.* However, of those at the Sea, the Torah relates that *(ibid. 14:31) Israel saw the great 'hand'*

Pharaoh's prophecy ◦§ *Arizal* notes that the numerical value of Rabbi Yehudah's acronym is 501, the same as that of the word אֲשֶׁר, *that.* When Moses made his first appearance before Pharaoh, the arrogant king said, מִי ה׳ אֲשֶׁר אֶשְׁמַע בְּקֹלוֹ, *Who is* HASHEM *that I should heed His voice? (ibid. 5:2).*

His impudent words contained a prophecy of which he was unaware: מִי ה׳, *Who is* HASHEM [now, I refuse to acknowledge Him, but —] אֲשֶׁר, when he afflicts me with the numerical value of 501 in the form of דְּצַ״ךְ עֲדַ״שׁ בְּאַחַ״ב — then אֶשְׁמַע בְּקֹלוֹ, *I will heed His voice.*

רַבִּי יוֹסֵי הַגְּלִילִי... — Rabbi Yose HaGalili ...

Understanding the pledge ◦§ The three Tannaim expounded on how many punishments were contained within each of the plagues. Why does it matter to us whether each plague included one, four, or five punishments?

Hashem promises that if Israel obediently observes the commandments, then the suffering of the Egyptians will not be inflicted upon us: כָּל הַמַּחֲלָה אֲשֶׁר שַׂמְתִּי בְמִצְרַיִם לֹא אָשִׂים עָלֶיךָ, *all the illness that I placed upon Egypt, I will not set upon you (Sh'mos 15:26);* and וְכָל מַדְוֵי מִצְרַיִם הָרָעִים אֲשֶׁר יָדַעְתָּ לֹא יְשִׂימָם בָּךְ, *all the evil suffering of Egypt which you knew, He will not set upon you (Devarim 7:15).* Thus, Israel's observance of the Torah will protect it from the suffering of the Egyptians — and vice-versa. Therefore it is important for us to visualize precisely what punishments are withheld from one who performs the commandments (*Vilna Gaon*).

יהוה בְּמִצְרַיִם וַיִּירְאוּ הָעָם אֶת־יהוה וַיַּאֲמִינוּ בַּיהוה וּבְמֹשֶׁה עַבְדּוֹ. כַּמָּה לָקוּ בְּאֶצְבַּע עֶשֶׂר מַכּוֹת. אֱמוֹר מֵעַתָּה בְּמִצְרַיִם לָקוּ עֶשֶׂר מַכּוֹת וְעַל־הַיָּם לָקוּ חֲמִשִּׁים מַכּוֹת:

רַבִּי אֱלִיעֶזֶר אוֹמֵר. מִנַּיִן שֶׁכָּל מַכָּה וּמַכָּה שֶׁהֵבִיא הַקָּדוֹשׁ בָּרוּךְ הוּא עַל הַמִּצְרִים בְּמִצְרַיִם הָיְתָה שֶׁל אַרְבַּע מַכּוֹת. שֶׁנֶּאֱמַר יְשַׁלַּח־בָּם חֲרוֹן אַפּוֹ עֶבְרָה וָזַעַם וְצָרָה מִשְׁלַחַת מַלְאֲכֵי רָעִים. עֶבְרָה אַחַת. וָזַעַם שְׁתַּיִם. וְצָרָה שָׁלֹשׁ. מִשְׁלַחַת מַלְאֲכֵי רָעִים אַרְבַּע: אֱמוֹר מֵעַתָּה בְּמִצְרַיִם לָקוּ אַרְבָּעִים מַכּוֹת וְעַל־הַיָּם לָקוּ מָאתַיִם מַכּוֹת:

רַבִּי עֲקִיבָא אוֹמֵר. מִנַּיִן שֶׁכָּל מַכָּה וּמַכָּה שֶׁהֵבִיא הַקָּדוֹשׁ בָּרוּךְ הוּא עַל הַמִּצְרִים בְּמִצְרַיִם הָיְתָה שֶׁל חָמֵשׁ מַכּוֹת. שֶׁנֶּאֱמַר יְשַׁלַּח־בָּם חֲרוֹן אַפּוֹ עֶבְרָה וָזַעַם וְצָרָה מִשְׁלַחַת מַלְאֲכֵי רָעִים. חֲרוֹן אַפּוֹ אַחַת. עֶבְרָה שְׁתַּיִם. וָזַעַם שָׁלֹשׁ. וְצָרָה אַרְבַּע. מִשְׁלַחַת מַלְאֲכֵי רָעִים חָמֵשׁ: אֱמוֹר מֵעַתָּה בְּמִצְרַיִם לָקוּ חֲמִשִּׁים מַכּוֹת וְעַל הַיָּם לָקוּ חֲמִשִּׁים וּמָאתַיִם מַכּוֹת:

Purpose of plagues ◄§ What is the basis for the difference of opinion between Rabbi Eliezer and Rabbi Akiva? There are two ways to understand the purpose of the ten plagues: as a kindness to Israel because it instilled in them the eternal lessons of faith in Hashem, or as a means of punishing the Egyptians for their inquities. Rabbi Eliezer holds that the plagues were intended primarily as a gesture of graciousness to Israel. Thus

which HASHEM laid upon the Egyptians, the people feared HASHEM and they believed in HASHEM and in His servant Moses. How many plagues did they receive with the finger? Ten! Then conclude that if they suffered ten plagues in Egypt [where they were struck with a *finger*, they must have been made to suffer fifty plagues at the Sea [where they were struck with a whole *hand*].

Rabbi Eliezer said: How does one derive that every plague that the Holy One, Blessed be He, inflicted upon the Egyptians in Egypt was equal to four plagues? — For it is written: *(Tehillim 78:49) He sent upon them His fierce anger: wrath, fury, and trouble, a band of emissaries of evil.* [Since each plague in Egypt consisted of] 1) *wrath*, 2) *fury*, 3) *trouble* and 4) *a band of emissaries of evil* . Therefore conclude that in Egypt they were struck by *forty* plagues and at the Sea by *two hundred!*

Rabbi Akiva said: How does one derive that each plague that God inflicted upon the Egyptians in Egypt was equal to *five* plagues? — For it is written: *He sent upon them His fierce anger, wrath, fury, and trouble, a band of emissaries of evil:* 1) *fierce anger*, 2) *wrath*, 3) *fury*, 4) *trouble*, and 5) *a band of emissaries of evil*. Conclude, therefore, that in Egypt they were struck by fifty plagues and at the sea by two hundred and fifty!

they were a gift of G-d in His manifestation of 'ה, the Four-Letter Name that represents the Attribute of Mercy. As products of the Four-Letter Name, they should be seen as taking a four-faceted form. Rabbi Akiva, on the other hand, interprets the plagues as retribution. Thus they manifest the Attribute of Justice represented by the *five*-lettered Name, אלקים, *Elokim.* Therefore, he interprets the plagues as being five-faceted.

כַּמָּה מַעֲלוֹת טוֹבוֹת לַמָּקוֹם עָלֵינוּ:

אִלּוּ הוֹצִיאָנוּ מִמִּצְרַיִם
דַּיֵּנוּ: וְלֹא־עָשָׂה בָהֶם שְׁפָטִים
אִלּוּ עָשָׂה בָהֶם שְׁפָטִים
דַּיֵּנוּ: וְלֹא־עָשָׂה בֵאלֹהֵיהֶם
אִלּוּ עָשָׂה בֵאלֹהֵיהֶם
דַּיֵּנוּ: וְלֹא־הָרַג אֶת־בְּכוֹרֵיהֶם
אִלּוּ הָרַג אֶת־בְּכוֹרֵיהֶם
דַּיֵּנוּ: וְלֹא־נָתַן לָנוּ אֶת־מָמוֹנָם
אִלּוּ נָתַן לָנוּ אֶת־מָמוֹנָם
דַּיֵּנוּ: וְלֹא־קָרַע לָנוּ אֶת־הַיָּם
אִלּוּ קָרַע לָנוּ אֶת־הַיָּם
דַּיֵּנוּ: וְלֹא־הֶעֱבִירָנוּ בְּתוֹכוֹ בֶּחָרָבָה
אִלּוּ הֶעֱבִירָנוּ בְּתוֹכוֹ בֶּחָרָבָה
דַּיֵּנוּ: וְלֹא־שִׁקַּע צָרֵינוּ בְּתוֹכוֹ
אִלּוּ שִׁקַּע צָרֵינוּ בְּתוֹכוֹ
דַּיֵּנוּ: וְלֹא־סִפֵּק צָרְכֵּנוּ בַּמִּדְבָּר אַרְבָּעִים שָׁנָה
אִלּוּ סִפֵּק צָרְכֵּנוּ בַּמִּדְבָּר אַרְבָּעִים שָׁנָה
דַּיֵּנוּ: וְלֹא־הֶאֱכִילָנוּ אֶת־הַמָּן

דַּיֵּנוּ — It would have sufficed us.

Infinite gratitude ⋗ We do not mean to suggest, חלילה, that we would have been content not to have received these blessings. How could we imagine not having been given the Torah, Sabbath, Eretz Yisrael, the Beis Hamikdash and

God has bestowed so many favors upon us.

Had He brought us out of Egypt,
and not executed judgments against the Egyptians,

it would have sufficed us!

Had He executed judgments against the Egyptians,
but not upon their gods, *it would have sufficed us!*

Had He executed judgments against their gods,
but not slain their firstborn, *it would have sufficed us!*

Had He slain their firstborn,
but not given us their wealth, *it would have sufficed us!*

Had He given us their wealth
and not split the Sea for us, *it would have sufficed us!*

Had He split the Sea for us
but not led us through it on dry land,

it would have sufficed us!

Had He led us through it on dry land
but not drowned our oppressors in it,

it would have sufficed us!

Had He drowned our oppressors in it
but not provided for our needs in the desert for forty
years, *it would have sufficed us!*

Had He provided for our needs in the desert for forty years,
but not fed us the Manna, *it would have sufficed us!*

everything else mentioned in this song of gratitude?
Rather the meaning is that any one of these gifts would
have been sufficient to require infinite expressions of
gratitude on our part. How much more grateful must
we be that He has given us all of those precious gifts!
(Malbim).

אִלּוּ הֶאֱכִילָנוּ אֶת הַמָּן
וְלֹא־נָתַן לָנוּ אֶת־הַשַּׁבָּת
דַּיֵּנוּ:
אִלּוּ נָתַן לָנוּ אֶת־הַשַּׁבָּת
וְלֹא־קֵרְבָנוּ לִפְנֵי הַר־סִינַי
דַּיֵּנוּ:
אִלּוּ קֵרְבָנוּ לִפְנֵי הַר־סִינַי
וְלֹא־נָתַן לָנוּ אֶת־הַתּוֹרָה
דַּיֵּנוּ:
אִלּוּ נָתַן לָנוּ אֶת הַתּוֹרָה
וְלֹא הִכְנִיסָנוּ לְאֶרֶץ יִשְׂרָאֵל
דַּיֵּנוּ:
אִלּוּ הִכְנִיסָנוּ לְאֶרֶץ יִשְׂרָאֵל
וְלֹא בָנָה לָנוּ אֶת בֵּית הַבְּחִירָה
דַּיֵּנוּ:

עַל אַחַת כַּמָּה וְכַמָּה טוֹבָה כְפוּלָה וּמְכֻפֶּלֶת
לַמָּקוֹם עָלֵינוּ. שֶׁהוֹצִיאָנוּ מִמִּצְרָיִם. וְעָשָׂה בָהֶם

Trust in G-d

◆§ אִלּוּ הֶאֱכִילָנוּ אֶת הַמָּן וְלֹא נָתַן לָנוּ אֶת הַשַּׁבָּת דַּיֵּנוּ ◆§ — *Had He fed us the manna and not given us the Sabbath, it would have sufficed us.*

The implication is that the manna would have been sufficient to offset the lack of Sabbath; what have the two in common?

Both manna and Sabbath teach בִּטָחוֹן, *trust*, in G-d. The person who forgoes the opportunity to work and profit on Sabbath shows trust that Hashem will provide for him, and that he will not suffer for having honored Sabbath.

Manna teaches a similar lesson. Jews gathered manna in the morning for that day only. They had to have faith that Hashem would give them more the next morning.

Therefore we say that without Sabbath, we would

Had He fed us the Manna,
but not given us the Shabbos,   *it would have sufficed us!*
Had He given us the Shabbos,
but not brought us before Mount Sinai,

it would have sufficed us!
Had He brought us before Mount Sinai,
but not given us the Torah,   *it would have sufficed us!*
Had He given us the Torah,
but not brought us into Eretz Yisrael,

it would have sufficed us!
Had He brought us into Eretz Yisrael,
and not built a Temple for us,   *it would have sufficed us!*

Thus, how much more so, should we be grateful to God for all the numerous favors He showered upon us: He brought us out of Egypt; executed judgments against the Egyptians; and

have been content with manna, because it, too, teaches the lesson of firm trust in Hashem.

A holy environment ∾§ אִלּוּ קֵרְבָנוּ לִפְנֵי הַר סִינַי וְלֹא נָתַן לָנוּ אֶת הַתּוֹרָה דַּיֵּנוּ §∾
Had He brought us before Mount Sinai but not given us the Torah it would have sufficed us.

But if the Torah was not to be given what purpose would there have been in gathering around a Sinai was not barren mountain?

Harav Avraham Pam likened this to the Talmudic parable of one who goes into a perfumery. Even if he buys nothing, he will leave the shop with a fragrance for having been in its sweet-smelling environs. So, too, with Israel. Being privileged to stand at Mount Sinai and see the cloud of Hashem's *Shechinah* atop it would have left a lasting impression.

שְׁפָטִים. וְעָשָׂה בֵאלֹהֵיהֶם. וְהָרַג אֶת־בְּכוֹרֵיהֶם. וְנָתַן
לָנוּ אֶת־מָמוֹנָם. וְקָרַע לָנוּ אֶת־הַיָּם. וְהֶעֱבִירָנוּ בְתוֹכוֹ
בֶּחָרָבָה. וְשִׁקַּע צָרֵינוּ בְּתוֹכוֹ. וְסִפֵּק צָרְכֵּנוּ בַּמִּדְבָּר
אַרְבָּעִים שָׁנָה. וְהֶאֱכִילָנוּ אֶת הַמָּן. וְנָתַן לָנוּ אֶת
הַשַּׁבָּת.וְקֵרְבָנוּ לִפְנֵי הַר־סִינַי. וְנָתַן לָנוּ אֶת־הַתּוֹרָה.
וְהִכְנִיסָנוּ לְאֶרֶץ יִשְׂרָאֵל. וּבָנָה לָנוּ אֶת בֵּית הַבְּחִירָה
לְכַפֵּר עַל־כָּל־עֲוֹנוֹתֵינוּ:

The cups should be refilled before commencing רַבָּן גַּמְלִיאֵל.

רַבָּן גַּמְלִיאֵל הָיָה אוֹמֵר. כָּל שֶׁלֹּא אָמַר שְׁלֹשָׁה
דְבָרִים אֵלּוּ בַּפֶּסַח לֹא־יָצָא יְדֵי חוֹבָתוֹ. וְאֵלּוּ הֵן.
פֶּסַח. מַצָּה. וּמָרוֹר:

פֶּסַח, מַצָּה, וּמָרוֹר — The Pesach sacrifice, matzah, and maror.

Bitterness is part of redemption

◄§ Matzah represents the redemption, for it is the reminder that when the time of the Exodus arrived, the Jews were taken out of exile so swiftly that their dough had no time to rise. Maror, obviously represents the bitterness of exile. That being the case, the maror should be mentioned and eaten first because the exile preceded the redemption.

However, as we have seen earlier, in order to bring about the redemption sooner than the 400 years mentioned to Abraham, Hashem took into consideration the intensity of the enslavement which was so harsh that the 210 years in Egypt were equivalent to what was envisioned for the full 400 years. Therefore, the very bitterness [מָרוֹר] of the exile became a device to hasten the redemption, and even while the servitude was in progress. G-d was already calculating its eventual end. Because redemption was uppermost in His mind, we eat matzah first (Noda BiYehudah).

◄§ The Sages teach כְּשֵׁם שֶׁמְּבָרְכִים עַל הַטּוֹב ,כָּךְ מְבָרְכִים עַל הָרָע — Just as one blesses [Hashem] for the good, so should he bless for the bad (Berachos 54a). The

against their gods; slew their firstborn; gave us their wealth; split the Sea for us; led us through it on dry land; sank our oppressors in it; sustained our needs in the desert for forty years; fed us the Manna; gave us the Sabbath; brought us before Mount Sinai; gave us the Torah; brought us to Eretz Yisrael; and built us a Temple to atone for all our sins.

The cups should be refilled before commencing רַבָּן גַּמְלִיאֵל.

Rabban Gamliel used to say: Whoever has not explained the following three things on Passover has not fulfilled his duty, namely:

Pesach — the Passover Offering;
Matzah — the Unleavened Bread
Maror — the Bitter Herbs.

Thanking for bitterness
proper realization that everything done by Hashem is for the ultimate good, requires that we bless Him equally no matter what befalls us. Therefore, we must thank Him not only for the Exodus, but for the exile even though the former is far more pleasant than the latter. If we were to mention *maror* before *matzah*, the impression would be left that the latter expressions of gratitude refer only to the *matzah* — symbolizing redemption. Therefore, the mention of *maror* is left for last to make it clear that we thank Hashem for everything — even the bitterness of exile *(Chasam Sofer)*.

Lest we forget
◆§ The Masters of Mussar, *Ethical Teaching,* stressed that human beings who have been the beneficiaries of good fortune often forget the suffering that preceded it. The result is that they lose their humility and become ungrateful to those who helped them when they were less fortunate. Therefore, we eat bitter herbs *after* eating matzah. We want the *maror* to be a reminder to us of the misfortunes of the past — and a warning that if we do not deserve to keep the new gifts which G-d has granted us, they can be taken away.

One should *not* point at the roasted bone on the *Seder* plate.

פֶּסַח שֶׁהָיוּ אֲבוֹתֵינוּ אוֹכְלִים בִּזְמַן שֶׁבֵּית־הַמִּקְדָּשׁ
הָיָה קַיָּם עַל־שׁוּם מָה. עַל־שׁוּם שֶׁפָּסַח הַקָּדוֹשׁ בָּרוּךְ
הוּא עַל בָּתֵּי אֲבוֹתֵינוּ בְּמִצְרַיִם. שֶׁנֶּאֱמַר וַאֲמַרְתֶּם
זֶבַח־פֶּסַח הוּא לַיהוה אֲשֶׁר פָּסַח עַל־בָּתֵּי בְנֵי־
יִשְׂרָאֵל בְּמִצְרַיִם בְּנָגְפּוֹ אֶת־מִצְרַיִם וְאֶת־בָּתֵּינוּ הִצִּיל
וַיִּקֹּד הָעָם וַיִּשְׁתַּחֲווּ:

Hold up the middle *matzah* while reciting the passage referring to it.

מַצָּה זוֹ שֶׁאָנוּ אוֹכְלִים עַל־שׁוּם מָה. עַל־שׁוּם שֶׁלֹּא
הִסְפִּיק בְּצֵקָם שֶׁל אֲבוֹתֵינוּ לְהַחֲמִיץ עַד שֶׁנִּגְלָה
עֲלֵיהֶם מֶלֶךְ מַלְכֵי הַמְּלָכִים הַקָּדוֹשׁ בָּרוּךְ הוּא
וּגְאָלָם. שֶׁנֶּאֱמַר וַיֹּאפוּ אֶת־הַבָּצֵק אֲשֶׁר הוֹצִיאוּ
מִמִּצְרַיִם עֻגֹת מַצּוֹת כִּי לֹא חָמֵץ כִּי גֹרְשׁוּ מִמִּצְרַיִם
וְלֹא יָכְלוּ לְהִתְמַהְמֵהַּ וְגַם־צֵדָה לֹא־עָשׂוּ לָהֶם:

מַצָּה זוֹ ... וְלֹא יָכְלוּ לְהִתְמַהְמֵהַּ ... — **This matzah ...
because they [our ancestors] could not delay ...**

**The
strength of
Torah**
&§ Had our ancestors delayed their leavetaking from
Egypt for even the few minutes needed to allow
their dough to rise, they could not have been redeemed
because they had already fallen to the forty-ninth level
of impurity and another moment in Egypt would have
sunk them inextricably into the morass of impurity.
How astounding! Before receiving the Torah, the Jews
had maintained their national identity for 210 years by
not changing their distinctive Jewish names, language,
or clothing, yet these trappings of nationalism were not
sufficient to prevent them from sinking beyond
redemption. But our present exile has endured for over

One should *not* point at the roasted bone on the *Seder* plate.

Pesach — Why did our fathers eat a Passover offering during the period when the Temple still stood? — Because the Holy One, Blessed be He, passed over the houses of our fathers in Egypt, as it is written: [Shemos 12:27]: *You shall say: 'It is a Passover offering for HASHEM, Who passed over the houses of the children in Israel in Egypt when He struck the Egyptians and spared our houses; and the people bowed down and prostrated themselves.'*

Hold up the middle *matzah* while reciting the passage referring to it.

Matzah — Why do we eat this matzah? — Because the King of Kings, the Holy One, revealed Himself to our fathers and redeemed them before their dough had time to leaven, as it is written: [Shemos 12:39]: *They baked the dough which they had brought out of Egypt into unleavened bread, for it had not fermented, because they were driven out of Egypt and could not delay, nor had they prepared any provision for the way.*

History conforms to Torah

19 centuries and we are still strong — such is the power of Torah! *(Rabbi Zalman Sorotzkin).*

⊷§ The Scriptural passage seems to imply that the Torah's commandment to eat *matzah* is based on the historical event of the Exodus; had the Exodus been leisurely enough to allow the dough to rise, there would be no reason to eat *matzah*. This, however, is the opposite of the truth. The Torah preceded creation. Indeed, the circumstances and events of the universe and its history were designed to make possible the fulfillment of the commandments. Thus, the haste of the Exodus was necessary to conform to the Torah's description of *matzah* as reflective of the speed with which Israel left the land of their enslavement. The mitzvah dictated the event, not vice-versa *(Bais Halevi).*

Hold up the *maror* while reciting the passage referring to it.

מָרוֹר זֶה שֶׁאָנוּ אוֹכְלִים עַל־שׁוּם מָה. עַל־שׁוּם
שֶׁמֵּרְרוּ הַמִּצְרִים אֶת־חַיֵּי אֲבוֹתֵינוּ בְּמִצְרָיִם. שֶׁנֶּאֱמַר
וַיְמָרְרוּ אֶת חַיֵּיהֶם בַּעֲבֹדָה קָשָׁה בְּחֹמֶר וּבִלְבֵנִים
וּבְכָל עֲבֹדָה בַּשָּׂדֶה אֵת כָּל־עֲבֹדָתָם אֲשֶׁר עָבְדוּ בָהֶם
בְּפָרֶךְ:

בְּכָל־דּוֹר וָדוֹר חַיָּב אָדָם לִרְאוֹת אֶת־עַצְמוֹ כְּאִלּוּ
הוּא יָצָא מִמִּצְרָיִם. שֶׁנֶּאֱמַר וְהִגַּדְתָּ לְבִנְךָ בַּיּוֹם הַהוּא
לֵאמֹר בַּעֲבוּר זֶה עָשָׂה יהוה לִי בְּצֵאתִי מִמִּצְרָיִם.לֹא
אֶת־אֲבוֹתֵינוּ בִּלְבָד גָּאַל הַקָּדוֹשׁ בָּרוּךְ הוּא אֶלָּא אַף

The trop tells the story ⇛§ וַיְמָרְרוּ אֶת חַיֵּיהֶם — *And they embittered their lives.*

As we have previously noted, the bitterness of the exile was a major factor in hastening its early end. *Vilna Gaon* finds an allusion to this in the *trop*, the cantillation, of the words וַיְמָרְרוּ אֶת חַיֵּיהֶם, *and they embittered their lives.* The *trop* is קַדְמָא וְאַזְלָא which can be translated as *precede and leave.* The inference is that because of the bitterness, they left early. Furthermore, the numerical value of קַדְמָא וְאַזְלָא is 190 — exactly equivalent to the number of years which the redemption was hastened.

When life was a horror ⇛§ Why does the verse stress that the Egyptians embittered their *lives?* It would have been sufficient to say that the Egyptians embittered אֹתָם, *them.*

People dread death and would prefer a miserable life to a peaceful death. Sometimes, however, suffering can be so great and unremitting that death would be a relief. This was the Jewish condition in Egypt. The Egyptians succeeded in embittering their *lives* to such an extent

Hold up the *maror* while reciting the passage referring to it.

Maror — Why do we eat this bitter herb? — Because the Egyptians embittered the lives of our fathers in Egypt, as it says *[Shemos 1:14]*: *'They embittered their lives with hard labor, with mortar and bricks, and with all manner of labor in the field: whatever service they made them perform was with hard labor.'*

In every generation it is one's duty to regard himself as though he *personally* had gone out of Egypt, as it is written *[Shemos 13:8]*: *You shall tell your son on that day: 'It was because of this that HASHEM did for me when I came out of Egypt.'* It was not only our fathers whom the Holy One redeemed from slavery; we, too, were redeemed with them, as

that they would have preferred death to life *(Chasam Sofer)*.

Most vital, but hardest

❧ A — חַיָב אָדָם לִרְאוֹת אֶת עַצְמוֹ כְּאִלוּ הוּא יָצָא מִמִצְרַיִם *person is required to consider himself as if he had gone out from Egypt.*

All the *mitzvos* of the *Seder* are relatively easy to perform — one can embellish upon the *Yetzias Mitzrayim* narrative, eat the required quantities of *matzah* and *maror*, and drink enough wine. But for a person to be wise enough and sensitive enought to feel as though he himself had been rescued from Egypt — that is exceedingly difficult *(Moadim U'Zmanim)*. But this is the main purpose of the *Seder*. Just as our forefathers came to accept G-d as their king when they left the sovereignty of Pharaoh to enter His, so must we utilize the experiences of the *Seder* and all it represents to proclaim our own redemption from the yoke of the transitory and accept upon ourselves the עוֹל מַלְכוּת שָׁמַיִם, *yoke of the Heavenly Kingdom (Chever Ma'amarim)*.

111   The Haggadah Treasury

אוֹתָנוּ גָּאַל עִמָּהֶם. שֶׁנֶּאֱמַר וְאוֹתָנוּ הוֹצִיא מִשָּׁם. לְמַעַן הָבִיא אֹתָנוּ לָתֶת לָנוּ אֶת הָאָרֶץ אֲשֶׁר נִשְׁבַּע לַאֲבוֹתֵינוּ:

The *matzos* should be covered and the cup lifted up and held until after the blessing of אֲשֶׁר גְּאָלָנוּ. According to some customs, however, the cup is put down before הַלְלוּיָהּ is begun, in which case the *matzos* should once more be uncovered. If this custom is followed, the *matzos* are to be covered and the cup raised again upon reaching the blessing אֲשֶׁר גְּאָלָנוּ.

לְפִיכָךְ אֲנַחְנוּ חַיָּבִים לְהוֹדוֹת לְהַלֵּל לְשַׁבֵּחַ לְפָאֵר לְרוֹמֵם לְהַדֵּר לְבָרֵךְ לְעַלֵּה וּלְקַלֵּס לְמִי שֶׁעָשָׂה לַאֲבוֹתֵינוּ וְלָנוּ אֶת־כָּל הַנִּסִּים הָאֵלוּ הוֹצִיאָנוּ מֵעַבְדוּת לְחֵרוּת מִיָּגוֹן לְשִׂמְחָה וּמֵאֵבֶל לְיוֹם טוֹב וּמֵאֲפֵלָה לְאוֹר גָּדוֹל וּמִשִּׁעְבּוּד לִגְאֻלָּה וְנֹאמַר לְפָנָיו שִׁירָה חֲדָשָׁה הַלְלוּיָהּ:

| Building to a climax | ∞§ לְפִיכָךְ אֲנַחְנוּ חַיָּבִים לְהוֹדוֹת — *Therefore we are obliged to thank.* |

The *Haggadah* enumerates nine expressions of praise, and concludes with the call to recite *Hallel*. The nine praises are in thanks for the first nine plagues that G-d brought upon the Egyptians. The call to sing *Hallel* is our response to the final plague, for it was the Plague of the First-Born that sealed the redemption and ended the exile. *Hallel* is the expression of gratitude for a complete deliverance. *(Vilna Gaon).*

הַלֵּל — Hallel

∞§ Only on *Pesach* is Hallel said at night — at the *Seder* by all Jews and also at the conclusion of *Ma'ariv* according to the custom of many communities. Normally,

it is written [*Devarim* 6:23]: *He brought **us** out from there so that He might take us to the land which He had promised to our fathers.*

The *matzos* should be covered and the cup lifted up and held until after the blessing of אֲשֶׁר גְּאָלָנוּ. According to some customs, however, the cup is put down before הַלְלוּיָהּ is begun, in which case the *matzos* should once more be uncovered. If this custom is followed, the *matzos* are to be covered and the cup raised again upon reaching the blessing אֲשֶׁר גְּאָלָנוּ.

Therefore it is our duty to thank, praise, pay tribute, glorify, exalt, honor, bless, and acclaim Him Who performed all these miracles for our fathers and for us. He brought us forth from slavery to freedom, from grief to joy, from mourning to festivity, from darkness to great light, and from servitude to redemption. Let us, therefore, recite a new song before Him! Halleluyah!

When night became day night represents darkness, fear, and exile — conditions that conflict with the jubilant feelings expressed by *Hallel*. The night of *Pesach*, however, is unique because at the time of the redemption, G-d *lit up the night like day* (*Tehillim* 139:12) — so great was the revelation of holiness. It is appropriate, therefore, that *Hallel* be recited.

The first two chapters of Hallel refer to the Exodus from Egypt; therefore, they are recited before the meal in conjunction with the *Haggadah* narrative. The balance of *Hallel* anticipates the redemption by Messiah; therefore, it is recited after the meal when we look ahead to the miracles that will eclipse even those of *Yetzias Mitzrayim*.

Netziv comments that we insert the festival meal into the midst of the Hallel to signify that on this night, even our meal is a form of praise to Hashem.

הַלְלוּיָהּ הַלְלוּ עַבְדֵי יהוה הַלְלוּ אֶת שֵׁם יהוה: יְהִי שֵׁם יהוה מְבֹרָךְ. מֵעַתָּה וְעַד־עוֹלָם: מִמִּזְרַח שֶׁמֶשׁ עַד־מְבוֹאוֹ מְהֻלָּל שֵׁם יהוה: רָם עַל־כָּל־גּוֹיִם יהוה. עַל הַשָּׁמַיִם כְּבוֹדוֹ: מִי כַּיהוה אֱלֹהֵינוּ. הַמַּגְבִּיהִי לָשָׁבֶת. הַמַּשְׁפִּילִי לִרְאוֹת בַּשָּׁמַיִם וּבָאָרֶץ: מְקִימִי מֵעָפָר דָּל. מֵאַשְׁפֹּת יָרִים אֶבְיוֹן: לְהוֹשִׁיבִי עִם־ נְדִיבִים. עִם נְדִיבֵי עַמּוֹ: מוֹשִׁיבִי עֲקֶרֶת הַבַּיִת אֵם־ הַבָּנִים שְׂמֵחָה הַלְלוּיָהּ:

הַלְלוּיָהּ – Halleluyah!

Always just

⇐§ מִמִּזְרַח שֶׁמֶשׁ עַד מְבוֹאוֹ — *From the rising of the sun until its setting.*

Sunrise is symbolic of good times and rising expectations. Sunset is symbolic of suffering and decline. Both the nation and the individual have experienced these two extremes. Nevertheless, whatever we undergo, whether Hashem seems to smile at us or frown — מְהֻלָּל שֵׁם ה', *praised be the Name of Hashem.* We always recognize that His ways are just, and we bless Him for the unpleasant as well as for the benevolent.

Rise from anywhere

⇐§ מְקִימִי מֵעָפָר דָּל מֵאַשְׁפֹּת יָרִים אֶבְיוֹן — *He raises the destitute from the dust, from the trash heaps He lifts the needy.*

Vilna Gaon gives a spiritual interpretation to the verse.

A דָּל has absolutely nothing while an אֶבְיוֹן, though in extreme need, is slightly better off.

Even a דָּל, one who is so spiritually destitute that he wallows in עָפָר, unproductive *dust,* can be raised up to a new and fruitful life. An אֶבְיוֹן, is one who may have some knowledge and good deeds, but who has sunk into the אַשְׁפּוֹת, the filthy *trash heaps* of sin — he, too, can be raised up to spiritual purity. So high can such people rise with sincere repentance, that they can take their

Halleluyah! Praise, you servants of HASHEM, praise the Name of HASHEM. Blessed be the Name of HASHEM from now and forever. From the rising of the sun to its setting, HASHEM's Name is praised. High above all nations is HASHEM, above the heavens is His glory. Who is like HASHEM, our God, Who is enthroned on high, yet deigns to look upon heaven and earth? He raises the destitute from the dust, from the trash heaps He lifts the needy — to seat them with nobles, with the nobles of His people. He transforms the barren wife into a glad mother of children. Halleluyah! [Tehillim 113].

place with נְדִיבִים, the *princes* [i.e. the Patriarchs, Abraham, Isaac, and Jacob], and with נְדִיבֵי עַמּוֹ, *the princes of his people*, [i.e. the prophets].

Definitions are relative

⊷§ מֵאַשְׁפֹּת יָרִים אֶבְיוֹן — *From the trash heaps, He lifts the needy.*

One's definition of a *trash heap* is relative. To the hungry, penniless pauper, a garbage dump is a source of food, and he feels no shame in scavenging there. The very wealthy person may be embarrassed to shop in even an ordinary store, much less scrounge for food in the dunghills. The higher one rises on the economic ladder, the loftier are his ideas of what is beneath his station, and he will come to feel disdain for his everyday practices of the past. So it is spiritually, as well. When a person elevates himself to a higher spiritual level, he looks at his past and is shocked at the activities that he once did routinely. 'How could I ever have allowed myself to be so degraded?' he will wonder. Such were the results of the Exodus. After Israel left Egypt, it looked back at its past and realized that, in comparison with its new aspirations, it had been living in trash heaps *(Sfas Emes)*. [We may add that during periods of spiritual downfall in the Desert, Israel spoke longingly of Egyptian past. When it was spiritually heightened, Israel regarded Egypt as a trash heap; when it fell into sin, it preferred Egypt to the proximity of G-d.]

בְּצֵאת יִשְׂרָאֵל מִמִּצְרָיִם בֵּית יַעֲקֹב מֵעַם לֹעֵז:
הָיְתָה יְהוּדָה לְקָדְשׁוֹ יִשְׂרָאֵל מַמְשְׁלוֹתָיו: הַיָּם רָאָה
וַיָּנֹס. הַיַּרְדֵּן יִסֹּב לְאָחוֹר: הֶהָרִים רָקְדוּ כְאֵילִים.
גְּבָעוֹת כִּבְנֵי צֹאן: מַה לְּךָ הַיָּם כִּי תָנוּס. הַיַּרְדֵּן תִּסֹּב
לְאָחוֹר: הֶהָרִים תִּרְקְדוּ כְאֵילִים. גְּבָעוֹת כִּבְנֵי צֹאן:
מִלִּפְנֵי אָדוֹן חוּלִי אָרֶץ. מִלִּפְנֵי אֱלוֹהַ יַעֲקֹב: הַהֹפְכִי
הַצּוּר אֲגַם מָיִם. חַלָּמִישׁ לְמַעְיְנוֹ מָיִם:

בְּצֵאת יִשְׂרָאֵל — When Israel went out

Israel's three virtues

⇠§ בְּצֵאת יִשְׂרָאֵל — *When Israel went out.*

According to the familiar teaching of the Sages, Israel merited redemption because:

לֹא שִׁנּוּ אֶת שְׁמָם, *they did not change their Jewish names;*

לֹא שִׁנּוּ אֶת לְשׁוֹנָם, *they did not change their holy tongue;* and

שֶׁהָיוּ גְדוּרִים בַּעֲרָיוֹת, *they were restrained against the prevailing immorality.*

The first two verses of this psalm allude to these three qualities. *When 'Israel' went out* — i.e., it had remained *'Israel'*, with its Jewish names; *from a people of 'alien tongue'* — i.e., the language of Egypt was still 'alien' to the Jewish people. *Judah became His 'sanctuary'* — i.e., despite the impurity and immorality of Egypt, Judah remained G-d's *sanctuary*, for, as our Sages taught (*Vayikra Rabbah* 24:6), restraint against sexual immorality is a precondition of holiness (*Chasam Sofer*).

When Judah showed the way

⇠§ הָיְתָה יְהוּדָה לְקָדְשׁוֹ יִשְׂרָאֵל מַמְשְׁלוֹתָיו — *Judah became His sanctuary, Israel His dominion.*

The *Midrash* relates that when Hashem told Israel to march into the sea, Nachshon ben Aminadav of the tribe of Judah led the way. He walked into the turbulent

When Israel went from Egypt, Jacob's household from a people of alien tongue, Judah became His sanctuary, Israel His dominion. The Sea saw and fled; the Jordan turned backward. The mountains skipped like rams, and the hills like young lambs. What ails you, O Sea, that you flee? O Jordan, that you turn backward? O mountains, that you skip like rams? O hills, like young lambs? Before HASHEM's presence – tremble, O earth, before the presence of the God of Jacob, Who turns the rock into a pond of water, the flint into a flowing fountain [Tehillim 113].

water until it reached his chin. Then he prayed, הוֹשִׁיעֵנִי אֱלֹקִים כִּי בָאוּ מַיִם עַד נָפֶשׁ, *'Save me, G-d, for the waters endanger my life (Tehillim 69:2).* At that point, Hashem told Moses to raise his staff — and the sea split. When that happened, Israel said, ה' יִמְלֹךְ לְעֹלָם וָעֶד, *HASHEM will reign forever! (Sh'mos 15:18).*

In the light of the *Midrash,* our verse can be interpreted: *When Judah* — in the person of its leader, Nachshon — *sanctified Him, Israel gained dominion,* over the sea and over its enemies *(Eretz HaChaim).*

Merit over seniority

⧼§ הַיָּם רָאָה וַיָּנֹס — *The sea saw and fled.*

What did it see that caused it to flee? — the casket of Joseph *(Midrash).*

HaDrash V'haEyun comments that the sea refused to split at first because the bodies of water were formed on the third day of creation while man was not created until the sixth day. Therefore, the sea contended that its seniority absolved it from rendering honor to human beings.

Then the sea saw Joseph's casket and understood that its reasoning had been in error. Joseph was next to the youngest of Jacob's sons, yet he excelled them all in scholarship and righteousness. Because he was so great, they all bowed to him. Seeing his casket, the sea realized that its seniority was not the determining factor in

בָּרוּךְ אַתָּה יהוה אֱלֹהֵינוּ מֶלֶךְ הָעוֹלָם אֲשֶׁר גְּאָלָנוּ
וְגָאַל אֶת אֲבוֹתֵינוּ מִמִּצְרַיִם וְהִגִּיעָנוּ הַלַּיְלָה הַזֶּה
לֶאֱכָל־בּוֹ מַצָּה וּמָרוֹר. כֵּן יהוה אֱלֹהֵינוּ וֵאלֹהֵי
אֲבוֹתֵינוּ יַגִּיעֵנוּ לְמוֹעֲדִים וְלִרְגָלִים אֲחֵרִים הַבָּאִים
לִקְרָאתֵנוּ לְשָׁלוֹם שְׂמֵחִים בְּבִנְיַן עִירֶךָ וְשָׂשִׂים
בַּעֲבוֹדָתֶךָ וְנֹאכַל שָׁם מִן הַזְּבָחִים וּמִן הַפְּסָחִים (שׁ
אומרים במוצאי שבת: מִן הַפְּסָחִים וּמִן הַזְּבָחִים) אֲשֶׁר יַגִּיעַ
דָּמָם עַל קִיר מִזְבַּחֲךָ לְרָצוֹן וְנוֹדֶה לְךָ שִׁיר חָדָשׁ עַל
גְּאֻלָּתֵנוּ וְעַל פְּדוּת נַפְשֵׁנוּ. בָּרוּךְ אַתָּה יהוה גָּאַל
יִשְׂרָאֵל:

deciding whether or not to honor Israel. Their trust in
G-d was more important.

Joseph's example ◦§ The waters were reluctant to halt their natural flow, maintaining that they were obliged to obey the natural law under which G-d had placed them. But Joseph's casket recalled the unbearable temptations under which Potiphar's wife had placed him. By any normal standards, Joseph should have surrendered to his passions. Nevertheless, his enormous powers of self-restraint kept him from sinning. If a frail human being could control his nature, then the sea, too, could restrain its natural flow for the sake of Israel.

To save the victim ◦§ Another *Midrash* states that the sea split because it saw בְּרַיְיתָא דְרַבִּי יִשְׁמָעֵאל, *a braisa taught by Rabbi Ishmael*. Which *braisa*?

Rabbi Yishmael taught that if one person is pursuing another with the intention of killing him, bystanders are obligated to rescue the intended victim even if they must kill the pursuer in the process (*Sanhedrin* 73a). The sea balked at splitting to save Israel and then

Blessed are thou, HASHEM our God, King of the universe, Who redeemed us and redeemed our ancestors from Egypt and enabled us to reach this night that we may eat matzah and maror. So, HASHEM our God and God of our fathers, bring us also to future festivals and holidays in peace, gladdened in the rebuilding of Your city, and joyful at Your service. There we shall eat of the offerings and Passover sacrifices *(On Saturday night some say: of the Passover sacrifices and offerings)* whose blood will gain the sides of Your altar for gracious acceptance. We shall then sing a new song of praise to You for our redemption and for the liberation of our souls. Blessed are You, HASHEM, Who has redeemed Israel.

returning to its flow to drown the Egyptians. Why does one nation deserve salvation more than the other? The *braisa* of Rabbi Ishmael provided the answer. The Egyptians were pursuing Israel and were prepared to murder them. Therefore the sea was obliged even to drown the Egytians in order to effect the rescue of the Jews *(Avnei Azel)*.

Surely for the rebbi ◄§ Or the *Midrash* may refer to a different *braisa* of Rabbi Yishmael. At the conclusion of the *Korbanos* section of *Shacharis*, we recite Rabbi Yishmael's י״ג מדות שהַתּוֹרָה נִדְרֶשֶׁת בָּהֶם, *Thirteen Principles of Torah Exegesis*. One of the principles is קַל וְחוֹמֶר, *a fortiori*. The sea knew that forty years later, the Jordan River would stop flowing in order to allow Joshua to lead the Jews into Eretz Yisrael. [That is why our verse concludes הַיַּרְדֵּן יִסּוֹב לְאָחוֹר, *the Jordan will turn back —* יִסּוֹב, *will turn*, is future tense.] The sea expounded a קַל וְחוֹמֶר, *a fortiori*, after the manner of Rabbi Ishmael: if the Jordan will stop flowing for Joshua who is merely a *disciple* of Moses, than surely I should split for Moses himself *(Kehilas Yitzchak)*.

119   **The Haggadah Treasury**

Over the second cup of wine, one recites:

בָּרוּךְ אַתָּה יהוה אֱלֹהֵינוּ מֶלֶךְ הָעוֹלָם בּוֹ
הַגָּפֶן:

ld be drunk while leaning on the left side — preferably the entire
cup, but at least most of it.

רחצה

washed for *matzah*. It is preferable to bring water and a basin
the head of the household at the *Seder* table.

בָּרוּךְ אַתָּה יהוה אֱלֹהֵינוּ מֶלֶךְ הָ
קִדְּשָׁנוּ בְּמִצְוֹתָיו וְצִוָּנוּ עַל נְטִילַת יָדָיִם

אֲשֶׁר

מוציא מצה

It should be borne in mind that the following blessings apply also to the כּוֹרֵךְ,
sandwich. Therefore, no interruption is permitted until after the 'sandwich' has
been eaten.
The head of the household lifts all the *matzos* on the *Seder* plate and recites the
הַמּוֹצִיא blessing.

בָּרוּךְ אַתָּה יהוה אֱלֹהֵינוּ מֶלֶךְ הָעוֹלָם הַמּוֹצִיא
לֶחֶם מִן־הָאָרֶץ:

The bottom *matzah* is put down and the following blessing is recited while the
top (whole) *matzah* and the broken piece are held. One should bear in mind that
the blessing refers also to the 'sandwich' and the *afikoman*.

בָּרוּךְ אַתָּה יהוה אֱלֹהֵינוּ מֶלֶךְ הָעוֹלָם אֲשֶׁר
קִדְּשָׁנוּ בְּמִצְוֹתָיו וְצִוָּנוּ עַל אֲכִילַת מַצָּה:

Each participant should eat an amount of *matzah* equivalent to two olives (see
Halachah section), one from each *matzah*. Obviously, it is impossible for a single

Over the second cup of wine, one recites:

Blessed are You, HASHEM our God, King of the universe, Who creates the fruit of the vine.

The cup should be drunk while leaning on the left side — preferably the entire cup, but at least most of it.

Rachtzah

— The hands are washed for *matzah*. It is preferable to bring water and a basin to the head of the household at the *Seder* table.

Blessed are You, HASHEM our God, King of the universe, Who has sanctified us by His commandments, and has commanded us concerning the washing of the hands.

Motzi Matzah

It should be borne in mind that the following blessings apply also to the כּוֹרֵךְ, *sandwich*. Therefore, no interruption is permitted until after the 'sandwich' has been eaten.
The head of the household lifts all the *matzos* on the *Seder* plate and recites the הַמּוֹצִיא blessing.

Blessed are You, HASHEM our God, King of the universe, Who brings forth bread from the earth.

The bottom *matzah* is put down and the following blessing is recited while the top (whole) *matzah* and the broken piece are held. One should bear in mind that the blessing refers also to the 'sandwich' and the *afikoman*.

Blessed are You, HASHEM our God, King of the universe, Who has sanctified us by His commandments, and has commanded us concerning the eating of the matzoh.

Each participant should eat an amount of *matzah* equivalent to two olives (see *Halachah* section), one from each *matzah*. Obviously, it is impossible for a single

matzah to provide a sufficient amount for each participant. Therefore, other matzos should be available from which to complete the required amount. Each participant should receive a small piece from each of the top two matzos, however. The matzos must be eaten while reclining and within the prescribed time-span (see Halachah section). The matzos need not be dipped into salt.

מרור

The head of the household takes the prescribed amount of Maror (see Halachah section), dips it into charoses, and shakes off the charoses. Each participant receives a like amount. The blessing applies to the maror of the sandwich , as well. Maror is eaten without reclining, and within the proper time-span.

בָּרוּךְ אַתָּה יהוה אֱלֹהֵינוּ מֶלֶךְ הָעוֹלָם אֲשֶׁר קִדְּשָׁנוּ בְּמִצְוֹתָיו וְצִוָּנוּ עַל אֲכִילַת מָרוֹר:

כורך

The bottom (thus far unbroken) matzah is now taken. From it, with the addition of other matzos, each participant receives and olive-sized portion of matzah along with an olive-sized portion of maror (dipped into charoses which is shaken off). The sandwich is eaten while reclining.

זֵכֶר לְמִקְדָּשׁ כְּהִלֵּל. כֵּן עָשָׂה הִלֵּל בִּזְמַן שֶׁבֵּית הַמִּקְדָּשׁ הָיָה קַיָּם. הָיָה כּוֹרֵךְ (פֶּסַח) מַצָּה וּמָרוֹר וְאוֹכֵל בְּיַחַד. לְקַיֵּם מַה שֶׁנֶּאֱמַר עַל-מַצוֹת וּמְרֹרִים יֹאכְלֻהוּ:

שלחן עורך

The meal should be eaten in a combination of joy and solemnity, for the meal, too, is part of the Seder ritual. While it is desirable that zemiros and discussion of the laws and events of Pesach be part of the meal, extraneous conversation should be avoided. It should be remembered that the Afikoman must be eaten while there is still some appetite for it. In fact, if one is so sated that he must

matzah to provide a sufficient amount for each participant. Therefore, other *matzos* should be available from which to complete the required amount. Each participant should receive a small piece from each of the top two *matzos*, however. The *matzos* must be eaten while reclining and within the prescribed time-span (see *Halachah* section). The *matzos* need not be dipped into salt.

Maror

The head of the household takes the prescribed amount of *Maror* (see *Halachah* section), dips it into *charoses*, and shakes off the *charoses*. Each participant receives a like amount. The blessing applies to the *maror* of the sandwich , as well. *Maror* is eaten *without* reclining, and within the proper time-span.

Blessed are You, HASHEM our God, King of the universe, Who has sanctified us by His commandments, and has commanded us concerning the eating of Maror.

Korech

The bottom (thus far unbroken) *matzah* is now taken. From it, with the addition of other *matzos*, each participant receives and olive-sized portion of *matzah* along with an olive-sized portion of *maror* (dipped into *charoses* which is shaken off). The sandwich is eaten while reclining.

In rememberance of the Temple we do as Hillel did in Temple times: he would combine Pesach, matzoh and marror in a sandwich and eat them together, to fulfill what is written in the Torah *(Bamidbar* 9:11): *"They shall eat it with matzos and bitter herbs."*

Shulchan Orech

The meal should be eaten in a combination of joy and solemnity, for the meal, too, is part of the *Seder* ritual. While it is desirable that *zemiros* and discussion of the laws and events of *Pesach* be part of the meal, extraneous conversation should be avoided. It should be remembered that the *Afikoman* must be eaten while there is still some appetite for it. In fact, if one is so sated that he must

literally force himself to eat it, he is not credited with the performance of the *mitzvah*. Therefore, it is unwise to eat more than a moderate amount during the meal.

It is customary to eat an egg during the meal. *Pri Megadim* explains that egg is a food of mourners, and we mourn the fact that we are as yet unable to offer the *Pesach* sacrifice. *Vilna Gaon* maintains that the egg from the *Seder* plate is eaten in memory of the *Chagigah* offering.

צפון

From the *Afikoman matzah*, an olive-sized portion — according to some, *two* olive-sized portions — is given to each participant. It should be eaten before midnight, while reclining, without delay, and uninterruptedly. Nothing may be eaten or drunk after the *Afikoman* (with the exception of water and the like) except for the last two *Seder* cups.

ברך

The third cup is poured and *Bircas Hamazon* recited. According to some customs, the כּוֹס שֶׁל אֵלִיָהוּ, *Cup of Elijah*, is poured at this point.

שִׁיר הַמַּעֲלוֹת בְּשׁוּב יהוה אֶת שִׁיבַת צִיוֹן הָיִינוּ
כְּחֹלְמִים: אָז יִמָּלֵא שְׂחוֹק פִּינוּ וּלְשׁוֹנֵנוּ רִנָּה אָז
יֹאמְרוּ בַגּוֹיִם הִגְדִּיל יהוה לַעֲשׂוֹת עִם אֵלֶּה: הִגְדִּיל
יהוה לַעֲשׂוֹת עִמָּנוּ הָיִינוּ שְׂמֵחִים: שׁוּבָה יהוה אֶת
שְׁבִיתֵנוּ כַּאֲפִיקִים בַּנֶּגֶב: הַזֹּרְעִים בְּדִמְעָה בְּרִנָּה
יִקְצֹרוּ: הָלוֹךְ יֵלֵךְ וּבָכֹה נֹשֵׂא מֶשֶׁךְ הַזָּרַע בֹּא־יָבֹא
בְרִנָּה נֹשֵׂא אֲלֻמֹּתָיו:

literally force himself to eat it, he is not credited with the performance of the *mitzvah*. Therefore, it is unwise to eat more than a moderate amount during the meal.

It is customary to eat an egg during the meal. *Pri Megadim* explains that egg is a food of mourners, and we mourn the fact that we are as yet unable to offer the *Pesach* sacrifice. *Vilna Gaon* maintains that the egg from the *Seder* plate is eaten in memory of the *Chagigah* offering.

Tzafun

From the *Afikoman matzah*, an olive-sized portion — according to some, *two* olive-sized portions — is given to each participant. It should be eaten before midnight, while reclining, without delay, and uninterruptedly. Nothing may be eaten or drunk after the *Afikoman* (with the exception of water and the like) except for the last two *Seder* cups.

Barech

The third cup is poured and *Bircas Hamazon* recited. According to some customs, the כּוֹס שֶׁל אֵלִיָּהוּ, *Cup of Elijah*, is poured at this point.

*A Song of Ascents. When HASHEM will return the captivity of Zion, we will be like dreamers. Then our mouth will be filled with laughter and our tongue with glad song. Then we will declare among nations, 'HASHEM has done greatly with these.' HASHEM has done greatly with us, we were gladdened. O HASHEM — return our captivity like springs in the desert. Those who tearfully will reap in glad joy. He who bears the worthy seed will walk on, weeping. He will return in exultation, a bearer of his sheaves. (Tehillim 126).

This translation of Grace After Meals is reprinted from the Artscroll Mesorah Series edition of Bircas HaMazon with the kind permission of the publishers; Copyright 1977 Mesorah Publications Ltd. N.Y.C.

If at least three males, aged thirteen or older eat together, one of them becomes
leader of the group in reciting *Bircas Hamazon*, beginning here:

The leader begins:

רַבּוֹתַי נְבָרֵךְ.

All respond:

יְהִי שֵׁם יהוה מְבֹרָךְ מֵעַתָּה וְעַד-עוֹלָם.

The leader continues:

יְהִי שֵׁם יהוה מְבֹרָךְ מֵעַתָּה וְעַד-עוֹלָם.

If 10 men join in the Zimun add 'our God'

בִּרְשׁוּת מָרָנָן וְרַבָּנָן וְרַבּוֹתַי נְבָרֵךְ (אֱלֹהֵינוּ) שֶׁאָכַלְנוּ מִשֶּׁלּוֹ.

The others respond:

בָּרוּךְ (אֱלֹהֵינוּ) שֶׁאָכַלְנוּ מִשֶּׁלּוֹ וּבְטוּבוֹ חָיִינוּ.

The leader concludes:

בָּרוּךְ (אֱלֹהֵינוּ) שֶׁאָכַלְנוּ מִשֶּׁלּוֹ וּבְטוּבוֹ חָיִינוּ.

בָּרוּךְ הוּא וּבָרוּךְ שְׁמוֹ

בָּרוּךְ אַתָּה יהוה אֱלֹהֵינוּ מֶלֶךְ הָעוֹלָם הַזָּן אֶת
הָעוֹלָם כֻּלּוֹ בְּטוּבוֹ בְּחֵן בְּחֶסֶד וּבְרַחֲמִים הוּא נֹתֵן
לֶחֶם לְכָל בָּשָׂר כִּי לְעוֹלָם חַסְדּוֹ. וּבְטוּבוֹ הַגָּדוֹל
תָּמִיד לֹא-חָסַר לָנוּ וְאַל-יֶחְסַר לָנוּ מָזוֹן לְעוֹלָם וָעֶד.

בָּרֵךְ — Bircas Hamazon

Only G-d gives nourishment 🍃 הוּא נוֹתֵן לֶחֶם לְכָל בָּשָׂר — *He gives nourishment to all flesh*

The Talmud says in *Ta'anis* 2a that Hashem makes use of angels to carry out nearly all functions on earth. An exception to this rule is פַּרְנָסָה, the provision of sustenance for which He holds the מַפְתְּחוֹת, *keys*,

If at least three males, aged thirteen or older eat together, one of them becomes leader of the group in reciting *Bircas Hamazon*, beginning here:

The leader begins:

Gentlemen let us bless.

All respond:

Blessed be the Name of HASHEM from this moment and forever!

The leader continues:

Blessed be the Name of HASHEM from this moment and forever!

If 10 men join in the *Zimun* add *'our God'*

With the permission of the distinguished people present let us bless [our God] for we have eaten from what is His.

The others respond:

Blessed be [our God] He of Whose we have eaten and through Whose goodness we live.

The leader concludes:

Blessed be [our God] He of Whose we have eaten and through Whose goodness we live.

Blessed be He and blessed be His Name.

Blessed are You, HASHEM, our God, King of the universe, Who nourishes the entire world; in His goodness, with grace, with lovingkindness, and with mercy. He gives nourishment to all flesh, for His lovingkindness is eternal. And through His great goodness nourishment was never lacking to us and may

Himself. The reason for this is that an angel would give food only to those who are deserving. G-d, however, in His infinite mercy provides even for people who are undeserving. Therefore, in thanking Him for food, we emphasize that הוּא נוֹתֵן לֶחֶם, *'He'* gives nourishment — we are grateful that it is He, Himself, Who provides for us *(Rif).*

בַּעֲבוּר שְׁמוֹ הַגָּדוֹל כִּי הוּא אֵל זָן וּמְפַרְנֵס לַכֹּל
וּמֵטִיב לַכֹּל וּמֵכִין מָזוֹן לְכָל בְּרִיּוֹתָיו אֲשֶׁר בָּרָא
(כָּאָמוּר פּוֹתֵחַ אֶת יָדֶךָ וּמַשְׂבִּיעַ לְכָל חַי רָצוֹן). בָּרוּךְ
אַתָּה יהוה הַזָּן אֶת־הַכֹּל:

נוֹדֶה לְךָ יהוה אֱלֹהֵינוּ עַל שֶׁהִנְחַלְתָּ לַאֲבוֹתֵינוּ
אֶרֶץ חֶמְדָּה טוֹבָה וּרְחָבָה וְעַל שֶׁהוֹצֵאתָנוּ יהוה
אֱלֹהֵינוּ מֵאֶרֶץ מִצְרַיִם וּפְדִיתָנוּ מִבֵּית עֲבָדִים וְעַל
בְּרִיתְךָ שֶׁחָתַמְתָּ בִּבְשָׂרֵנוּ וְעַל תּוֹרָתְךָ שֶׁלִּמַּדְתָּנוּ וְעַל
חֻקֶּיךָ שֶׁהוֹדַעְתָּנוּ וְעַל חַיִּים חֵן וָחֶסֶד שֶׁחוֹנַנְתָּנוּ וְעַל
אֲכִילַת מָזוֹן שָׁאַתָּה זָן וּמְפַרְנֵס אוֹתָנוּ תָּמִיד בְּכָל יוֹם
וּבְכָל עֵת וּבְכָל שָׁעָה:

The strength to accept	ﭏ פּוֹתֵחַ אֶת יָדֶךָ וּמַשְׂבִּיעַ לְכָל חַי רָצוֹן ﭏ — *You open Your hand and satisfy the desire of every living thing.*

Hashem does not bring suffering on people unless they have the spiritual resources to accept it willingly and learn from it. Thus, we may be confident that if He gives someone a full measure of travail, He also provides a commensurate measure of strength to cope with the affliction. This is implied by our verse: You open Your hand to satisfy every living person with the רָצוֹן, *willingness*, to accept and say [*Berachos* 60b]: כָּל דְּעָבִיד רַחֲמָנָא לְטָב עָבִיד, *whatever the Merciful One does, He does for the good (Baal Shem Tov).*

The gift of satisfaction — ﭏ Why was David so ambiguous — instead of saying that G-d satisfies a vague *desire*, why didn't he say that G-d provides כֶּסֶף וְזָהָב, *gold and silver?*

As our Sages say, מִי שֶׁיֵּשׁ לוֹ מָנָה רוֹצֶה מָאתַיִם, *one who has a hundred wants to have two hundred (Koheles Rabbah 1:3).* Thus, the gift of prosperity is not an unmixed blessing because the recipient of material good merely has his appetite whetted for more. The greatest

it never be lacking to us forever. For the sake of His Great Name, because He is the God Who nourishes and sustains all, and benefits all, and He prepares food for all of His creatures which He has created; (as it is said, 'You open Your Hand and satisfy the desire of every living thing'). Blessed are You, HASHEM, Who nourishes all.

We thank You, HASHEM, our God, because You have given to our forefathers as a heritage a desirable, good and spacious land; because You removed us, HASHEM, our God, from the land of Egypt and You redeemed us from the house of bondage; for Your covenant which You sealed in our flesh; for Your Torah which You taught us and for Your statutes which You made known to us; for life, grace, and lovingkindness which You granted us; and for the provision of food with which You nourish and sustain us constantly, in every day, in every season, and in every hour.

of all blessings is what David specifies: רָצוֹן, that a person be satisfied with what he has *(Rabbi Zalman Sorotzkin).*

Exodus and covenant

וְעַל שֶׁהוֹצֵאתָנוּ ... מֵאֶרֶץ מִצְרַיִם ... וְעַל בְּרִיתְךָ שֶׁחָתַמְתָּ ᵉ৯ בִּבְשָׂרֵנוּ — *Because You removed us ... from the land of Egypt ... and for Your covenant which You sealed in our flesh.*

As we have seen above, the Jews at the threshold of the Exodus lacked the merits without which they could not be redeemed. Hashem gave them two commandments which they could perform immediately — the *Pesach* sacrifice and circumcision. Thus circumcision was instrumental in making the Exodus possible. That is why the covenant of circumcision is mentioned in conjunction with the Exodus. [The *Pesach* sacrifice is not mentioned because it is not a constant phenomenon like the others for which we thank Hashem after every meal] *(E'is l'Daber).*

וְעַל הַכֹּל יהוה אֱלֹהֵינוּ אֲנַחְנוּ מוֹדִים לָךְ וּמְבָרְכִים
אוֹתָךְ יִתְבָּרַךְ שִׁמְךָ בְּפִי כָּל חַי תָּמִיד לְעוֹלָם וָעֶד.
כַּכָּתוּב וְאָכַלְתָּ וְשָׂבָעְתָּ וּבֵרַכְתָּ אֶת יהוה אֱלֹהֶיךָ עַל
הָאָרֶץ הַטֹּבָה אֲשֶׁר נָתַן לָךְ. בָּרוּךְ אַתָּה יהוה עַל
הָאָרֶץ וְעַל הַמָּזוֹן:

רַחֵם יהוה אֱלֹהֵינוּ עַל יִשְׂרָאֵל עַמֶּךָ וְעַל יְרוּשָׁלַיִם
עִירֶךָ וְעַל צִיּוֹן מִשְׁכַּן כְּבוֹדֶךָ וְעַל מַלְכוּת בֵּית דָּוִד
מְשִׁיחֶךָ וְעַל הַבַּיִת הַגָּדוֹל וְהַקָּדוֹשׁ שֶׁנִּקְרָא שִׁמְךָ
עָלָיו. אֱלֹהֵינוּ אָבִינוּ רְעֵנוּ זוּנֵנוּ פַּרְנְסֵנוּ וְכַלְכְּלֵנוּ
וְהַרְוִיחֵנוּ וְהַרְוַח לָנוּ יהוה אֱלֹהֵינוּ מְהֵרָה מִכָּל
צָרוֹתֵינוּ. וְנָא אַל תַּצְרִיכֵנוּ יהוה אֱלֹהֵינוּ לֹא לִידֵי
מַתְּנַת בָּשָׂר וָדָם וְלֹא לִידֵי הַלְוָאָתָם כִּי אִם לְיָדְךָ
הַמְּלֵאָה הַפְּתוּחָה הַקְּדוֹשָׁה וְהָרְחָבָה שֶׁלֹּא נֵבוֹשׁ
וְלֹא נִכָּלֵם לְעוֹלָם וָעֶד:

On Shabbos add the following paragraph:

רְצֵה וְהַחֲלִיצֵנוּ יהוה אֱלֹהֵינוּ בְּמִצְוֹתֶיךָ וּבְמִצְוַת יוֹם
הַשְּׁבִיעִי הַשַּׁבָּת הַגָּדוֹל וְהַקָּדוֹשׁ הַזֶּה כִּי יוֹם זֶה גָּדוֹל וְקָדוֹשׁ
הוּא לְפָנֶיךָ לִשְׁבָּת בּוֹ וְלָנוּחַ בּוֹ בְּאַהֲבָה כְּמִצְוַת רְצוֹנֶךָ
וּבִרְצוֹנְךָ הָנִיחַ לָנוּ יהוה אֱלֹהֵינוּ שֶׁלֹּא תְהֵא צָרָה וְיָגוֹן
וַאֲנָחָה בְּיוֹם מְנוּחָתֵנוּ וְהַרְאֵנוּ יהוה אֱלֹהֵינוּ בְּנֶחָמַת צִיּוֹן
עִירֶךָ וּבְבִנְיַן יְרוּשָׁלַיִם עִיר קָדְשֶׁךָ כִּי אַתָּה הוּא בַּעַל
הַיְשׁוּעוֹת וּבַעַל הַנֶּחָמוֹת:

אֱלֹהֵינוּ וֵאלֹהֵי אֲבוֹתֵינוּ יַעֲלֶה וְיָבֹא וְיַגִּיעַ וְיֵרָאֶה
וְיֵרָצֶה וְיִשָּׁמַע וְיִפָּקֵד וְיִזָּכֵר זִכְרוֹנֵנוּ וּפִקְדוֹנֵנוּ וְזִכְרוֹן
אֲבוֹתֵינוּ וְזִכְרוֹן מָשִׁיחַ בֶּן דָּוִד עַבְדֶּךָ וְזִכְרוֹן יְרוּשָׁלַיִם

For all, HASHEM, our God, we thank You and bless You. May Your Name be blessed continuously forever by the mouth of all the living. As it is written, 'And you shall eat and be satisfied and bless HASHEM, your God, for the good land which He gave you.' Blessed are You, HASHEM, for the land and for the food.

Have mercy (we beg You) HASHEM, our God, on Your people Israel, on Your city Jerusalem, on Zion the resting place of Your Glory, on the monarchy of the house of David, Your anointed, and on the great and holy House upon which Your Name is called. Our God, our Father — tend us, nourish us, sustain us, support us, relieve us; HASHEM, our God, grant us speedy relief from all our troubles. Please, HASHEM, our God, make us not needful of the gifts of human hands nor of their loans — but only of Your Hand that is full, open, holy, and generous, that we not feel inner shame or be humiliated for ever and ever.

On Shabbos add the following paragraph:

May it please You, HASHEM, our God — give us rest through Your commandments and through the commandment of the seventh day, this great and holy Sabbath. For this day is great and holy before You to rest on it and be content on it in love, as ordained by Your will. May it be Your will, HASHEM, our God, that there be no distress, grief, or lament on this day of our contentment. And show us, HASHEM, our God, the consolation of Zion, Your city, and the rebuilding of Jerusalem, city of Your holiness, for You are the Master of salvations and Master of consolations.

Our God and God of our fathers, may there rise, come, reach, be noted, be favored, be heard, be considered, and be remembered before You — the remembrance and considera- tion of ourselves, the remembrance of our fathers, the remembrance of Messiah, son of David, Your servant, the remembrance of Jerusalem, Your holy city, and the remembrance of Your entire people, the House of Israel — for

131 **The Haggadah Treasury**

עִיר קָדְשֶׁךָ וְזִכְרוֹן כָּל עַמְּךָ בֵּית יִשְׂרָאֵל לְפָנֶיךָ לִפְלֵיטָה לְטוֹבָה לְחֵן וּלְחֶסֶד וּלְרַחֲמִים לְחַיִּים וּלְשָׁלוֹם בְּיוֹם חַג הַמַּצּוֹת הַזֶּה. זָכְרֵנוּ יהוה אֱלֹהֵינוּ בּוֹ לְטוֹבָה וּפָקְדֵנוּ בוֹ לִבְרָכָה וְהוֹשִׁיעֵנוּ בוֹ לְחַיִּים טוֹבִים וּבִדְבַר יְשׁוּעָה וְרַחֲמִים חוּס וְחָנֵּנוּ וְרַחֵם עָלֵינוּ וְהוֹשִׁיעֵנוּ כִּי אֵלֶיךָ עֵינֵינוּ כִּי אֵל (מֶלֶךְ) חַנּוּן וְרַחוּם אָתָּה:

וּבְנֵה יְרוּשָׁלַיִם עִיר הַקֹּדֶשׁ בִּמְהֵרָה בְיָמֵינוּ. בָּרוּךְ אַתָּה יהוה בּוֹנֶה בְרַחֲמָיו יְרוּשָׁלָיִם. אָמֵן:

בָּרוּךְ אַתָּה יהוה אֱלֹהֵינוּ מֶלֶךְ הָעוֹלָם הָאֵל אָבִינוּ מַלְכֵּנוּ אַדִּירֵנוּ בּוֹרְאֵנוּ גּוֹאֲלֵנוּ יוֹצְרֵנוּ קְדוֹשֵׁנוּ קְדוֹשׁ יַעֲקֹב רוֹעֵנוּ רוֹעֵה יִשְׂרָאֵל הַמֶּלֶךְ הַטּוֹב וְהַמֵּטִיב לַכֹּל שֶׁבְּכָל יוֹם וָיוֹם הוּא הֵטִיב הוּא מֵטִיב הוּא יֵיטִיב לָנוּ. הוּא גְמָלָנוּ הוּא גוֹמְלֵנוּ הוּא יִגְמְלֵנוּ לָעַד לְחֵן וּלְחֶסֶד וּלְרַחֲמִים וּלְרֶוַח הַצָּלָה וְהַצְלָחָה בְּרָכָה וִישׁוּעָה נֶחָמָה פַּרְנָסָה וְכַלְכָּלָה וְרַחֲמִים וְחַיִּים וְשָׁלוֹם וְכָל טוֹב וּמִכָּל טוּב לְעוֹלָם אַל יְחַסְּרֵנוּ:

הָרַחֲמָן הוּא יִמְלוֹךְ עָלֵינוּ לְעוֹלָם וָעֶד. הָרַחֲמָן הוּא יִתְבָּרַךְ בַּשָּׁמַיִם וּבָאָרֶץ. הָרַחֲמָן הוּא יִשְׁתַּבַּח לְדוֹר דּוֹרִים וְיִתְפָּאַר בָּנוּ לָעַד וּלְנֵצַח נְצָחִים וְיִתְהַדַּר בָּנוּ לָעַד וּלְעוֹלְמֵי עוֹלָמִים. הָרַחֲמָן הוּא יְפַרְנְסֵנוּ בְּכָבוֹד. הָרַחֲמָן הוּא יִשְׁבּוֹר עֻלֵּנוּ מֵעַל צַוָּארֵנוּ וְהוּא יוֹלִיכֵנוּ קוֹמְמִיּוּת לְאַרְצֵנוּ. הָרַחֲמָן הוּא יִשְׁלַח לָנוּ

deliverance, for well-being, for grace, for lovingkindness, and for mercy, for life and for peace on this day of the Festival of Matzos. Remember us on it, HASHEM our God, for goodness, consider us on it for blessing, and help us on it for good life. Concerning salvation and mercy, have pity, show grace and be merciful upon us and help us. For our eyes are turned to You; for You are the Almighty, gracious, and merciful (King).

Rebuild Jerusalem, the Holy City, soon in our days. Blessed are You, HASHEM, Who rebuilds Jerusalem in His mercy. Amen.

Blessed are You, HASHEM our God, King of the Universe, the Almighty, our Father, our King, our Sovereign, our Creator, our Redeemer, our Maker, our Holy One, Holy One of Jacob, our Shepherd, the Shepherd of Israel, the good and beneficent King. For every single day He did good, does good, and will do good to us. He was bountiful with us, is bountiful with us, and will forever be bountiful with us — with grace and with lovingkindness and with mercy, with relief, salvation, success, blessing, help, consolation, sustenance, support, mercy, life, peace, and all good; and of all good things may He never deprive us.

The compassionate One! May He reign over us forever.

The compassionate One! May He be blessed on heaven and on earth.

The compassionate One! May He be praised throughout all generations; may He be glorified through us to the ultimate ends, and be honored through us to the inscrutable everlasting.

The compassionate One! May He sustain us in honor.

The compassionate One! May He break the yoke of oppression from our necks and guide us erect to our Land.

בְּרָכָה מְרֻבָּה בַּבַּיִת הַזֶּה וְעַל שֻׁלְחָן זֶה שֶׁאָכַלְנוּ עָלָיו.
הָרַחֲמָן הוּא יִשְׁלַח לָנוּ אֶת אֵלִיָּהוּ הַנָּבִיא זָכוּר לַטּוֹב
וִיבַשֶּׂר לָנוּ בְּשׂוֹרוֹת טוֹבוֹת יְשׁוּעוֹת וְנֶחָמוֹת. הָרַחֲמָן
הוּא יְבָרֵךְ

Guests start here, adding the words in parentheses in their parents' home:

אֶת (אָבִי מוֹרִי) בַּעַל הַבַּיִת הַזֶּה וְאֶת (אִמִּי מוֹרָתִי)
בַּעֲלַת הַבַּיִת הַזֶּה.

The host and the hostess start here
adding the words in parentheses if applicable:

אוֹתִי (וְאֶת אִשְׁתִּי / בַּעֲלִי וְאֶת זַרְעִי) וְאֶת כָּל אֲשֶׁר
לִי וְאֶת כָּל הַמְסֻבִּין כָּאן. אוֹתָם וְאֶת בֵּיתָם וְאֶת
זַרְעָם וְאֶת כָּל אֲשֶׁר לָהֶם אוֹתָנוּ וְאֶת כָּל אֲשֶׁר לָנוּ
כְּמוֹ שֶׁנִּתְבָּרְכוּ אֲבוֹתֵינוּ אַבְרָהָם יִצְחָק וְיַעֲקֹב בַּכֹּל
מִכֹּל כֹּל כֵּן יְבָרֵךְ אוֹתָנוּ כֻּלָּנוּ יַחַד בִּבְרָכָה שְׁלֵמָה
וְנֹאמַר אָמֵן:

בַּמָּרוֹם יְלַמְּדוּ עֲלֵיהֶם וְעָלֵינוּ זְכוּת שֶׁתְּהֵא
לְמִשְׁמֶרֶת שָׁלוֹם. וְנִשָּׂא בְרָכָה מֵאֵת יהוה וּצְדָקָה
מֵאֱלֹהֵי יִשְׁעֵנוּ וְנִמְצָא חֵן וְשֵׂכֶל טוֹב בְּעֵינֵי אֱלֹהִים
וְאָדָם:

On Shabbos add:

הָרַחֲמָן הוּא יַנְחִילֵנוּ יוֹם שֶׁכֻּלּוֹ שַׁבָּת וּמְנוּחָה לְחַיֵּי
הָעוֹלָמִים:

הָרַחֲמָן הוּא יַנְחִילֵנוּ יוֹם שֶׁכֻּלּוֹ טוֹב. יוֹם שֶׁכֻּלּוֹ
אָרוּךְ. יוֹם שֶׁצַּדִּיקִים יוֹשְׁבִים וְעַטְרוֹתֵיהֶם בְּרָאשֵׁיהֶם
וְנֶהֱנִים מִזִּיו הַשְּׁכִינָה וִיהִי חֶלְקֵנוּ עִמָּהֶם:

The compassionate One! May He send us abundant blessing to this house and upon the table which we have eaten.

The compassionate One! May He send us Elijah, the Prophet — may he be remembered for good — to proclaim to us good tidings, salvations, and consolations.

The compassionate One! May He bless —

Guests start here, adding the words in parentheses in their parents' home:
(my father, my teacher) the master of this house, and (my mother, my teacher) lady of this house,

The host and the hostess start here
adding the words in parentheses if applicable:

me (my wife/husband and family) and all that is mine, and all that sit here; them, their house, their family, and all that is theirs, ours and all that is ours — just as our forefathers Abraham, Isaac and Jacob were blessed in everything, from everything, with everything. So may He bless us all together with a perfect blessing. And let us say: Amen!

On high, may merit be pleaded upon them and upon us, for a safeguard of peace. May we receive a blessing from Hashem and just kindness from the God of our salvation, and find favor and understanding in the eyes of God and man.

(On Shabbos): The compassionate One! May He cause us to inherit the day which will be completely a Sabbath and rest day for eternal life.

The compassionate One! May he cause us to inherit that day which is altogether good, that everlasting day, the day when the just will sit with crowns on their heads, enjoying the reflection of God's Majesty — and may our portion be with them!

הָרַחֲמָן הוּא יְזַכֵּנוּ לִימוֹת הַמָּשִׁיחַ וּלְחַיֵּי הָעוֹלָם הַבָּא. מַגְדִּיל יְשׁוּעוֹת מַלְכּוֹ וְעֹשֶׂה חֶסֶד לִמְשִׁיחוֹ לְדָוִד וּלְזַרְעוֹ עַד עוֹלָם. עֹשֶׂה שָׁלוֹם בִּמְרוֹמָיו הוּא יַעֲשֶׂה שָׁלוֹם עָלֵינוּ וְעַל כָּל יִשְׂרָאֵל וְאִמְרוּ אָמֵן:

יְראוּ אֶת יהוה קְדֹשָׁיו כִּי אֵין מַחְסוֹר לִירֵאָיו. כְּפִירִים רָשׁוּ וְרָעֵבוּ וְדֹרְשֵׁי יהוה לֹא יַחְסְרוּ כָל טוֹב. הוֹדוּ לַיהוה כִּי טוֹב כִּי לְעוֹלָם חַסְדּוֹ. פּוֹתֵחַ אֶת יָדֶךָ וּמַשְׂבִּיעַ לְכָל חַי רָצוֹן. בָּרוּךְ הַגֶּבֶר אֲשֶׁר יִבְטַח בַּיהוה וְהָיָה יהוה מִבְטַחוֹ. נַעַר הָיִיתִי גַּם זָקַנְתִּי וְלֹא רָאִיתִי צַדִּיק נֶעֱזָב וְזַרְעוֹ מְבַקֶּשׁ לָחֶם. יהוה עֹז לְעַמּוֹ יִתֵּן יהוה יְבָרֵךְ אֶת עַמּוֹ בַשָּׁלוֹם:

The third cup is drunk while reclining.

בָּרוּךְ אַתָּה יהוה אֱלֹהֵינוּ מֶלֶךְ הָעוֹלָם בּוֹרֵא פְּרִי הַגָּפֶן:

יראו את ה' — Fear Hashem

Fear of too much good

◆§ יִרְאוּ אֶת ה' קְדֹשָׁיו כִּי אֵין מַחְסוֹר לִירֵאָיו — *Fear HASHEM, His holy ones, for those who fear Him feel no deprivation*

Righteous people have always feared that good for-tune in this world may be an indication that they have been drawing on their store of merit that should be in-suring their share in the world to come. So it was that after his defeat of the Four Kings, Abraham feared that the miracle had been at the cost of his accumulated merit (*Bereishis* 15:1); similarly Jacob feared that his safe departure from Laban had left him ill-equipped spiritually to survive the ordeal of a confrontation with Esau (*ibid* 32:10). In a like vein King David said יִרְאוּ

The compassionate One! May He make us worthy to attain the days of Messiah and the life of the World to Come. He who is a tower of salvations to His king and shows lovingkindness to His anointed, to David and his descendants forever. He Who makes harmony in His heavenly heights, may He make harmony for us and all Israel. Say: Amen!

Fear HASHEM, His holy ones, for those who fear Him feel no deprivation. Young lions may feel want and hunger, but those who seek HASHEM will not lack any good. Give thanks to God, for He is good; His kindness is eternal. You open Your hand and satisfy the desire of every living thing. Blessed is the man who trusts in HASHEM, and HASHEM will be his trust. I was a youth and also have aged, and I have not seen a righteous man forsaken, with his children begging for bread. HASHEM will give might to His nation; HASHEM will bless His nation with peace.

The third cup is drunk while reclining.

Blessed are You, HASHEM our God, King of the universe, Who creates the fruit of the vine.

אֶת ה' קְדוֹשָׁיו, *holy people fear HASHEM*, i.e., they consider themselves undeserving, *especially* כִּי אֵין מַחְסוֹר לִירֵאָיו, *when those who fear Him are not deprived of anything* — for if they seem to be granted limitless blessing, they are afraid that they will be left devoid of merit (*Kedushas Levi*).

Lacking nothing ◦§ וְדֹרְשֵׁי ה' לֹא יַחְסְרוּ כָל טוֹב — *They who seek HASHEM will not lack any good.*

Truly righteous may indeed lack many luxuries and comforts — even necessities. But in their *own* minds they lack nothing because they are satisfied and happy with their lot (*Rabbi Zalman Sorotzkin*).

The fourth cup is poured. Acording to most customs, the כּוֹס שֶׁל אֵלִיָּהוּ, *Cup of Elijah* is poured, at this point after which the door is opened and שְׁפֹךְ חֲמָתְךָ recited.

שְׁפֹךְ חֲמָתְךָ אֶל הַגּוֹיִם אֲשֶׁר לֹא יְדָעוּךָ וְעַל

כּוֹס שֶׁל אֵלִיָּהוּ — The Cup of Eliyahu

Elijah and fulfillment

◆§ According to some opinions, there is a requirement to drink a fifth cup at the *Seder* in commemoration of the Divine pledge of וְהֵבֵאתִי אֶתְכֶם אֶל הָאָרֶץ, *and I will bring you to the Land (Sh'mos 6:8).* According to others, there is no cup commemorating that pledge because its final fulfillment has not yet come (see *Pesachim* 118a, *Rif* and *Tos.* ad loc.). We do not drink a fifth cup, because the halachah is in doubt, but we pour it and leave it on the table to await the coming of the prophet Elijah whose advent will presage Messiah and the fulfillment of the pledge. Further, we have a tradition that Elijah will provide the conclusive answers to all undecided halachic questions. Therefore, the Cup of Eliyahu symbolizes both our hope that he will come soon — even tonight — and our trust that Messiah will bring the final and eternal fulfillment of the promise that exile will become a thing of the past *(Hafla'ah).*

שְׁפֹךְ חֲמָתְךָ — Pour Your wrath

The final cup

◆§ It is customary to open the front door at this point to demonstrate our confidence in G-d's promise that the night of Pesach is לֵיל שִׁמֻּרִים, *a night of watching (S'hmos 12:42)* for all generations, a night when G-d extends special protection to his people. Thus we open the door, unafraid of whatever may be on its other side.

Meiri interprets the Four Cups as symbolic of the four cups of punishment that are the eventual lot of the Four Monarchies who have subjugated Israel since the destruction of the First Bais Hamikdash — Babylonia, Persia, Greece, and Rome. The first three kingdoms have already been wiped from the stage of power, but

The fourth cup is poured. Acording to most customs, the כּוֹס שֶׁל אֵלִיָּהוּ, *Cup of Elijah* is poured, at this point after which the door is opened and שְׁפֹךְ חֲמָתְךָ recited.

Pour Your wrath upon the nations that do not recognize

the fourth, who represents all the forces responsible for the present exile, is still ascendant and still threatens Israel. Thus we pour the fourth cup with a prayer that G-d's wrath be unleashed against these final forces of darkness in the form of the cup of punishment that will accompany the final redemption.

No fear of pairs ◈§ If the open door represents our faith in G-d's promised protection, then why was it not opened at the very beginning of the *Seder*?

The Talmud states that the use of זוּגוֹת, *a combination of pairs*, is a source of danger under certain circumstances (*Pesachim* 109b). [See there and commentaries *ad loc.* for elucidation of the concept of 'pairs'.] If so, why do we use four cups — a multiple of two — at the *Seder*? Because the night of *Pesach* is לֵיל שִׁמּוּרִים, a night when Hashem protects Israel; therefore, we have no fear of 'pairs'. Therefore, the pouring of the fourth cup, which might be interpreted as a dangerous act because it makes *two pairs* of cups, is the proper time to show that on this night we fear no danger (*Bais Halevi*).

When we will watch ◈§ During the final stage of the ten plagues, when the first-born were killed and Pharaoh's resistance crumbled, the Jews followed the command לֹא תֵצְאוּ אִישׁ מִפֶּתַח בֵּיתוֹ עַד בֹּקֶר, *no man may go out from the door of his house until dawn* (*Sh'mos* 12:22). Although the Jews were to be saved, they did not deserve to see the punishments that were to be inflicted upon the Egyptians. [This is similar to the case of Lot and his family who were saved from Sodom but were forbidden to watch the destruction of the city (*Bereishis* 19:17).] However, when the final redemption arrives with the coming of Messiah, Israel *will* be permitted to watch the destruction of evil. Therefore, when we beseech G-d to

139 **The Haggadah Treasury**

מַמְלָכוֹת אֲשֶׁר בְּשִׁמְךָ לֹא קָרָאוּ: כִּי אָכַל אֶת יַעֲקֹב
וְאֶת נָוֵהוּ הֵשַׁמּוּ: שְׁפָךְ עֲלֵיהֶם זַעְמֶךָ וַחֲרוֹן אַפְּךָ
יַשִּׂיגֵם: תִּרְדֹּף בְּאַף וְתַשְׁמִידֵם מִתַּחַת שְׁמֵי יהוה:

pour out His wrath upon the evildoers, we open the
door to symbolize our hope that He will speedily bring
that longed-for time (S'fas Emes).

**To
remember
Jacob**
◄§ The custom of the open door may be derived from a
Midrash quoted in part by Da'as Zekeinim to
Bereishis 27:30. Jacob received the Abrahamitic blessings from Isaac on the Seder night. For that reason, he
prepared two lambs for Isaac, one to represent the
Pesach offering and the other to represent the Chagigah
offering. After Isaac had eaten and blessed Jacob, Esau
threw open the door and entered. Thereupon Jacob hid
behind the open door and escaped the room before Esau
could notice him. To commemorate Jacob's escape at
this juncture of the Seder thanks to the open door, we
open our doors at this point (Menachem Zion).

**The Seder
watch**
◄§ The custom of opening the doors has been based on
medieval history. Beginning with the time of the
Crusaders, it was a common practice for Christians to
place a body in Jewish courtyards during the Seder
night, and then accuse the Jews of murdering him to
secure blood for the baking of matzos and the preparation of wine. These blood libels would become the
pretext for pogroms that cost the lives of countless
Jews. During those periods of danger, Jews would constantly open their doors to see if such a plot was being
executed. As they looked out, they would implore G-d
to pour out His wrath against those who sought to
devour Israel. We maintain the custom although,
Baruch Hashem, we need not share their dread (Ziv
HaMinhagim).

You and upon the kingdoms that do not invoke Your Name. For they have devoured Jacob and destroyed His Habitation. Pour Your anger upon them and let Your fiery wrath overtake them. Pursue them with wrath and annihilate them from beneath the heavens of HASHEM.

Proof of their evil

§ כִּי אָכַל אֶת יַעֲקֹב וְאֶת נָוֵהוּ הֵשַׁמּוּ — *For they have devoured Jacob and destroyed His Habitation.*

This prayer refers to those who destroyed the *Bais Hamikdosh*. By its dual reference to them as the murderers of Jews and as the destroyers of the Temple, it provides the answer to a troubling question: If, as many verses for the Prophets make clear, it was G-d's will that the Bais Hamikdosh be destroyed, why should He punish the nation that carried out the Divine command? One answer, as suggested in our verse, is that they were to be G-d's agents only in destroying the *Bais Hamikdosh*, but they were given no license to murder indiscriminately. That they shed so much Jewish blood in so vicious a manner proves that everything they did — including the destruction of the Temple — was motivated by evil *(Rabbi Mordechai Benet).*

A product of His wrath

§ כִּי אָכַל ... הֵשַׁמּוּ — [lit. *For 'he' devoured ... 'they' destroyed.*]

Why is the first verb in the singular and the second in the plural?

The word אָכַל, *He has devoured,* may refer to G-d. It was G-d Who ordained that Israel must suffer at the hands of its enemies. The nations were merely the tools to carry out the Divine decree. [see above] *(Rabbi Marcus Lehmann).*

[We may go a step further. The destruction perpetrated by the enemies of Israel was made possible only because Israel's sins had turned the wrath of G-d against it. Had not G-d decreed the destruction and the exile, no designs of the nations could have succeeded.]

הלל

לֹא לָנוּ יהוה לֹא לָנוּ כִּי לְשִׁמְךָ תֵּן כָּבוֹד עַל חַסְדְּךָ
עַל אֲמִתֶּךָ: לָמָּה יֹאמְרוּ הַגּוֹיִם אַיֵּה נָא אֱלֹהֵיהֶם:
וֵאלֹהֵינוּ בַשָּׁמַיִם כֹּל אֲשֶׁר חָפֵץ עָשָׂה: עֲצַבֵּיהֶם כֶּסֶף
וְזָהָב מַעֲשֵׂה יְדֵי אָדָם: פֶּה לָהֶם וְלֹא יְדַבֵּרוּ עֵינַיִם
לָהֶם וְלֹא יִרְאוּ: אָזְנַיִם לָהֶם וְלֹא יִשְׁמָעוּ אַף לָהֶם
וְלֹא יְרִיחוּן: יְדֵיהֶם וְלֹא יְמִישׁוּן רַגְלֵיהֶם וְלֹא יְהַלֵּכוּ
לֹא יֶהְגּוּ בִּגְרוֹנָם: כְּמוֹהֶם יִהְיוּ עֹשֵׂיהֶם כֹּל אֲשֶׁר בֹּטֵחַ
בָּהֶם: יִשְׂרָאֵל בְּטַח בַּיהוה עֶזְרָם וּמָגִנָּם הוּא: בֵּית
אַהֲרֹן בִּטְחוּ בַיהוה עֶזְרָם וּמָגִנָּם הוּא: יִרְאֵי יהוה
בִּטְחוּ בַיהוה עֶזְרָם וּמָגִנָּם הוּא:

לֹא לָנוּ — Not for our own sake.

Sad Shortsightedness

§ עֲצַבֵּיהֶם כֶּסֶף וְזָהָב מַעֲשֵׂה יְדֵי אָדָם — *Their idols are silver and gold, the handiwork of man.*

The verse has been interpreted homiletically as follows: עֲצַבֵּיהֶם is related to עַצְבוּת, sadness. It is a sad tragedy that people believe that their amassing of *silver and gold* is a result of their *own handiwork*. People fail to realize that whatever they achieve is only thanks to the goodness of G-d (*Tzemach Tzedek*).

Integral parts of the idol

§ פֶּה לָהֶם ... עֵינַיִם לָהֶם ... אַף לָהֶם ... יְדֵיהֶם ... רַגְלֵיהֶם — *They have a mouth ... they have eyes ... they have a nose ... their hands ... their feet.*

The change of expression is noteworthy — *hands* and *feet* are described as *theirs*, but in connection with the other organs, the verse says, *they have*. The choice of words is based on the Mishnah (*Avodah Zarah* 41a). Pieces broken off an idol may be used because they are no longer considered part of the idol. Thus פֶּה לָהֶם, they [the idols] *have a mouth*, but the mouth is not considered an integral part of them. The hands and eyes,

Hallel

Not for our sake, O Lord, not for our sake, but for Your Name's sake give glory, for the sake of Your kindness and Your truth! Why should the nations say: 'Where is their God?' Our God is in the heavens; whatever He pleases, He does! Their idols are silver and gold, the handiwork of man. They have a mouth, but cannot speak; they have eyes, but cannot see; they have ears, but cannot hear; they have a nose, but cannot smell; their hands — they cannot feel; their feet — they cannot walk; nor can they utter a sound with their throat. Those who make them should become like them, whoever trusts in them! O Israel! Trust in HASHEM — He is their help and shield! House of Aaron! Trust in HASHEM! He is their help and shield. You who fear HASHEM! — trust in HASHEM, He is their help and shield! *(Tehillim* 115:1-11).

however, are judged differently. Even when they are removed from the idol, they remain forbidden. Thus: יְדֵיהֶם, they are *'their' hands,* the implication being that the hands always are considered as if they are still part of the idol *(Chanukas HaTorah).*

Three categories ⮜ יִשְׂרָאֵל בְּטַח בַּה' ... בֵּית אַהֲרֹן ... יִרְאֵי ה' — *Israel! — trust in* HASHEM *... House of Aaron! ... You who fear* HASHEM! *...*

The Talmud *(Pesachim* 118a) interprets this verse as a reference to מִלְחֶמֶת גּוֹג וּמָגוֹג, *The War of Gog and Magog,* or חֶבְלֵי מָשִׁיחַ, *the suffering of the period of Messiah's coming* — times that will test the faith of Israel. However, why does the Psalmist divide Israel into the three categories of Israel, Kohanim, and those who fear Hashem?

The *Chofetz Chaim* explained that the three represent different levels of spiritual greatness. 'Israel' refers to the nation as a whole, the ordinary dedicated Jews. *The House of Aaron,* Kohanim, are those who teach

143 **The Haggadah Treasury**

יהוה זְכָרָנוּ יְבָרֵךְ יְבָרֵךְ אֶת בֵּית יִשְׂרָאֵל יְבָרֵךְ אֶת
בֵּית אַהֲרֹן: יְבָרֵךְ יִרְאֵי יהוה הַקְּטַנִּים עִם הַגְּדֹלִים:
יֹסֵף יהוה עֲלֵיכֶם עֲלֵיכֶם וְעַל בְּנֵיכֶם: בְּרוּכִים אַתֶּם
לַיהוה עֹשֵׂה שָׁמַיִם וָאָרֶץ: הַשָּׁמַיִם שָׁמַיִם לַיהוה
וְהָאָרֶץ נָתַן לִבְנֵי אָדָם: לֹא הַמֵּתִים יְהַלְלוּ־יָהּ וְלֹא
כָּל יֹרְדֵי דוּמָה: וַאֲנַחְנוּ נְבָרֵךְ יָהּ מֵעַתָּה וְעַד עוֹלָם
הַלְלוּיָהּ:

and guide the people in the wisdom of Torah and the observance of its commandments. *Those who fear Hashem* are the greatest and noblest of the nation. Each group will be sorely tested during the period leading up to the coming of Messiah, for that will be a time when the Attribute of Justice will hover over the nation inflicting ordeals that will weed out those who sincerely trust in Hashem from those who will fall by the wayside. Everyone's faith will be challenged according to his own level; the Psalmist exhorts each class of Jews to hold fast to its faith. Then it will merit the blessings enumerated in the next paragraph of *Hallel* — blessings that are conferred upon each group commensurate with the strength it marshals in facing its challenge.

Furthermore, the groups are enumerated separately because each has its own form of merit. Ordinary Jews have bravely sacrificed and even gone to their death to sanctify Hashem's Name. The Kohanim have the merit of the quintessential children of Aaron — the Chashmonaim who saved the nation from spiritual disintegration. Those who fear Hashem to the greatest extent have the enormous merit of inculcating fear and love of G-d in their brethren.

ה' זְכָרָנוּ — HASHEM has remembered us

⧉ הַשָּׁמַיִם שָׁמַיִם לַה' וְהָאָרֶץ נָתַן לִבְנֵי אָדָם — *As for heaven — the heaven is HASHEM's, but the earth He has given to mankind.*

HASHEM Who has remembered us will bless — He will bless the House of Israel; He will bless the House of Aaron; He will bless those who fear HASHEM, the small as well as the great. May HASHEM add upon you, upon you and your children! You are blessed of HASHEM, maker of heaven and earth. As for the heaven — the heaven is HASHEM's, but the earth He has given to mankind. Neither the dead can praise HASHEM, nor any who descend into silence; but we will bless HASHEM henceforth and forever. *Halleluyah! (Tehillim* 115:12-18).

Heaven on earth   *Rabbi Mordechai of Kobrin* and many others have explained the verse homiletically: The heaven is already 'heavenly' and dedicated to the holiness of G-d. Man is not required to perfect the heavens. But the earth is the province of man. It was given to us with the injunction that we perfect it and transform its material nature into something spiritual — indeed, that we make the earth 'heavenly.'

The proper concern   ◄§ The masters of מוּסָר, *Ethics*, give another homiletical interpretation to the verse. Man lives in two realms, the spiritual and the material. In his activities בֵּין אָדָם לַמָּקוֹם, *between man and God*, he may seek the highest levels of spirituality and make ever increasing demands on himself. It is proper and even desirable for one to deny himself all but the absolute material necessities in order to strive for greater and greater spiritual attainment; he may set heaven itself as his goal. But in his relationships בֵּין אָדָם לַחֲבֵרוֹ, *between man and his fellow man*, he should realize that the *earth* was given to man. His comrade may well worry about money, prestige, food, or clothing — concerns that seem hopelessly mundane to the 'heavenly' person. But in dealings with other human beings, *their* concerns must be uppermost. As Rabbi Yisrael Salanter put it: 'To help satisfy someone else's *material* needs is my *spiritual* concern.'

Begin anew   ◄§ וַאֲנַחְנוּ נְבָרֵךְ קָהּ מֵעַתָּה וְעַד עוֹלָם — *But we will bless HASHEM henceforth and forever.*
Often a person's prayers will be disturbed by

אָהַבְתִּי כִּי יִשְׁמַע יהוה אֶת קוֹלִי תַּחֲנוּנָי: כִּי הִטָּה
אָזְנוֹ לִי וּבְיָמַי אֶקְרָא: אֲפָפוּנִי חֶבְלֵי מָוֶת וּמְצָרֵי
שְׁאוֹל מְצָאוּנִי צָרָה וְיָגוֹן אֶמְצָא: וּבְשֵׁם יהוה אֶקְרָא
אָנָּה יהוה מַלְּטָה נַפְשִׁי: חַנּוּן יהוה וְצַדִּיק וֵאלֹהֵינוּ
מְרַחֵם: שֹׁמֵר פְּתָאִים יהוה דַּלּוֹתִי וְלִי יְהוֹשִׁיעַ: שׁוּבִי
נַפְשִׁי לִמְנוּחָיְכִי כִּי יהוה גָּמַל עָלָיְכִי: כִּי חִלַּצְתָּ נַפְשִׁי
מִמָּוֶת אֶת עֵינִי מִן דִּמְעָה אֶת רַגְלִי מִדֶּחִי: אֶתְהַלֵּךְ
לִפְנֵי יהוה בְּאַרְצוֹת הַחַיִּים: הֶאֱמַנְתִּי כִּי אֲדַבֵּר אֲנִי
עָנִיתִי מְאֹד: אֲנִי אָמַרְתִּי בְחָפְזִי כָּל הָאָדָם כֹּזֵב:

memories of the many sins he has committed — and he
wonders, 'How can I pray to Hashem?' This is the work
of the evil inclination; it is a device to prevent a person
from bettering himself, for as long as someone is
depressed he cannot raise himself to higher spiritual
levels. To the contrary, one who is beset by thoughts of
his deficiencies should resolve to begin anew and put to
rest the troubling thoughts of earlier failures. This is
the Psalmist's call: We will bless Hashem *from now on*,
even though we have failed previously *(Bais Avraham)*.

אָהַבְתִּי — I love

Act while there is time

◆§ אֲפָפוּנִי חֶבְלֵי מָוֶת ... וּבְשֵׁם ה' אֶקְרָא ... שֹׁמֵר פְּתָאִים ה'
— *The ropes of death encompassed me ... Then I called
upon the Name of HASHEM ... HASHEM protects the
simple*

These verses refer to the human soul. It originates in
the highest spiritual realms and then descends through
level after level of holiness until it finally arrives on
earth. Surely, the soul which is forced to undergo such
an ordeal and spend a lifetime so far beneath its station
must have a very great mission — otherwise why was it
sent here? Therefore it should be unthinkable for one to
waste his life on trifles and ignore the truly significant.
If someone were to undertake a dangerous trek across

I love Him for HASHEM hears my voice, my supplications. For He has inclined His ear to me, all my days I will call upon Him. The ropes of death encompassed me; the confines of the grave have found me; trouble and sorrow have I found. Then I called upon the Name of HASHEM: 'Please HASHEM, save my soul', Gracious is HASHEM and righteous, our God is merciful. HASHEM protects the simple; I was brought low but He saved me. Return to your rest, my soul, for HASHEM has been kind to you. You delivered my soul from death, my eyes from tears and my feet from stumbling. I shall walk before the Lord in the lands of the living. I kept faith although I say: 'I suffer exceedingly.' I said in my haste: 'All mankind is deceitful.' *(Tehillim* 116:1-11).

mountain and desert for the sake of smelling a few grains of snuff, he would be regarded as a fool, and justly so. He who allows his soul to while away its years on earth is no less foolish.

But if someone were to waste his years that way, with the result that his soul were to return through all those spiritual worlds back to its home naked of merit and devoid of *mitzvos*, it will find itself surrounded by the fiery angels who will tolerate no such abuse of its mission. *Ropes of death will encompass it*, because it will lack the merit to survive the Heavenly judgment. It will *call in the Name of Hashem*, beseeching Him as the *Protector of fools* to have mercy upon it. But then it will be too late *(Chafetz Chaim).*

David can comfort &ᵊ הֶאֱמַנְתִּי כִּי אֲדַבֵּר אֲנִי עָנִיתִי מְאֹד — *I kept faith although I say 'I suffer exceedingly.'*

A pauper would not be impressed by the consolations of a magnate. The hungry, ragged poor man will say to himself, 'What can he know of my plight — he who has never been hungry, he who has everything he could ever dream of having?' But it is different if the consolation comes from one who was once poor himself

מָה אָשִׁיב לַיהוה כָּל תַּגְמוּלוֹהִי עָלָי: כּוֹס יְשׁוּעוֹת
אֶשָּׂא וּבְשֵׁם יהוה אֶקְרָא: נְדָרַי לַיהוה אֲשַׁלֵּם נֶגְדָה
נָּא לְכָל־עַמּוֹ: יָקָר בְּעֵינֵי יהוה הַמָּוְתָה לַחֲסִידָיו: אָנָּה
יהוה כִּי אֲנִי עַבְדֶּךָ אֲנִי עַבְדְּךָ בֶּן אֲמָתֶךָ פִּתַּחְתָּ
לְמוֹסֵרָי: לְךָ אֶזְבַּח זֶבַח תּוֹדָה וּבְשֵׁם יהוה אֶקְרָא:
נְדָרַי לַיהוה אֲשַׁלֵּם נֶגְדָה נָּא לְכָל עַמּוֹ: בְּחַצְרוֹת בֵּית
יהוה בְּתוֹכֵכִי יְרוּשָׁלָיִם הַלְלוּיָהּ:

but who can now say, 'Do not despair. I too, was once
destitute, but Hashem helped me and made me wealthy.
The same thing can happen to you if you trust in
Hashem!' That is a worthwhile consolation, for it
comes from one who understands the problem and has
experienced the solution. With such words, King David
spread hope in Hashem. For David was despised and
derided when he was young. Even after Sh'muel
anointed him as the future king, Saul still pursued him
seeking to kill him. In his despair he even called out
כָּל הָאָדָם כֹּזֵב, *all mankind is deceitful.* Nevertheless,
Hashem saved him. David can say, 'Trust in Him and
he will help you just as He helped me!' Thus: הֶאֱמַנְתִּי, *I
caused people to have faith, because* כִּי אֲדַבֵּר, *when I
spoke,* אֲנִי עָנִיתִי מְאֹד *I had suffered exceedingly* — my
experience made my words more meaningful.

מָה אָשִׁיב — How can I repay

**Always
asking for
more**

◆§ מָה אָשִׁיב לַה' כָּל תַּגְמוּלוֹהִי עָלָי — *How can I repay
HASHEM for all His kindness to me?*

Chesed L'Avraham explained the verse with a
parable. Someone borrowed money for a specific period
of time. When the due date arrived, he went to the
home of his lender, but instead of repaying the loan, he
explained that he was involved in a business transaction
which not only forced him to ask for an extension of

How can I repay HASHEM for all His kindness to me? I will raise the cup of salvations, and invoke the Name of HASHEM. My vows to HASHEM will I pay in the presence of His entire people. Precious in the eyes of HASHEM is the death of His devout ones. Please, HASHEM — for I am Your servant, I am Your servant, son of Your handmaid — You have released my bonds. To You I sacrifice thanksgiving offerings, and the Name of HASHEM will I invoke. My vows to HASHEM will I pay in the presence of His entire people; in the courtyards of the House of HASHEM, in your midst, O Jerusalem. *Halleluyah! (Tehillim* 116:12-19).

the loan, but also compelled him to request additional money. The lender agreed to both requests. When the time of payment came, the same scene was repeated, and this happened a third and a fourth time. Finally the borrower realized that he was so indebted to the lender — morally and financially — that he could never hope to repay him. Thus, the Psalmist says: *How can I repay* HASHEM *for all His kindness to me?* He has helped me over and over although I have been undeserving. What is more, כּוֹס יְשׁוּעוֹת אֶשָּׂא, when it is time to *lift up the cup of salvations* to repay Him by doing something to earn His past kindnesses — וּבְשֵׁם ה' אֶקְרָא, *I call upon the Name of* HASHEM to plead for further mercy.

Maintaining Credit ◆§ The *Chafetz Chaim* expressed a similar thought. People can buy on credit continuously as long as they make payments on their outstanding balance. If they make even partial payments, their credit remains acceptable even though they may be increasing their total debt by taking more goods. However, the customer who never makes a payment loses his credit rating. This is the Psalmist's lament — Hashem has done so much for me that I can never repay him even partially for what He has given me. How, then, can I ever hope to deserve His further graciousness?

הַלְלוּ אֶת יהוה כָּל גּוֹיִם שַׁבְּחוּהוּ כָּל הָאֻמִּים: כִּי
גָבַר עָלֵינוּ חַסְדּוֹ וֶאֱמֶת יהוה לְעוֹלָם הַלְלוּיָהּ:

כִּי לְעוֹלָם חַסְדּוֹ:	הוֹדוּ לַיהוה כִּי טוֹב
כִּי לְעוֹלָם חַסְדּוֹ:	יֹאמַר נָא יִשְׂרָאֵל
כִּי לְעוֹלָם חַסְדּוֹ:	יֹאמְרוּ נָא בֵית אַהֲרֹן
כִּי לְעוֹלָם חַסְדּוֹ:	יֹאמְרוּ נָא יִרְאֵי יהוה

מִן הַמֵּצַר קָרָאתִי יָּהּ עָנָנִי בַמֶּרְחַב יָהּ: יהוה לִי לֹא

הַלְלוּ אֶת ה' — Praise Hashem

Only You know the truth

⋦§ *הַלְלוּ ה' כָּל גּוֹיִם ... כִּי גָבַר עָלֵינוּ חַסְדּוֹ* §⋧ — *Praise HASHEM, all You nations ... for His kindness to us was overwhelming.*

⋦§ During the reign of the infamous Czar Nikolai whose hatred of the Jews knew no bounds, the rabbinic leaders of Russia were frequently forced to go to St. Petersburg, the capital, to make pleas and exert influence against antisemitic decrees.

During one of these visits, Reb Itzel [*Rabbi Yitzchok Berlin*], Rosh Hayeshiva of Volozhin, was asked by a Czarist minister with reference to our verse: 'How is it that the non-Jewish peoples are expected to praise G-d for the kindness He shows Israel? *You*, not we, are the ones who should be praising Him!'

Reb Itzel answered, 'If it were up to you and your colleagues in St. Petersburg our lives would be even more miserable than they already are. I have no doubt that you planned countless decrees against us of a harshness far worse than those you have attempted to carry out, but Hashem arranges affairs so that you cannot put them into effect. That is why *you* must praise Him — for only you are aware of the full extent of His mercy. Who knows better than you what would have been our fate were it not for Hashem's kindness?'

Praise HASHEM, all you nations; praise Him, all you peoples! For His kindness to us was overwhelming, and the truth of HASHEM is eternal, *Halleluyah! (Tehillim 117).*

Psalm 118:1-4

Give thanks to HASHEM for He is good;

His kindness endures forever!

Let Israel say:

His kindness endures forever!

Let the House of Aaron say:

His kindness endures forever!

Let them who fear HASHEM say:

His kindness endures forever!

From the straits did I call to God; God answered me with ex-pansiveness. HASHEM is with me, I have no fear; how can man

Thanking for failure	◆§ The *Chafetz Chaim* explained that when Messiah comes, all those who sought to harm Israel will be punished. The more suffering they caused, the greater will be their punishment. Then they will feel an enormous sense of gratitude to Hashem for not having permitted them to implement even more of their cruel intentions, for, had they been able to commit even more atrocities, their punishments would have been that much greater. Then *they will praise Hashem for His kindness to us* — for even our enemies will have been the beneficiaries of His concern for us.

מִן הַמֵּצַר — **From the straits**

Give Your blessings	◆§ A person's requests depend on his own horizons. One who has lived in abject poverty all his life will pray fervently for a warm blanket and complete loaf of fresh bread. A wealthy magnate will pray for the suc-

151   **The Haggadah Treasury**

אִירָא מַה יַּעֲשֶׂה לִי אָדָם: יהוה לִי בְּעֹזְרָי וַאֲנִי אֶרְאֶה
בְשֹׂנְאָי: טוב לַחֲסוֹת בַּיהוה מִבְּטֹחַ בָּאָדָם: טוב
לַחֲסוֹת בַּיהוה מִבְּטֹחַ בִּנְדִיבִים: כָּל גּוֹיִם סְבָבוּנִי
בְּשֵׁם יהוה כִּי אֲמִילַם: סַבּוּנִי גַם סְבָבוּנִי בְּשֵׁם יהוה
כִּי אֲמִילַם: סַבּוּנִי כִדְבֹרִים דֹּעֲכוּ כְּאֵשׁ קוֹצִים בְּשֵׁם
יהוה כִּי אֲמִילַם: דָּחֹה דְחִיתַנִי לִנְפֹּל וַיהוה עֲזָרָנִי:
עָזִּי וְזִמְרָת יָהּ וַיְהִי לִי לִישׁוּעָה: קוֹל רִנָּה וִישׁוּעָה
בְּאָהֳלֵי צַדִּיקִים יְמִין יהוה עֹשָׂה חָיִל: יְמִין יהוה

cess of business venture involving millions. Hashem's
horizons, of course, are limitless. We should realize that
whatever may seem important to us is negligible to
Him. Therefore, though we pray from our own narrow,
straitened perception of what is truly desirable and
beneficial, we hope that He will answer us commensurate with His own infinite greatness. This is why
great people attempt to avoid praying for specific
needs; better to ask Hashem to be good to us in general
terms, for only He understands what is *truly* good
(*Toldos Chaim*).

Known by his enemies

⋖§ ה׳ לִי בְּעֹזְרָי וַאֲנִי אֶרְאֶה בְשֹׂנְאָי §⋗ — *HASHEM is for me through my helpers; therefore I can face my foes.*

Rabbi Yosaif Leib Bloch of Telshe interpreted the
verse homiletically: It is a famous folk saying that one
is known by his enemies. If one's enemies are righteous
people, then surely he must be lacking; but if one is
hated by the wicked, then he must be highly commen-
dable. King David expresses his confidence that
Hashem will become his Helper. How does he know he
deserves such heavenly regard? Because he looks about
him *and sees the character of his enemies.* They are
people who have thrown off the yoke of Torah and
mitzvos. If David has the privilege of being hated by

affect me? HASHEM is for me through my helpers; therefore I can face my foes. It is better to take refuge in HASHEM than to rely on man. It is better to take refuge in HASHEM than to rely on princes. All nations encompass me; but in the Name of HASHEM I cut them down. They encompass me. They swarm around me; but in the Name of HASHEM, I cut them down! They swarm around me like bees, but they are extinguished as a fire does thorns; in the Name of HASHEM I cut them down! You pushed me hard that I might fall, but HASHEM assisted me. My strength and song is HASHEM; He became my salvation. The sound of rejoicing and salvation is in the tents of the righteous: 'The right hand of HASHEM does valiantly. HASHEM's right hand is raised triumphantly; HASHEM's right

such people, then he can feel confident that he is serving G-d and will merit His help.

Deserving to see
⋘§ As we know from the episode of Lot, one who is saved despite the lack of compelling personal merit, does not have the right to watch the destruction of his enemies. On the other hand, the *tzaddik* would not be so restricted. Thus: if Hashem is for me בְּעֹזְרָי, in *my* [well-earned, deserved] *assistance*, then I may *watch* the fate of *my enemies*.

The best security
⋘§ טוֹב לַחֲסוֹת בַּה' מִבְּטוֹחַ בָּאָדָם — *It is better to take refuge in HASHEM than to rely on man*
Vilna Gaon explains the difference between the two closely related words חִסָּיוֹן, *taking refuge*, and בִּטָחוֹן, *reliance*. The former denotes absolute confidence even though no guarantees have been given. Thus, one may seek מַחֲסֶה, *protection*, behind a boulder or under a sturdy roof — neither the boulder nor the roof have pledged shelter, but one has confidence in their indestructability. The latter [בִּטָחוֹן, *reliance*] presupposes a promise of protection. Thus one may seek a הַבְטָחָה, *a pledge*, from a powerful military or political power, or rely on an insurance company to protect him from

153   The Haggadah Treasury

רוֹמְמָה יְמִין יהוה עֹשָׂה חָיִל: לֹא אָמוּת כִּי אֶחְיֶה
וַאֲסַפֵּר מַעֲשֵׂי יָהּ: יַסֹּר יִסְּרַנִּי יָּהּ וְלַמָּוֶת לֹא נְתָנָנִי:
פִּתְחוּ לִי שַׁעֲרֵי צֶדֶק אָבֹא בָם אוֹדֶה יָהּ: זֶה הַשַּׁעַר
לַיהוה צַדִּיקִים יָבֹאוּ בוֹ: אוֹדְךָ כִּי עֲנִיתָנִי וַתְּהִי לִי
לִישׁוּעָה:אודך אֶבֶן מָאֲסוּ הַבּוֹנִים הָיְתָה לְרֹאשׁ פִּנָּה:
אבן מֵאֵת יהוה הָיְתָה זֹּאת הִיא נִפְלָאת בְּעֵינֵינוּ:מאת
זֶה הַיּוֹם עָשָׂה יהוה נָגִילָה וְנִשְׂמְחָה בוֹ:זה

אָנָּא יהוה הוֹשִׁיעָה נָּא: אָנָּא יהוה הוֹשִׁיעָה נָּא:
אָנָּא יהוה הַצְלִיחָה נָּא: אָנָּא יהוה הַצְלִיחָה נָּא:

בָּרוּךְ הַבָּא בְּשֵׁם יהוה בֵּרַכְנוּכֶם מִבֵּית יהוה:ברוך
אֵל יהוה וַיָּאֶר לָנוּ אִסְרוּ חַג בַּעֲבֹתִים עַד קַרְנוֹת
הַמִּזְבֵּחַ:אל אֵלִי אַתָּה וְאוֹדֶךָּ אֱלֹהַי אֲרוֹמְמֶךָּ:אלי
הוֹדוּ לַיהוה כִּי טוֹב כִּי לְעוֹלָם חַסְדּוֹ:הודו

According to the *Ashkenaz* order of the *Seder*, יְהַלְלוּךְ (without the concluding blessing) is recited at this point.

financial ruination. The Psalmist says that it is far better to put one's blind trust in Hashem's protection than to rely on the most profuse assurance of human beings. How much more so when Hashem has promised to protect those who trust in Him!

The true life ◆§ לֹא אָמוּת כִּי אֶחְיֶה — *I shall not die! I shall live.*

To understand the apparent redundancy, we must seek a true definition of life. Our Sages teach that רְשָׁעִים בְּחַיֵּיהֶם קְרוּאִים מֵתִים, *the wicked are considered dead even while they are alive.* One may breathe, eat, vegetate, and propagate, but he is not considered to be *truly* alive in a meaningful way, unless the purpose of life is to accomplish G-d's will. Therefore the Psalmist

hand does valiantly!' I shall not die! I shall live and relate the deeds of God. God chastened me exceedingly but He did not let me die. Open for me the gates of righteousness, I will enter them and thank God. This is the gate of HASHEM; the righteous shall enter through it.

Each of the following four verses is recited twice:

I thank You for You answered me and became my salvation!

The stone which the builders despised has become the cornerstone!

This emanated from HASHEM; it is wondrous in our eyes!

This is the day HASHEM has made; we will rejoice and be glad in Him!

O HASHEM, please save us!

O HASHEM, please save us!

O HASHEM, please make us prosper!

O HASHEM, please make us prosper!

Each of the following four verses is recited twice:

Blessed be he who comes, in the Name of HASHEM; we bless you from the House of HASHEM.

HASHEM is God and He given illuminated for us; bind the festival offering with cords to the corners of the altar.

You are my God, and I thank You; my God, and I exalt You.

Give thanks to HASHEM, for He is good;

His kindness endures forever.

According to the *Ashkenaz* order of the *Seder,* יְהַלְלוּךְ (without the concluding blessing) is recited at this point.

כִּי לְעוֹלָם חַסְדּוֹ:	הוֹדוּ לַיהוה כִּי טוֹב
כִּי לְעוֹלָם חַסְדּוֹ:	הוֹדוּ לֵאלֹהֵי הָאֱלֹהִים
כִּי לְעוֹלָם חַסְדּוֹ:	הוֹדוּ לַאֲדֹנֵי הָאֲדֹנִים
כִּי לְעוֹלָם חַסְדּוֹ:	לְעֹשֵׂה נִפְלָאוֹת גְּדֹלוֹת לְבַדּוֹ
כִּי לְעוֹלָם חַסְדּוֹ:	לְעֹשֵׂה הַשָּׁמַיִם בִּתְבוּנָה
כִּי לְעוֹלָם חַסְדּוֹ:	לְרֹקַע הָאָרֶץ עַל הַמָּיִם
כִּי לְעוֹלָם חַסְדּוֹ:	לְעֹשֵׂה אוֹרִים גְּדֹלִים
כִּי לְעוֹלָם חַסְדּוֹ:	אֶת הַשֶּׁמֶשׁ לְמֶמְשֶׁלֶת בַּיּוֹם
כְּלַ"חַ:	אֶת הַיָּרֵחַ וְכוֹכָבִים לְמֶמְשְׁלוֹת בַּלָּיְלָה
כִּי לְעוֹלָם חַסְדּוֹ:	לְמַכֵּה מִצְרַיִם בִּבְכוֹרֵיהֶם
כִּי לְעוֹלָם חַסְדּוֹ:	וַיּוֹצֵא יִשְׂרָאֵל מִתּוֹכָם

refers to both levels of life: *I shall not die* — but I am not content merely to maintain my animal life. *I shall live* — in the only meaningful way: by serving G-d! (*Rabbi Zalman Sorotzkin*).

הַלֵּל הַגָּדוֹל – The Great Hallel

Twenty-six generations until Torah

◂§ In this psalm there are twenty-six verses extolling the kindess of G-d and concluding כִּי לְעוֹלָם חַסְדּוֹ, *for His kindness is eternal.* The *Midrash* explains that these twenty-six expressions of Divine goodness represent the twenty-six generations before the Torah was given. During all of that time, the universe was sustained by virtue of G-d's mercy. After the Torah was given, however, the very survival and the quality of the world's survival became dependent on the performance of Israel in its struggle to live up to the obligations imposed upon it by G-d in His Torah. This explains why the gift of the Torah is not mentioned in the psalm's lengthy catalog of G-d's graciousness. The instances of mercy mentioned by the Psalmist all repre-

Give thanks to HASHEM, for He is good;

His kindness endures forever.

Give thanks to the God of gods;

His kindness endures forever.

Give thanks to the Master of masters;

His kindness endures forever.

To Him Who alone does great wonders;

His kindness endures forever.

To Him Who made the heaven with understanding;

His kindness endures forever.

To Him Who stretched out the earth over the waters;

His kindness endures forever.

To Him Who made great luminaries;

His kindness endures forever.

The sun for the reign of day;

His kindness endures forever.

The moon and the stars for the reign of night;

His kindness endures forever.

To Him Who struck Egypt through their firstborn;

His kindness endures forever.

And removed Israel from their midst;

His kindness endures forever.

sent cases of undeserved mercy. The gift of Torah,
however, was made to render unnecessary such
manifestations of mercy for the Torah was given to
enable man to *earn* G-d's blessings.

בְּיָד חֲזָקָה וּבִזְרוֹעַ נְטוּיָה   כִּי לְעוֹלָם חַסְדּוֹ:

לְגֹזֵר יַם סוּף לִגְזָרִים   כִּי לְעוֹלָם חַסְדּוֹ:

וְהֶעֱבִיר יִשְׂרָאֵל בְּתוֹכוֹ   כִּי לְעוֹלָם חַסְדּוֹ:

וְנִעֵר פַּרְעֹה וְחֵילוֹ בְיַם סוּף   כִּי לְעוֹלָם חַסְדּוֹ:

לְמוֹלִיךְ עַמּוֹ בַּמִּדְבָּר   כִּי לְעוֹלָם חַסְדּוֹ:

לְמַכֵּה מְלָכִים גְּדֹלִים   כִּי לְעוֹלָם חַסְדּוֹ:

וַיַּהֲרֹג מְלָכִים אַדִּירִים   כִּי לְעוֹלָם חַסְדּוֹ:

לְסִיחוֹן מֶלֶךְ הָאֱמֹרִי   כִּי לְעוֹלָם חַסְדּוֹ:

וּלְעוֹג מֶלֶךְ הַבָּשָׁן   כִּי לְעוֹלָם חַסְדּוֹ:

Twelve paths   ∾§ לְגֹזֵר יַם סוּף לִגְזָרִים — *Who divided the Sea of Reeds into parts.*

Why was it necessary to divide the sea into twelve parts — would one large path through the sea have been sufficient? The reason for the twelve paths was to establish clearly that each tribe was worthy enough to have the sea split for its sake alone (*Rabbi Zalman Sorotzkin*).

To fit the crime   ∾§ וְנִעֵר פַּרְעֹה וְחֵילוֹ בְיַם סוּף — *And threw Pharaoh and his army into the Sea of Reeds.*

The treatment meted out to Pharaoh and his cohorts by the sea was מִדָּה כְּנֶגֶד מִדָּה, *measure for measure*, in accordance with their behavior toward Israel. The Egyptians graciously opened their doors to welcome Joseph's brothers when they came to Egypt to escape the Canaanite famine — but then slammed shut their doors when Israel wanted to leave. So, too, the sea allowed the Egyptians to enter its bed in pursuit of Israel — but then crashed down its watery walls upon them so that they could not escape death. Furthermore, by pursuing the Jews after having allowed them to go free, the Egytians were guilty of breaking their word. So, too, the sea 'changed its mind,' so to speak, for it allowed

With strong hand and outstretched arm;

His kindness endures forever.

Who divided the Sea of Reeds into parts;

His kindness endures forever.

And caused Israel to pass through it;

His kindness endures forever.

And threw Pharaoh and his army into the Sea of Reeds;

His kindness endures forever.

To Him Who led His people through the wilderness;

His kindness endures forever.

To Him Who smote great kings;

His kindness endures forever.

And slew mighty kings;

His kindness endures forever.

Sichon, king of the Emorites;

His kindness endures forever.

And Og, King of Bashan;

His kindness endures forever.

them to enter in safety, but then destroyed them. This treachery of the Egyptians in engaging in an attempt to re-impose slavery upon Israel, finds expression in a Talmudic curse. Of one who reneges on an agreement, the *Mishnah (Bava Metziah* 48a) says מִי שֶׁפָּרַע מִמִּצְרָיִם בַּיָּם, הוּא יִפָּרַע מִמִּי שֶׁאֵינוֹ עוֹמֵד בְּדִבּוּרוֹ — *He Who exacted punishment from Egypt at the sea, may He ex-act punishment from the one who did not keep his word.*

וְנָתַן אַרְצָם לְנַחֲלָה כִּי לְעוֹלָם חַסְדּוֹ:
נַחֲלָה לְיִשְׂרָאֵל עַבְדּוֹ כִּי לְעוֹלָם חַסְדּוֹ:
שֶׁבְּשִׁפְלֵנוּ זָכַר לָנוּ כִּי לְעוֹלָם חַסְדּוֹ:
וַיִּפְרְקֵנוּ מִצָּרֵינוּ כִּי לְעוֹלָם חַסְדּוֹ:
נֹתֵן לֶחֶם לְכָל בָּשָׂר כִּי לְעוֹלָם חַסְדּוֹ:
הוֹדוּ לְאֵל הַשָּׁמָיִם כִּי לְעוֹלָם חַסְדּוֹ:

נִשְׁמַת כָּל חַי תְּבָרֵךְ אֶת שִׁמְךָ יהוה אֱלֹהֵינוּ וְרוּחַ
כָּל בָּשָׂר תְּפָאֵר וּתְרוֹמֵם זִכְרְךָ מַלְכֵּנוּ תָּמִיד. מִן
הָעוֹלָם וְעַד הָעוֹלָם אַתָּה אֵל וּמִבַּלְעָדֶיךָ אֵין לָנוּ מֶלֶךְ
גּוֹאֵל וּמוֹשִׁיעַ פּוֹדֶה וּמַצִּיל וּמְפַרְנֵס וְעוֹנֶה וּמְרַחֵם
בְּכָל עֵת צָרָה וְצוּקָה. אֵין לָנוּ מֶלֶךְ עוֹזֵר וְסוֹמֵךְ אֶלָּא
אָתָּה. אֱלֹהֵי הָרִאשׁוֹנִים וְהָאַחֲרוֹנִים אֱלוֹהַּ כָּל בְּרִיּוֹת
אֲדוֹן כָּל תּוֹלָדוֹת הַמְהֻלָּל בְּכָל הַתִּשְׁבָּחוֹת הַמְנַהֵג
עוֹלָמוֹ בְּחֶסֶד וּבְרִיּוֹתָיו בְּרַחֲמִים וַיהוה עֵר הִנֵּה לֹא
יָנוּם וְלֹא יִישָׁן הַמְעוֹרֵר יְשֵׁנִים וְהַמֵּקִיץ נִרְדָּמִים
וְהַמֵּשִׂיחַ אִלְּמִים וְהַמַּתִּיר אֲסוּרִים וְהַסּוֹמֵךְ נוֹפְלִים
וְהַזּוֹקֵף כְּפוּפִים וְהַמְפַעֲנֵחַ נֶעֱלָמִים לְךָ לְבַדְּךָ אֲנַחְנוּ
מוֹדִים. וְאִלּוּ פִינוּ מָלֵא שִׁירָה כַּיָּם וּלְשׁוֹנֵנוּ רִנָּה
כַּהֲמוֹן גַּלָּיו וְשִׂפְתוֹתֵינוּ שֶׁבַח כְּמֶרְחֲבֵי רָקִיעַ וְעֵינֵינוּ

נִשְׁמַת — The soul

For
Himself
alone

§ וּלְךָ לְבַדְּךָ אֲנַחְנוּ מוֹדִים — *To You alone do we give
thanks.*
   We have lauded Hashem for his universal acceptance
— He is the G-d of first and last, of all creatures and all
generations, and so on. Then we praise Him for all He
has done for us and for all humanity. But in the final

And gave their land as an inheritance;

> His kindness endures forever.

An inheritance to Israel His servant;

> His kindness endures forever.

Who remembered us in our lowliness;

> His kindness endures forever.

And released us from our foes;

> His kindness endures forever.

He gives food to all living creatures;

> His kindness endures forever.

Give thanks to God of heaven;

His kindness endures forever! *(Tehillim* 136).

The soul of every living being shall bless Your Name, HASHEM our God; the spirit of all flesh shall always glorify and exalt Your remembrance, our King. From eternity to eternity, You are God, and except for You we have no king, redeemer or helper. O Rescuer, and Redeemer, Sustainer and Merciful One in every time of trouble and distress. We have no King, Helper and Supporter but You — God of the first and of the last, God of all creatures, Master of all generations, Who is extolled through a multitude of praises, Who guides His world with kindness and His creatures with mercy. HASHEM is awake, He neither slumbers nor sleeps; Who rouses the sleepers and awakens the slumbers; He makes the mute speak and frees the bound; He supports the falling and raises erect the bowed down and uncovers the hidden, To You alone we give thanks.

Were our mouth as full of song as the sea, and our tongue as full of jubilation as its multitudes of waves, and our lips as full of praise as the breadth of the heavens, and our eyes as

מְאִירוֹת כַּשֶּׁמֶשׁ וְכַיָּרֵחַ וְיָדֵינוּ פְרוּשׂוֹת כְּנִשְׁרֵי שָׁמָיִם
וְרַגְלֵינוּ קַלּוֹת כָּאַיָּלוֹת אֵין אֲנַחְנוּ מַסְפִּיקִים לְהוֹדוֹת
לְךָ יהוה אֱלֹהֵינוּ וֵאלֹהֵי אֲבוֹתֵינוּ וּלְבָרֵךְ אֶת שְׁמָךְ
מַלְכֵּנוּ עַל אַחַת מֵאֶלֶף אֶלֶף אַלְפֵי אֲלָפִים וְרִבֵּי
רְבָבוֹת פְּעָמִים הַטּוֹבוֹת נִסִּים וְנִפְלָאוֹת שֶׁעָשִׂיתָ עִם
אֲבוֹתֵינוּ וְעִמָּנוּ. מִלְּפָנִים מִמִּצְרַיִם גְּאַלְתָּנוּ יהוה
אֱלֹהֵינוּ וּמִבֵּית עֲבָדִים פְּדִיתָנוּ בְּרָעָב זַנְתָּנוּ וּבְשָׂבָע
כִּלְכַּלְתָּנוּ מֵחֶרֶב הִצַּלְתָּנוּ וּמִדֶּבֶר מִלַּטְתָּנוּ וּמֵחֳלָיִם
רָעִים רַבִּים וְנֶאֱמָנִים דִּלִּיתָנוּ. עַד הֵנָּה עֲזָרוּנוּ רַחֲמֶיךָ
וְלֹא עֲזָבוּנוּ חֲסָדֶיךָ יהוה אֱלֹהֵינוּ וְאַל תִּטְּשֵׁנוּ יהוה
אֱלֹהֵינוּ לָנֶצַח. עַל כֵּן אֵבָרִים שֶׁפִּלַּגְתָּ בָּנוּ וְרוּחַ
וּנְשָׁמָה שֶׁנָּפַחְתָּ בְּאַפֵּינוּ וְלָשׁוֹן אֲשֶׁר שַׂמְתָּ בְּפִינוּ הֵן
הֵם יוֹדוּ וִיבָרְכוּ וִישַׁבְּחוּ וִיפָאֲרוּ וִישׁוֹרְרוּ וִירוֹמְמוּ
וְיַעֲרִיצוּ וְיַקְדִּישׁוּ וְיַמְלִיכוּ אֶת שִׁמְךָ מַלְכֵּנוּ תָּמִיד. כִּי
כָל פֶּה לְךָ יוֹדֶה וְכָל לָשׁוֹן לְךָ תִשָּׁבַע וְכָל עַיִן לְךָ
תְצַפֶּה וְכָל בֶּרֶךְ לְךָ תִכְרַע וְכָל קוֹמָה לְפָנֶיךָ
תִשְׁתַּחֲוֶה וְכָל הַלְּבָבוֹת יִירָאוּךְ וְכָל קֶרֶב וּכְלָיוֹת
יְזַמְּרוּ לִשְׁמֶךָ. כַּדָּבָר שֶׁכָּתוּב כָּל עַצְמֹתַי תֹּאמַרְנָה
יהוה מִי כָמוֹךָ מַצִּיל עָנִי מֵחָזָק מִמֶּנּוּ וְעָנִי וְאֶבְיוֹן
מִגֹּזְלוֹ שַׁוְעַת עֲנִיִּים אַתָּה תִשְׁמַע צַעֲקַת הַדַּל
תַּקְשִׁיב וְתוֹשִׁיעַ. מִי יִדְמֶה לָּךְ וּמִי יִשְׁוֶה לָּךְ וּמִי
יַעֲרֹךְ לָךְ הָאֵל הַגָּדוֹל הַגִּבּוֹר וְהַנּוֹרָא אֵל עֶלְיוֹן קֹנֵה

analysis, we acknowledge that our allegiance to Him
does not depend on this extensive list of His achieve-
ments. *To You alone do we give thanks* — for Himself

brilliant as the sun and the moon, and our hands as outspread in prayer as the eagles of the sky and our feet as swift as deer — we still could not sufficiently thank You HASHEM our God and God of our fathers, and bless Your Name, our King, for even one of the thousands upon thousands and myriads upon myriads of favors, miracles and wonders, which You performed for our fathers and for us. Firstly, You liberated us from Egypt, HASHEM our God, and redeemed us from the house of bondage. In famine You nourished us and in plenty You supported us. From the sword You saved us; from the plague You let us escape; and You spared us from severe, numerous, and enduring diseases. Until now Your mercy has helped us, and Your kindness has not forsaken us, O HASHEM, our God. Do not abandon us, HASHEM our God, to the ultimate end.

Therefore, the limbs which You set within us, and the spirit and soul which You breathed into our nostrils, and the tongue which You have placed in our mouth — they shall all thank and bless, praise and glorify, exalt and revere, be devoted, sanctify and do homage to Your Name, our King forever. For every mouth shall offer thanks to You; every tongue shall vow allegiance to You; every eye shall long for You; every knee shall bend to You and all who stand erect shall bow before You. All hearts shall fear You, and men's innermost feelings and thoughts shall sing praises to Your name, as it is written [*Tehillim* 35:10]: *all my bones shall say: HASHEM, who is like You?* You save the poor man from one stronger than him, the poor and needy from one who would rob him. The cries of the needy do You hear, to the scream of the destitute do You attend — and You save. Who may be likened to You? Who is equal to You? Who can be compared to You? O great, mighty, and awesome God, supreme God, Maker of heaven and earth.

alone are we grateful to Him. We do not require Him to 'purchase' our gratitude *(Chidushei HaRim).*

שָׁמַיִם וָאָרֶץ. נְהַלֶּלְךָ וּנְשַׁבֵּחֲךָ וּנְפָאֶרְךָ וּנְבָרֵךְ אֶת
שֵׁם קָדְשֶׁךָ כָּאָמוּר לְדָוִד בָּרְכִי נַפְשִׁי אֶת יהוה וְכָל
קְרָבַי אֶת שֵׁם קָדְשׁוֹ:

הָאֵל בְּתַעֲצֻמוֹת עֻזֶּךָ הַגָּדוֹל בִּכְבוֹד שְׁמֶךָ הַגִּבּוֹר
לָנֶצַח וְהַנּוֹרָא בְּנוֹרְאוֹתֶיךָ הַמֶּלֶךְ הַיּוֹשֵׁב עַל כִּסֵּא רָם
וְנִשָּׂא:

שׁוֹכֵן עַד מָרוֹם וְקָדוֹשׁ שְׁמוֹ. וְכָתוּב רַנְּנוּ צַדִּיקִים
בַּיהוה לַיְשָׁרִים נָאוָה תְהִלָּה: בְּפִי יְשָׁרִים תִּתְרוֹמָם
וּבְשִׂפְתֵי צַדִּיקִים תִּתְבָּרַךְ וּבִלְשׁוֹן חֲסִידִים תִּתְקַדָּשׁ
וּבְקֶרֶב קְדוֹשִׁים תִּתְהַלָּל:

וּבְמַקְהֲלוֹת רִבְבוֹת עַמְּךָ בֵּית יִשְׂרָאֵל בְּרִנָּה
יִתְפָּאֵר שִׁמְךָ מַלְכֵּנוּ בְּכָל דּוֹר וָדוֹר שֶׁכֵּן חוֹבַת כָּל
הַיְצוּרִים לְפָנֶיךָ יהוה אֱלֹהֵינוּ וֵאלֹהֵי אֲבוֹתֵינוּ
לְהוֹדוֹת לְהַלֵּל לְשַׁבֵּחַ לְפָאֵר לְרוֹמֵם לְהַדֵּר וּלְנַצֵּחַ
לְבָרֵךְ לְעַלֵּה וּלְקַלֵּס עַל כָּל דִּבְרֵי שִׁירוֹת וְתִשְׁבְּחוֹת
דָּוִד בֶּן יִשַׁי עַבְדְּךָ מְשִׁיחֶךָ:

In the *Ashkenaz* order, יִשְׁתַּבַּח is said with its concluding blessing, and
יְהַלְלוּךָ is omitted.

וּבְכֵן יִשְׁתַּבַּח שִׁמְךָ לָעַד מַלְכֵּנוּ הָאֵל הַמֶּלֶךְ הַגָּדוֹל
וְהַקָּדוֹשׁ בַּשָּׁמַיִם וּבָאָרֶץ כִּי לְךָ נָאֶה יהוה אֱלֹהֵינוּ
וֵאלֹהֵי אֲבוֹתֵינוּ שִׁיר וּשְׁבָחָה הַלֵּל וְזִמְרָה עֹז
וּמֶמְשָׁלָה נֶצַח גְּדֻלָּה וּגְבוּרָה תְּהִלָּה וְתִפְאֶרֶת קְדֻשָּׁה
וּמַלְכוּת בְּרָכוֹת וְהוֹדָאוֹת לְשִׁמְךָ הַגָּדוֹל וְהַקָּדוֹשׁ
וּמֵעוֹלָם וְעַד־עוֹלָם אַתָּה אֵל.

We shall praise, acclaim, and glorify You and bless Your holy Name, as it is said [*Tehillim* 103:1]: *A Psalm of David: Bless HASHEM, O my soul, and let my whole inner being bless His holy Name!*

O God in the omnipotence of Your strength, great in the honor of Your name, powerful forever and awesomehhrough Your awesome deeds, O King enthroned upon a high and lofty throne!

He Who abides forever, exalted and holy is His Name. And it is written [*Tehillim* 33:1]: *Rejoice in HASHEM, you righteous; His praise is pleasant for the upright.* By the mouth of the upright shall You be exalted; by the lips of the righteous You shall be blessed; by the tongue of the pious You shall be sanctified; and amid the holy shall You be praised.

And in the assemblies of the myriads of Your people, the House of Israel, with jubilation shall Your name, our King, be glorified in every generation. For such is the duty of all creatures — before You, HASHEM, our God, God of our fathers, to thank, praise, laud, extol, exalt, adore, ascribe eternity, bless, raise high, and sing praises — even beyond all expressions of the songs and praises of David the son of Jesse, Your servant, Your anointed.

In the *Ashkenaz* order, יִשְׁתַּבַּח is said with its concluding blessing, and יְהַלְלוּךְ is omitted.

And thus, may Your Name be praised forever, our King, the God and King Who is great and holy in heaven and on earth; for to You, HASHEM our God and God of our fathers, it is fitting to render song and praise, *hallel* and hymns, power and dominion, victory, greatness and might, praise and glory, holiness and sovereignty, blessings and thanksgiving, to Your great and Holy Name. And for ever and ever proclaim You as Almighty.

יְהַלְלוּךָ יהוה אֱלֹהֵינוּ עַל כָּל מַעֲשֶׂיךָ וַחֲסִידֶיךָ
צַדִּיקִים עוֹשֵׂי רְצוֹנֶךָ וְכָל עַמְּךָ בֵּית יִשְׂרָאֵל כֻּלָּם
בְּרִנָּה יוֹדוּ וִיבָרְכוּ וִישַׁבְּחוּ וִיפָאֲרוּ וִישׁוֹרְרוּ וִירוֹמְמוּ
וְיַעֲרִיצוּ וְיַקְדִּישׁוּ וְיַמְלִיכוּ אֶת שִׁמְךָ מַלְכֵּנוּ תָּמִיד כִּי
לְךָ טוֹב לְהוֹדוֹת וּלְשִׁמְךָ נָאֶה לְזַמֵּר כִּי מֵעוֹלָם וְעַד
עוֹלָם אַתָּה אֵל: בָּרוּךְ אַתָּה יהוה מֶלֶךְ מְהֻלָּל
בַּתִּשְׁבָּחוֹת:

The fourth cup should be drunk while reclining.
It is preferable that the entire cup be drunk.

בָּרוּךְ אַתָּה יהוה אֱלֹהֵינוּ מֶלֶךְ הָעוֹלָם בּוֹרֵא פְּרִי
הַגָּפֶן:

After drinking the fourth cup, recite the following

בָּרוּךְ אַתָּה יהוה אֱלֹהֵינוּ מֶלֶךְ הָעוֹלָם עַל הַגֶּפֶן
וְעַל פְּרִי הַגֶּפֶן וְעַל תְּנוּבַת הַשָּׂדֶה וְעַל אֶרֶץ חֶמְדָּה
טוֹבָה וּרְחָבָה שֶׁרָצִיתָ וְהִנְחַלְתָּ לַאֲבוֹתֵינוּ לֶאֱכוֹל
מִפִּרְיָהּ וְלִשְׂבּוֹעַ מִטּוּבָהּ. רַחֶם נָא יהוה אֱלֹהֵינוּ עַל
יִשְׂרָאֵל עַמֶּךָ וְעַל יְרוּשָׁלַיִם עִירֶךָ וְעַל צִיּוֹן מִשְׁכַּן
כְּבוֹדֶךָ וְעַל מִזְבְּחֶךָ וְעַל הֵיכָלֶךָ וּבְנֵה יְרוּשָׁלַיִם עִיר
הַקֹּדֶשׁ בִּמְהֵרָה בְיָמֵינוּ וְהַעֲלֵנוּ לְתוֹכָהּ וְשַׂמְּחֵנוּ
בְּבִנְיָנָהּ וְנֹאכַל מִפִּרְיָהּ וְנִשְׂבַּע מִטּוּבָהּ וּנְבָרֶכְךָ עָלֶיהָ
בִּקְדֻשָּׁה וּבְטָהֳרָה (בשבת וּרְצֵה וְהַחֲלִיצֵנוּ בְּיוֹם הַשַּׁבָּת
הַזֶּה) וְשַׂמְּחֵנוּ בְּיוֹם חַג הַמַּצּוֹת הַזֶּה כִּי אַתָּה יהוה
טוֹב וּמֵטִיב לַכֹּל וְנוֹדֶה לְּךָ עַל הָאָרֶץ וְעַל פְּרִי הַגָּפֶן:
בָּרוּךְ אַתָּה יהוה עַל הָאָרֶץ וְעַל פְּרִי הַגָּפֶן:

They shall praise You, HASHEM our God for all Your works, along with Your pious followers, the righteous, who do Your will, and Your entire people, the House of Israel, with joy will thank, praise, bless, glorify, extol, exalt, revere, sanctify, and coronate Your name, our King always! For to You it is fitting to give thanks, and unto Your name it is proper to sing praises, for from eternity to eternity You are God. Blessed are You HASHEM, the King Who is lauded with praises.

The fourth cup should be drunk here.
It is preferable that the entire cup be drunk.

Blessed are You, HASHEM our God, King of the universe, Who creates the fruit of the vine,

After drinking the fourth cup, recite the following

Blessed are You, HASHEM our God King of the universe, for the vine and the fruit of the vine, and for the produce of the field. For the desirable, good, and spacious land that You were pleased to give our forefathers as a heritage to eat of its fruit and to be satisfied with its goodness. Have mercy, we beg You, HASHEM our God, on Israel Your people; on Jerusalem, Your city; on Zion, resting place of Your glory; Your altar, and Your Temple. Rebuild Jerusalem the city of holiness, speedily in our days. Bring us up into it and gladden us in its rebuilding and let us eat from its fruit and be satisfied with its goodness and bless You upon it in holiness and purity. *(On Sababth add:* Favor us and strengthen us on this Sabbath day) and grant us happiness on this Festival of Matzos; for You, HASHEM, are good and do good to all, and we thank You for the land and for the fruit of the vine. Blessed are You, HASHEM, for the land and the fruit of the vine.

חֲסַל סִדּוּר פֶּסַח כְּהִלְכָתוֹ. כְּכָל מִשְׁפָּטוֹ וְחֻקָּתוֹ. כַּאֲשֶׁר זָכִינוּ לְסַדֵּר אוֹתוֹ. כֵּן נִזְכֶּה לַעֲשׂוֹתוֹ: זָךְ שׁוֹכֵן מְעוֹנָה. קוֹמֵם קְהַל עֲדַת מִי מָנָה. בְּקָרוֹב נַהֵל נִטְעֵי כַנָּה. פְּדוּיִם לְצִיּוֹן בְּרִנָּה:

לְשָׁנָה הַבָּאָה בִּירוּשָׁלָיִם:

On the first night recite the following:
On the second night recite וּבְכֵן וַאֲמַרְתֶּם זֶבַח פֶּסַח, on page 176.

וּבְכֵן וַיְהִי בַּחֲצִי הַלַּיְלָה

אָז רוֹב נִסִּים הִפְלֵאתָ   בַּלַּיְלָה.

בְּרֹאשׁ אַשְׁמוּרוֹת זֶה   הַלַּיְלָה.

גֵּר צֶדֶק נִצַּחְתּוֹ כְּנֶחֱלַק לוֹ   לַיְלָה.

וַיְהִי בַּחֲצִי הַלַּיְלָה:

וַיְהִי בַּחֲצִי הַלַּיְלָה — And it came to pass at midnight.

At the darkest moment   •§ The question is raised how the night, which represents the forces of darkness and exile, could have become the time for redemption. That should more logically have come with the dawn. To explain why, the *Haggadah* includes this song which lists a long series of

Nirtzah

The Seder observance is accepted by God:

The Seder is now concluded in accordance with its laws, with all its ordinances and statutes. Just as we were privileged to arrange it, so may we merit to perform it. O Pure One, Who dwells on high, raise up the countless congregation, soon — guide the offshoots of Your plants, redeemed, to Zion with glad song.

NEXT YEAR IN JERUSALEM

On the first night, recite the following:
On the second night recite וּבְכֵן וַאֲמַרְתֶּם זֶבַח פֶּסַח, on page 176.

It came to pass at midnight.

You have, of old, performed many wonders by night.
   At the head of the watches of this night.
To the righteous convert, (Abraham),
   You gave triumph by dividing
   for him the night.

It came to pass at midnight.

miracles which took place at midnight. That moment, coming as it does at the very darkest and inauspicious moment of all, is a particular עֵת רָצוֹן וּשְׁעַת רַחֲמִים, *time of Divine favor and mercy.* For that reason, too, תִּקּוּן חֲצוֹת, prayers for the end of the exile, are recited at that moment. G-d's greatest mercy is awakened just when all hope seems to be lost *(Lail Shimurim).*

דַּנְתָּ מֶלֶךְ גְּרָר בַּחֲלוֹם   הַלַּיְלָה.
הִפְחַדְתָּ אֲרַמִּי בְּאֶמֶשׁ   לַיְלָה.
וַיָּשַׂר יִשְׂרָאֵל לְמַלְאָךְ וַיּוּכַל לוֹ   לַיְלָה.
וַיְהִי בַּחֲצִי הַלַּיְלָה:

זֶרַע בְּכוֹרֵי פַתְרוֹס מָחַצְתָּ בַּחֲצִי   הַלַּיְלָה.
חֵילָם לֹא מָצְאוּ בְּקוּמָם   בַּלַּיְלָה.
טִיסַת נְגִיד חֲרֹשֶׁת סִלִּיתָ בְּכוֹכְבֵי   לַיְלָה.
וַיְהִי בַּחֲצִי הַלַּיְלָה:

יָעֵץ מְחָרֵף לְנוֹפֵף אִוּוּי הוֹבַשְׁתָּ פְגָרָיו   בַּלַּיְלָה.
כָּרַע בֵּל וּמַצָּבוֹ בְּאִישׁוֹן   לַיְלָה.
לְאִישׁ חֲמוּדוֹת נִגְלָה רָז חֲזוֹת   לַיְלָה.
וַיְהִי בַּחֲצִי הַלַּיְלָה:

The missing proof

◆§ זֶרַע בְּכוֹרֵי פַתְרוֹס מָחַצְתָּ בַּחֲצִי הַלַּיְלָה — *The first-born offspring of Egypt You crushed in the middle of the night.*

In warning Pharaoh about the plague of the first-born, Moses said it would occur בַּחֲצֹת הַלַּיְלָה, at 'about' midnight (Sh'mos 11:4). As *Rashi* explains, Moses feared that the Egyptians might miscalculate the precise moment of midnight. Thus they would claim that Moses was a charlatan for the plague struck either a little before or a little after midnight according to their reckoning. Therefore, in order not to give them an excuse for further defiance of G-d, Moses said that the plague would strike at *about* midnight, but not necessarily at the exact moment.

Rabbi Yonasan Eybescheutz asks why there should have been any doubt as the exact *moment of midnight* in view of the Talmudic statement that dogs bark at the

You judged the king of Gerar, (Abimelech),
   in a dream by night.
You frightened the Aramean, (Laban),
   in the dark of night.
Israel (Jacob) fought with an angel
   and overcame him by night.

                              It came to pass at midnight.

Egypt's first-born You crushed at midnight.
Their host they found not upon arising
   at night.
The army of the prince of Charoshes, (Sisera)
   You swept away with stars of the night.

                              It came to pass at midnight.

The blasphemer, (Sancherib), planned to raise
   his hand against Jerusalem
   — but You withered his corpses by night.
Baal was overturned with its pedestal,
   in the darkness of night.
To the man of Your delights (Daniel),
   was revealed the mystery of the visions of night.

                              It came to pass at midnight.

midpoint of the night. That would have been the moment when the first-born died, thus validating Moses'
prophecy. The answer is, however, that Hashem
promised Israel that the Divine protection extended
over it that night would be so far reaching that not even
a dog would bark at a Jew all through the night. Thus
the proof of midnight would be lacking and the Egyptians would be able to concoct their fantasies about the
lack of accuracy in Moses' prophecy.

מִשְׁתַּכֵּר בִּכְלֵי קֹדֶשׁ נֶהֱרַג בּוֹ   בַּלַּיְלָה.
נוֹשַׁע מִבּוֹר אֲרָיוֹת פּוֹתֵר בְּעָתוּתֵי   לַיְלָה.
שִׂנְאָה נָטַר אֲגָגִי וְכָתַב סְפָרִים   בַּלַּיְלָה.
וַיְהִי בַּחֲצִי הַלַּיְלָה:

עוֹרַרְתָּ נִצְחֲךָ עָלָיו בְּנֶדֶד שְׁנַת   לַיְלָה.
פּוּרָה תִדְרוֹךְ לְשׁוֹמֵר מַה   מִלַּיְלָה.
צָרַח כַּשּׁוֹמֵר וְשָׂח אָתָא בֹקֶר וְגַם   לַיְלָה.
וַיְהִי בַּחֲצִי הַלַּיְלָה:

The Seder vacuum

◆§ עוֹרַרְתָּ נִצְחֲךָ עָלָיו בְּנֶדֶד שְׁנַת לַיְלָה — *You began Your triumph over him when You disturbed the king's sleep of night.*

The reference is to the triumph over Haman which began when Ahasuerus' sleep was disturbed. Thereupon, he ordered that the royal chronicle be read, he learned that Mordechai had saved his life and gone unrewarded, and thus began the chain of events which led to Haman's execution and the salvation of the Jews. That happened on the night of *Pesach*. which was during the three-day fast that Esther had asked the Jews to observe (*Megillah* 15a). The question arises why Esther should have wanted a fast which prevented Israel from observing the commandments of *Pesach*. The planned extermination of the Jews was eleven months off — why couldn't the fast be later?

Tiferes Shlomo explained that for a proper understanding of Esther's action, we must realize that the good deeds of *tzaddikim* are precious and significant to G-d, especially the love which Israel evinces for Him during its *Seder* observances. When it relives the Exodus and rededicates itself to Hashem's service, it gains a new measure of His love. Esther wanted G-d's mercy

He, (Belshazzar), who caroused from the holy vessels
  was killed that very night.
From the lions' den was rescued (Daniel),
  he who interpreted the 'terrors' of the night.
The Aggagite nursed hatred and wrote decrees at night.
                    It came to pass at midnight.

You began Your triumph over him when You
  disturbed the (King's) sleep of night.
Trample the wine-press to help those who ask
  the watchman, 'What of the long night?'
He will shout, like a watchman, and say:
  'Morning comes after night.'
                    It came to pass at midnight.

upon Israel to be awakened by the *vacuum* that would
be.created on that *Seder* night. If the Jews would forgo
their usual *mitzvos* of the evening, the Heavenly
Famalia would realize how precious were the good
deeds of the righteous, for the spiritual fulfillment of
even the heavens would suffer by the lack of Jewish
mitzvos.

So it was. The verses of the Megillah telling that
Ahasuerus' sleep was troubled can be interpreted as a
reference to הַמֶּלֶךְ, *'The* King' — Hashem *(Megillah*
15b). Hashem was troubled because the *Seder* commandments were not being fulfilled. He ordered that
the 'Chronicles' listing the good deeds of Israel be
brought before Him. It was read to Him, so to speak,
that Mordechai always told about the Exodus that night
— but now he was fasting and praying for deliverance
from Haman. Thus was G-d's mercy awakened as
Esther has hoped.

קָרֵב יוֹם אֲשֶׁר הוּא לֹא יוֹם וְלֹא   לַיְלָה.

רָם הוֹדַע כִּי לְךָ הַיּוֹם אַף לְךָ   הַלַּיְלָה.

שׁוֹמְרִים הַפְקֵד לְעִירְךָ כָּל הַיּוֹם וְכָל   הַלַּיְלָה.

תָּאִיר כְּאוֹר יוֹם חֶשְׁכַּת   לַיְלָה.

וַיְהִי בַּחֲצִי הַלָּיְלָה:

A
summary
of the
song

❧ The following is a stanza-by-stanza review of the song וַיְהִי בַּחֲצִי הַלַּיְלָה, **And it came to pass at midnight:**

א — You performed many miracles at night.

ב — They were done at the beginning of an אַשְׁמוּרָה *[one of the 'watches' into which the night is divided]* of this night.

ג — You made Abraham — who was a גֵּר צֶדֶק, *a righteous convert*, victorious when he defeated the four kings at night.

ד — You judged Abimelech the king of Gerar in a dream at night.

ה — You frightened Laban in the darkness of the night.

ו — Israel [i.e., Jacob] fought against an angel and overcame him, at night.

ז — The first-born of Egypt were destroyed at midnight.

ח — The Egyptians could not find their wealth and treasures when they arose that night.

ט — You waged war against the army of Sisera, the ruler of Charoshes, with the stars of the night.

י — You humbled those who worshiped Baal, the idol of Babylonia, at night.

כ — Sancherib who had planned to raise his hand against Jerusalem was cast down and his army fell dead, at night.

ל — To Daniel, wo was called אִישׁ חֲמוּדוֹת, *the man of [G-d's] delights*, was revealed the secret of the dream which Nevuchadnezzar dreamt at night.

Hasten the day (of Messiah),
   that is neither day nor night.
Most High — make known that Yours are day and night.
Appoint guards for Your city, all the day and all the night
   Brighten like the light of day the darkness of night.

It came to pass at midnight.

מ — Belshazzar, who became drunk while drinking from the holy vessels of the Temple, was killed at night.

נ — Daniel, who was saved from the lion's den, interpreted the frightening dream of which Nevuchadnezzar dreamt at night.

ס — Haman, the Aggagite, who hated the Jews, wrote letters at night to destroy them.

ע — You aroused Your strength against Haman by not allowing Ahasuerus to sleep at night.

פ — 'Tread on the nations as if they were grapes' — may Hashem give this reply to the guardian angel of Israel who asks, 'What will be the outcome of this long exile night?'

צ — At that time Hashem will roar and command the light of the day to shine for the righteous, and the darkness of night to enshroud the wicked.

ק — Hasten the time of redemption when there will be only day and no night.

ר — Hashem, the Exalted One, let it be known through our redemption that both the day and the night are Yours.

ש — Appoint guards to stand around Your city, Jerusalem, all day and all night.

ת — Let the darkness of the exile be brightened by the light of day.

On the second night recite the following:
On the first night recite וּבְכֵן וַיְהִי בַּחֲצִי הַלַּיְלָה, on page 168.

וּבְכֵן וַאֲמַרְתֶּם זֶבַח פֶּסַח

אִמֵּץ גְּבוּרוֹתֶיךָ הִפְלֵאתָ   בַּפֶּסַח.

בְּרֹאשׁ כָּל מוֹעֲדוֹת נִשֵּׂאתָ   פֶּסַח.

גִּלִּיתָ לְאֶזְרָחִי חֲצוֹת לֵיל   פֶּסַח.

וַאֲמַרְתֶּם זֶבַח פֶּסַח:

דְּלָתָיו דָּפַקְתָּ כְּחֹם הַיּוֹם   בַּפֶּסַח.

הִסְעִיד נוֹצְצִים עָגוֹת מַצּוֹת   בַּפֶּסַח.

וְאֶל הַבָּקָר רָץ זֵכֶר לְשׁוֹר עֵרֶךְ   פֶּסַח.

וַאֲמַרְתֶּם זֶבַח פֶּסַח:

וּבְכֵן וַאֲמַרְתֶּם זֶבַח פֶּסַח — And you shall say, 'This is the feast of Pesach'

A
halachic
Erev
Pesach

◆§ הִסְעִיד נוֹצְצִים עָגוֹת מַצּוֹת בַּפֶּסַח — *He satisfied the angels with matzah-cakes on Pesach.*

The reference is to Abraham who asked Sarah to prepare *matzah* cakes for the angels who came on *Pesach* to inform them of the prophecy that Isaac was to be born by the next year. There are difficulties in the narrative. First, why does the Torah describe Abraham's *matzos* as עֻגוֹת, *cakes* (*Bereishis* 18:6), while those that Lot baked for them are called מַצּוֹת, *matzos* (*ibid.* 19:3). Secondly, after Abraham's *matzah* cakes became impure and thus unusable (see *Rashi* to 18:8), why did he not bake others? Finally, how is it that Lot served wine to the angels while Abraham did not (*ibid.*)?

Rabbi Zalman Sorotzkin explains the entire sequence of events in consonance with the laws of *Pesach*. The angels came to Abraham at mid-day (18:1) of *Erev*

On second night recite the following:
On the first night recite וַיְהִי בַּחֲצִי הַלַּיְלָה, on page 168.

And You shall say: This is the feast of Pesach.

You displayed wondrously Your mighty powers on Pesach
Above all festivals You elevated Pesach.
To the Oriental, (Abraham), You revealed
  the future midnight of Pesach.
      And you shall say: This is the feast of Pesach.

At his door You knocked in the heat of the day
  on Pesach;
He satiated the angels with matzah-cakes on Pesach
And he ran to the herd — symbolic of the
  sacrificial beast of Pesach.
      And you shall say: This is the feast of Pesach.

Pesach. Since Abraham observed even Rabbinic enact-
ments and the Sages forbade the eating of *matzos* on
Erev Pesach, he could not offer them *matzos*. Instead,
he prepared עֻגּוֹת, *matzah-cakes* made with eggs or fruit
juice [i.e., מַצָּה עֲשִׁירָה] which may be eaten on *Eruv
Pesach* because they are not acceptable for the performance of the commandment of eating *matzah* even
though they are not *chametz*. Nevertheless, such food
may be eaten only until early afternoon [סָמוּךְ לְמִנְחָה] of
Erev Pesach. That explains why Abraham was in such a
hurry to prepare the food for the angels — had there
been any delay, it would have been too late to serve
cakes. By the same token, after the original cakes
became impure, it was too late to prepare new ones.
Wine, too, may not be used *Erev Pesach* and for that
reason, Abraham could not offer wine to the angels.
    By the time the angels arrived at Lot's home,
however, it was already the *Seder* night. Then, not only

בַּפֶּסַח.   זוֹעֲמוּ סְדוֹמִים וְלוֹהֲטוּ בָּאֵשׁ
פֶּסַח.   חֻלַּץ לוֹט מֵהֶם וּמַצּוֹת אָפָה בְּקֵץ
בַּפֶּסַח.   טֵאטֵאתָ אַדְמַת מוֹף וְנוֹף בְּעָבְרְךָ
    וַאֲמַרְתֶּם זֶבַח פֶּסַח:

פֶּסַח.   יָהּ רֹאשׁ כָּל אוֹן מָחַצְתָּ בְּלֵיל שִׁמּוּר
פֶּסַח.   כַּבִּיר עַל בֵּן בְּכוֹר פָּסַחְתָּ בְּדַם
בַּפֶּסַח.   לְבִלְתִּי תֵּת מַשְׁחִית לָבֹא בִּפְתָחַי
    וַאֲמַרְתֶּם זֶבַח פֶּסַח:

פֶּסַח.   מְסֻגֶּרֶת סֻגָּרָה בְּעִתּוֹתֵי
פֶּסַח.   נִשְׁמְדָה מִדְיָן בִּצְלִיל שְׂעוֹרֵי עֹמֶר
פֶּסַח.   שֹׂרְפוּ מִשְׁמַנֵּי פּוּל וְלוּד בִּיקַד יְקוֹד
    וַאֲמַרְתֶּם זֶבַח פֶּסַח:

could *matzos* be offered them, but wine as well was flowing freely because the Four Cups were used in observance of the *Seder*.

A summary of the song   ❧ The following is a stanza-by-stanza review of the song וּבְכֵן וַאֲמַרְתֶּם זֶבַח פֶּסַח, And you shall say: 'This is the feast of Pesach':

א — You have exhibited Your awesome might on Pesach.

ב — You have set Pesach as the first of all the festivals.

ג — You revealed to Abraham on the night of Pesach what would occur.

ד — You knocked on his door to visit Abraham in the heat of the day, on Pesach.

ה — Abraham fed the angels *matzos* on *Pesach*.

The Sodomites provoked (God) and were devoured by fire
   on Pesach;
Lot was withdrawn from them — he had baked matzos at the
time of Pesach.
You swept clean the soil of Moph and Noph (in Egypt) when
You passed through on Pesach.
                    And you shall say: This is the feast of Pesach.

God, You crushed every first-born of On (in Egypt)
   on the watchful night of Pesach.
But Master — Your own first-born, You skipped by merit of the
blood of Pesach,
Not to allow the Destroyer to enter my doors on Pesach.
                    And you shall say: This is the feast of Pesach.

The beleaguered (Jericho) was besieged on Pesach.
Midian was destroyed with a barley cake,
   from the Omer of Pesach.
The mighty nobles of Pul and Lud (Assyria) were consumed
   in a great conflagration on Pesach.
                    And you shall say: This is the feast of Pesach.

ו — Abraham ran to the cattle — a remembrance to the
ox which was to be sacrificed for the Chagigah offering
of Pesach.
ז — The people of Sodom angered Hashem and were
burnt by fire on Pesach.
ח — Lot separated himself from the people of Sodom,
and he baked *matzos* on Pesach.
ט — You destroyed the land of Moph and Noph, the
Egyptian provinces, as You passed there on Pesach.
י — Hashem, You destroyed the first-born on the night
of watchfulness.

עוֹד הַיּוֹם בְּנֹב לַעֲמוֹד עַד גָּעָה עוֹנַת   פֶּסַח.

פַּס יַד כָּתְבָה לְקַעֲקֵעַ צוּל   בְּפֶסַח.

צָפֹה הַצָּפִית עָרוֹךְ הַשֻּׁלְחָן   בְּפֶסַח.

וַאֲמַרְתֶּם זֶבַח פֶּסַח:

קָהָל כִּנְּסָה הֲדַסָּה צוֹם לְשַׁלֵּשׁ   בְּפֶסַח.

רֹאשׁ מִבֵּית רָשָׁע מָחַצְתָּ בְּעֵץ חֲמִשִּׁים   בְּפֶסַח.

שְׁתֵּי אֵלֶּה רֶגַע תָּבִיא לְעוּצִית   בְּפֶסַח.

תָּעֹז יָדְךָ וְתָרוּם יְמִינְךָ כְּלֵיל הִתְקַדֶּשׁ חַג פֶּסַח

וַאֲמַרְתֶּם זֶבַח פֶּסַח:

כ — You passed over the first-born of Israel in the merit of the blood of Pesach offering.

ל — You didn't permit the destroyer to enter the homes of Israel on Pesach.

מ — Jericho, the fortified and sealed city, was conquered during the time of Pesach.

נ — Midian was destroyed because of the merit of the Omer which was sacrificed on Pesach.

ס — Sancherib, and his strong army were consumed by the fire of the angel on Pesach.

ע — Today we will be in Nob, and tomorrow we will conquer Jerusalem, said Sancherib and he waited until the time of Pesach arrived.

פ — A hand wrote on the wall, telling Belshazzar about the destruction of Babylonia on Pesach.

He (Sancherib) would have stood that day at Nob,
   but for the advent of Pesach.
A hand inscribed the destruction of Zul (Babylon)
   on Pesach,
As the watch was set, and the royal table decked, on Pesach.
               And you shall say: This is the feast of Pesach.

Hadassah gathered a congregation for a three-day fast
   on Pesach.
You caused the head of the evil clan (Haman)
   to be hanged on a fifty-cubit gallows on Pesach.
Doubly, will You bring in an instant
   upon Utsis (Edom) on Pesach;
Let Your hand be strong, and Your right arm exalted,
   as on that night when You hallowed
   the festival of Pesach.
               And you shall say: This is the feast of Pesach.

צ — Belshazzar waited for the arrival of his enemies
when he arranged his table on Pesach.
ק — Esther gathered the Jews to fast for three days during Pesach.
ר — The wicked Haman was killed and hanged from a
tree which was fifty cubits high on Pesach.
ש — May You bring a double misfortune upon the nation of Edom on Pesach.
ת — May You show the strength that You showed on
the night that Pesach became sanctified.

כִּי לוֹ נָאֶה. כִּי לוֹ יָאֶה:

אַדִּיר בִּמְלוּכָה. בָּחוּר כַּהֲלָכָה. גְּדוּדָיו יֹאמְרוּ לוֹ.
לְךָ וּלְךָ. לְךָ כִּי לְךָ. לְךָ אַף לְךָ. לְךָ יהוה הַמַּמְלָכָה. כִּי
לוֹ נָאֶה. כִּי לוֹ יָאֶה:

דָּגוּל בִּמְלוּכָה. הָדוּר כַּהֲלָכָה. וָתִיקָיו יֹאמְרוּ לוֹ.
לְךָ וּלְךָ. לְךָ כִּי לְךָ. לְךָ אַף לְךָ. לְךָ יהוה הַמַּמְלָכָה. כִּי
לוֹ נָאֶה. כִּי לוֹ יָאֶה:

זַכַּאי בִּמְלוּכָה. חָסִין כַּהֲלָכָה. טַפְסְרָיו יֹאמְרוּ לוֹ.
לְךָ וּלְךָ. לְךָ כִּי לְךָ. לְךָ אַף לְךָ. לְךָ יהוה הַמַּמְלָכָה. כִּי
לוֹ נָאֶה. כִּי לוֹ יָאֶה:

יָחִיד בִּמְלוּכָה. כַּבִּיר כַּהֲלָכָה. לִמּוּדָיו יֹאמְרוּ לוֹ.
לְךָ וּלְךָ. לְךָ כִּי לְךָ. לְךָ אַף לְךָ. לְךָ יהוה הַמַּמְלָכָה. כִּי
לוֹ נָאֶה. כִּי לוֹ יָאֶה:

מוֹשֵׁל בִּמְלוּכָה. נוֹרָא כַּהֲלָכָה. סְבִיבָיו יֹאמְרוּ
לוֹ.לְךָ וּלְךָ. לְךָ כִּי לְךָ. לְךָ אַף לְךָ. לְךָ יהוה הַמַּמְלָכָה.
כִּי לוֹ נָאֶה. כִּי לוֹ יָאֶה:

עֲנָיו בִּמְלוּכָה. פּוֹדֶה כַּהֲלָכָה. צַדִּיקָיו יֹאמְרוּ לוֹ.
לְךָ וּלְךָ. לְךָ כִּי לְךָ. לְךָ אַף לְךָ. לְךָ יהוה הַמַּמְלָכָה. כִּי
לוֹ נָאֶה. כִּי לוֹ יָאֶה:

קָדוֹשׁ בִּמְלוּכָה. רַחוּם כַּהֲלָכָה. שִׁנְאַנָּיו יֹאמְרוּ

To Him praise is due!
To Him praise is fitting!

Powerful in majesty, perfectly distinguished, His companies of angels say to him:

Yours and only Yours; Yours, yes Yours; Yours, surely Yours; Yours, HASHEM, is the sovereignty. To Him praise is due. To Him praise is fitting.

Supreme in kingship, perfectly glorious, His faithful say to Him:

Yours and only Yours; Yours, yes Yours; Yours, surely Yours; Yours, HASHEM, is the sovereignty. To Him praise is due. To Him praise is fitting.

Pure in kingship, perfectly mighty, His angels say unto him:

Yours and only Yours; Yours, yes Yours; Yours, surely Yours; Yours, HASHEM, is the sovereignty. To Him praise is due. To Him praise is fitting.

Alone in kingship, perfectly omnipotent, His scholars say unto Him:

Yours and only Yours; Yours, yes Yours; Yours, surely Yours; Yours, HASHEM, is the sovereignty. To Him praise is due. To Him praise is fitting.

Commanding in kingship, perfectly wondrous, His surrounding (angels) say to Him:

Yours and only Yours; Yours, yes Yours; Yours, surely Yours; Yours, HASHEM, is the sovereignty. To Him praise is due. To Him praise is fitting.

Gentle in Kingship, perfectly the Redeemer, His righteous say to Him:

Yours and only Yours; Yours, yes Yours; Yours, surely Yours; Yours, HASHEM, is the sovereignty. To Him praise is due. To Him praise is fitting.

Holy in kingship, perfectly merciful, His troops of angels say to Him:

לוֹ.לְךָ וּלְךָ. לְךָ כִּי לְךָ. לְךָ אַף לְךָ. לְךָ יהוה הַמַּמְלָכָה.
כִּי לוֹ נָאֶה. כִּי לוֹ יָאֶה:

תַּקִּיף בִּמְלוּכָה. תּוֹמֵךְ כַּהֲלָכָה. תְּמִימָיו יֹאמְרוּ לוֹ.
לְךָ וּלְךָ. לְךָ כִּי לְךָ. לְךָ אַף לְךָ. לְךָ יהוה הַמַּמְלָכָה. כִּי
לוֹ נָאֶה. כִּי לוֹ יָאֶה:

אַדִּיר הוּא

אַדִּיר הוּא יִבְנֶה בֵיתוֹ בְּקָרוֹב. בִּמְהֵרָה בִּמְהֵרָה
בְּיָמֵינוּ בְּקָרוֹב. אֵל בְּנֵה אֵל בְּנֵה. בְּנֵה בֵיתְךָ בְּקָרוֹב:

בָּחוּר הוּא. גָּדוֹל הוּא. דָּגוּל הוּא. יִבְנֶה בֵיתוֹ
בְּקָרוֹב. בִּמְהֵרָה בִּמְהֵרָה בְּיָמֵינוּ בְּקָרוֹב. אֵל בְּנֵה אֵל
בְּנֵה. בְּנֵה בֵיתְךָ בְּקָרוֹב:

אַדִּיר הוּא — He Who is most mighty

Hashem's definition and ours

◆§ בִּמְהֵרָה בִּמְהֵרָה בְּיָמֵינוּ בְּקָרוֹב — *Speedily, yes speedily in our days, soon!*

The Talmud expounds that מְהֵרָה דְמָרֵי עָלְמָא הֲנָה תתנ״ב שָׁנִים, *to the Master of the universe, the word* מְהֵרָה, *quickly, can mean* [as much as] *852 years* (*Gittin* 68), for we see that He warned: כִּי אָבֹד תֹּאבֵדוּן מַהֵר, *you will quickly become lost* [i.e., for your sins you will be driven from the Land *'quickly'*] (*Devarim* 4:26), but the destruction of the Temple and the exile did not occur for 850 years. [See *Rashi* to *Devarim* 4:26 for the discrepancy of 850 years to 852 years.] Thus, if we were

Yours and only Yours; Yours, yes Yours; Yours, surely Yours; Yours, HASHEM, is the sovereignty. To Him praise is due. To Him praise is fitting.

Almighty is He in kingship, perfectly sustaining, His perfect ones say to Him:

Yours and only Yours; Yours, yes Yours; Yours, surely Yours; Yours, HASHEM, is the sovereignty. To Him praise is due. To Him praise is fitting.

He is mighty.

He is most mighty. *May He soon rebuild His House, speedily, yes speedily, in our days, soon. God, rebuild, God, rebuild, rebuild Your House soon!*

He is distinguished, He is great, He is exalted. *May He soon rebuild His House, speedily, yes speedily, in our days, soon. God, rebuild, God, rebuild, rebuild Your House soon!*

simply to pray that Hashem rebuild the *Bais Hamikdosh* בִּמְהֵרָה, *speedily*, we might be forced to wait many centuries for the fulfillment of our request. Therefore, we add בִּמְהֵרָה בְיָמֵינוּ בְּקָרוֹב, *yes, speedily in our days, soon! (Machatzis HaShekel).*

His eternal handiwork

◆§ קֵל בְּנֵה קֵל בְּנֵה בְּנֵה בֵיתְךָ בְּקָרוֹב — *Rebuild, G-d; rebuild, G-d; rebuild Your House soon.*

The Sages declare the man's handiwork is transitory, but G-d's deeds are eternal. The first two Temples were built by human beings, therefore they could be destroyed, but the Third Temple will be eternal because it will be built by Hashem. Thus we stress in our prayer, אֵל בְּנֵה — let it be built by Hashem so that it will surely endure forever *(Ephod Bad).*

185   The Haggadah Treasury

הֶדּוּר הוּא. וָתִיק הוּא. זַכַּאי הוּא. חָסִיד הוּא. יִבְנֶה בֵּיתוֹ בְּקָרוֹב. בִּמְהֵרָה בִּמְהֵרָה בְּיָמֵינוּ בְּקָרוֹב. אֵל בְּנֵה אֵל בְּנֵה. בְּנֵה בֵּיתְךָ בְּקָרוֹב:

טָהוֹר הוּא. יָחִיד הוּא. כַּבִּיר הוּא. לָמוּד הוּא. מֶלֶךְ הוּא. נוֹרָא הוּא. סַגִּיב הוּא. עִזּוּז הוּא. פּוֹדֶה הוּא. צַדִּיק הוּא. יִבְנֶה בֵּיתוֹ בְּקָרוֹב. בִּמְהֵרָה בִּמְהֵרָה בְּיָמֵינוּ בְּקָרוֹב. אֵל בְּנֵה אֵל בְּנֵה. בְּנֵה בֵּיתְךָ בְּקָרוֹב.

קָדוֹשׁ הוּא. רַחוּם הוּא. שַׁדַּי הוּא. תַּקִּיף הוּא. יִבְנֶה בֵּיתוֹ בְּקָרוֹב. בִּמְהֵרָה בִּמְהֵרָה בְּיָמֵינוּ בְּקָרוֹב. אֵל בְּנֵה אֵל בְּנֵה. בְּנֵה בֵּיתְךָ בְּקָרוֹב:

אֶחָד מִי יוֹדֵעַ

אֶחָד מִי יוֹדֵעַ. אֶחָד אֲנִי יוֹדֵעַ. אֶחָד אֱלֹהֵינוּ שֶׁבַּשָּׁמַיִם וּבָאָרֶץ:

שְׁנַיִם מִי יוֹדֵעַ. שְׁנַיִם אֲנִי יוֹדֵעַ. שְׁנֵי לֻחוֹת הַבְּרִית. אֶחָד אֱלֹהֵינוּ שֶׁבַּשָּׁמַיִם וּבָאָרֶץ:

אֶחָד מִי יוֹדֵעַ — Who knows one?

A list of merits ✑ *Eteres Yeshuah* interprets the song as a list of the merits which resulted in the redemption of our forefathers. It is composed in the form of someone asking Who knows one merit; Who knows a second merit, and so on. The answers are as follows:

He is all glorious, He is faithful, He is faultless, He is righteous. *May He soon rebuild His House, speedily, yes speedily, in our days, soon. God, rebuild, God, rebuild, rebuild Your House soon!*

He is pure, He is unique, He is powerful, He is all-wise, He is King, He is awesome, He is sublime, He is all-powerful, He is the Redeemer, He is the all-righteous. *May He soon rebuild His House, speedily, yes speedily, in our days, soon. God, rebuild, God, rebuild, rebuild Your House soon!*

He is holy, He is compassionate, He is Almighty, He is omnipotent. *May He soon rebuild His House, speedily, yes speedily, in our days, soon. God, rebuild, God, rebuild, rebuild Your House soon!*

Who Knows One?

Who knows one? I know one: One is our God, in heaven and on earth.

Who knows two? I know two: two are the Tablets of the Covenant; One is our God, in heaven and on earth.

1 — The first merit of Israel was its faith in Hashem, the G-d of heaven and earth: וַיַּאֲמֵן הָעָם, *and the nation believed (Sh'mos 4:31).*

2 — The two tablets containing the Ten Commandments which our forefathers were ready to accept upon themselves: בְּהוֹצִיאֲךָ אֶת הָעָם מִמִּצְרַיִם תַּעַבְדוּן אֶת הָאֱלֹקִים עַל הָהָר הַזֶּה, *When you take this nation out from Egypt, you will all serve G-d at this mountain (Sh'mos 3:12).*

שְׁלֹשָׁה מִי יוֹדֵעַ. שְׁלֹשָׁה אֲנִי יוֹדֵעַ. שְׁלֹשָׁה אָבוֹת. שְׁנֵי לְחוֹת הַבְּרִית. אֶחָד אֱלֹהֵינוּ שֶׁבַּשָּׁמַיִם וּבָאָרֶץ:

אַרְבַּע מִי יוֹדֵעַ. אַרְבַּע אֲנִי יוֹדֵעַ. אַרְבַּע אִמָּהוֹת. שְׁלֹשָׁה אָבוֹת. שְׁנֵי לְחוֹת הַבְּרִית. אֶחָד אֱלֹהֵינוּ שֶׁבַּשָּׁמַיִם וּבָאָרֶץ:

חֲמִשָּׁה מִי יוֹדֵעַ. חֲמִשָּׁה אֲנִי יוֹדֵעַ. חֲמִשָּׁה חֻמְשֵׁי תוֹרָה. אַרְבַּע אִמָּהוֹת. שְׁלֹשָׁה אָבוֹת. שְׁנֵי לְחוֹת הַבְּרִית. אֶחָד אֱלֹהֵינוּ שֶׁבַּשָּׁמַיִם וּבָאָרֶץ:

שִׁשָּׁה מִי יוֹדֵעַ. שִׁשָּׁה אֲנִי יוֹדֵעַ. שִׁשָּׁה סִדְרֵי מִשְׁנָה. חֲמִשָּׁה חֻמְשֵׁי תוֹרָה. אַרְבַּע אִמָּהוֹת. שְׁלֹשָׁה אָבוֹת. שְׁנֵי לְחוֹת הַבְּרִית. אֶחָד אֱלֹהֵינוּ שֶׁבַּשָּׁמַיִם וּבָאָרֶץ.

שִׁבְעָה מִי יוֹדֵעַ. שִׁבְעָה אֲנִי יוֹדֵעַ. שִׁבְעָה יְמֵי שַׁבַּתָּא. שִׁשָּׁה סִדְרֵי מִשְׁנָה. חֲמִשָּׁה חֻמְשֵׁי תוֹרָה. אַרְבַּע אִמָּהוֹת. שְׁלֹשָׁה אָבוֹת. שְׁנֵי לְחוֹת הַבְּרִית. אֶחָד אֱלֹהֵינוּ שֶׁבַּשָּׁמַיִם וּבָאָרֶץ:

3 — The covenant that Hashem made with the three Patriarchs וַיִּזְכֹּר אֱלֹקִים אֶת בְּרִיתוֹ אֶת אַבְרָהָם אֶת יִצְחָק וְאֵת יַעֲקֹב, *and God remembered His covenant with Abraham, with Isaac, and with Jacob* (Sh'mos 2:24).

4 — The merit of the four Matriarchs: מְקַפֵּץ עַל הַגְּבָעוֹת, *He skipped over the hills,* (Shir HaShirim 2:8) this refers to G-d's zeal to redeem Israel in the merit of the Matriarchs (*Midrash Shir Hashirim*).

5 — The Five Books of Moses which Israel was to receive.

Who knows three? I know three: three are the Patriarchs; two are the Tablets of the Covenant; One is our God, in heaven and on earth.

Who knows four? I know four: four are the Matriarchs; three are the Patriarchs; two are the Tablets of the Covenant; One is our God, in heaven and on earth.

Who knows five? I know five: five are the books of Torah; four are the Matriarchs; three are the Patriarchs; two are the Tablets of the Covenant; One is our God, in heaven and on earth.

Who knows six? I know six: six are the Orders of the Mishnah; five are the books of Torah; four are the Matriarchs; three are the Patriarchs; two are the Tablets of the Covenant; One is our God, in heaven and on earth.

Who knows seven? I know seven: seven are the days of the week; six are the Orders of the Mishnah; five are the books of the Torah; four are the Matriarchs; three are the Patriarchs; two are the Tablets of the Covenant; One is our God, in heaven and on earth.

6 — The Oral Torah which is contained in the Six Orders of the Mishnah: לֹא כָּרַת הקב״ה בְּרִית עִם יִשְׂרָאֵל אֶלָּא בִּשְׁבִיל דְּבָרִים שֶׁבְּעַל פֶּה, *The Holy One Blessed be He, did not seal a covenant with Israel except because of the Oral Law (Gittin 60b).*

7 — The Jews observed Sabbath even in Egypt: הקב״ה גוֹאֲלָן לְפִי שֶׁהָיוּ נוֹחִין בְּשַׁבָּת — *The Holy One Blessed be He redeemed them because they rested on Sabbath (Midrash).*

שְׁמוֹנָה מִי יוֹדֵעַ. שְׁמוֹנָה אֲנִי יוֹדֵעַ. שְׁמוֹנָה יְמֵי
מִילָה. שִׁבְעָה יְמֵי שַׁבַּתָּא. שִׁשָּׁה סִדְרֵי מִשְׁנָה. חֲמִשָּׁה
חֻמְשֵׁי תוֹרָה. אַרְבַּע אִמָּהוֹת. שְׁלֹשָׁה אָבוֹת. שְׁנֵי
לֻחוֹת הַבְּרִית. אֶחָד אֱלֹהֵינוּ שֶׁבַּשָּׁמַיִם וּבָאָרֶץ:

תִּשְׁעָה מִי יוֹדֵעַ. תִּשְׁעָה אֲנִי יוֹדֵעַ. תִּשְׁעָה יַרְחֵי
לֵדָה. שְׁמוֹנָה יְמֵי מִילָה. שִׁבְעָה יְמֵי שַׁבַּתָּא. שִׁשָּׁה
סִדְרֵי מִשְׁנָה. חֲמִשָּׁה חֻמְשֵׁי תוֹרָה. אַרְבַּע אִמָּהוֹת.
שְׁלֹשָׁה אָבוֹת. שְׁנֵי לֻחוֹת הַבְּרִית. אֶחָד אֱלֹהֵינוּ
שֶׁבַּשָּׁמַיִם וּבָאָרֶץ:

עֲשָׂרָה מִי יוֹדֵעַ. עֲשָׂרָה אֲנִי יוֹדֵעַ. עֲשָׂרָה דִבְּרַיָּא.
תִּשְׁעָה יַרְחֵי לֵדָה. שְׁמוֹנָה יְמֵי מִילָה. שִׁבְעָה יְמֵי
שַׁבַּתָּא. שִׁשָּׁה סִדְרֵי מִשְׁנָה. חֲמִשָּׁה חוּמְשֵׁי תוֹרָה.
אַרְבַּע אִמָּהוֹת. שְׁלֹשָׁה אָבוֹת. שְׁנֵי לֻחוֹת הַבְּרִית.
אֶחָד אֱלֹהֵינוּ שֶׁבַּשָּׁמַיִם וּבָאָרֶץ:

אַחַד עָשָׂר מִי יוֹדֵעַ. אַחַד עָשָׂר אֲנִי יוֹדֵעַ. אַחַד
עָשָׂר כּוֹכְבַיָּא. עֲשָׂרָה דִבְּרַיָּא. תִּשְׁעָה יַרְחֵי לֵדָה.
שְׁמוֹנָה יְמֵי מִילָה. שִׁבְעָה יְמֵי שַׁבַּתָּא. שִׁשָּׁה סִדְרֵי
מִשְׁנָה. חֲמִשָּׁה חֻמְשֵׁי תוֹרָה. אַרְבַּע אִמָּהוֹת. שְׁלֹשָׁה
אָבוֹת. שְׁנֵי לֻחוֹת הַבְּרִית. אֶחָד אֱלֹהֵינוּ שֶׁבַּשָּׁמַיִם
וּבָאָרֶץ:

8 — The Jews finally left Egypt thanks to their performance of מִילָה, *circumcision*, for, prior to the Exodus, they were given the commandments of *milah* and
Pesach (see *comm.* to וָאֹמַר לָךְ בְּדָמַיִךְ חֲיִי)
9 — Despite the Egyptian decrees that were designed

Who knows eight? I know eight: eight are the days of circumcision; seven are the days of the week; six are the Orders of the Mishnah; five are the books of Torah; four are the Matriarchs; three are the Patriarchs; two are the Tablets of the Covenant; One is our God, in heaven and on the earth.

Who knows nine? I know nine: nine are the months of pregnancy; eight are the days of circumcision; seven are the days of the week; six are the Orders of the Mishnah; five are the books of the Torah; four are the Matriarchs; three are the Patriarchs; two are the Tablets of the Covenant; One is our God, in heaven and on the earth.

Who knows ten? I know ten: ten are the Ten Commandments; nine are the months of pregnancy; eight are the days of circumcision; seven are the days of the week; six are the Orders of the Mishnah; five are the books of the Torah; four are the Matriarchs; three are the Patriarchs; two are the Tablets of the Covenant; One is our God, in heaven and on earth.

Who knows eleven? I know eleven: eleven are the stars (in Joseph's dream); ten are the Ten Commandments; nine are the months of pregnancy; eight are the days to circumcision; seven are the days of the week; six are the Orders of the Mishnah; five are the books of the Torah; four are the Matriarchs; three are the Patriarchs; two are the Tablets of the Covenant; One is our God, in heaven and on earth.

to disrupt family life, Israel kept itself sacred and continued to give birth to new generations.

10 — The Jews were determined to accept the Ten Commandments upon leaving Egypt.

11 — The eleven stars that Joseph saw in his dream (*Bereishis* 37:9) represented his eleven brothers who came to Egypt and whose descendants left it without

שְׁנֵים עָשָׂר מִי יוֹדֵעַ. שְׁנֵים עָשָׂר אֲנִי יוֹדֵעַ. שְׁנֵים
עָשָׂר שִׁבְטַיָּא. אַחַד עָשָׂר כּוֹכְבַיָּא. עֲשָׂרָה דִבְּרַיָּא.
תִּשְׁעָה יַרְחֵי לֵדָה. שְׁמוֹנָה יְמֵי מִילָה. שִׁבְעָה יְמֵי
שַׁבַּתָּא. שִׁשָּׁה סִדְרֵי מִשְׁנָה. חֲמִשָּׁה חֻמְשֵׁי תוֹרָה.
אַרְבַּע אִמָּהוֹת. שְׁלֹשָׁה אָבוֹת. שְׁנֵי לֻחוֹת הַבְּרִית.
אֶחָד אֱלֹהֵינוּ שֶׁבַּשָּׁמַיִם וּבָאָרֶץ:

שְׁלֹשָׁה עָשָׂר מִי יוֹדֵעַ. שְׁלֹשָׁה עָשָׂר אֲנִי יוֹדֵעַ.
שְׁלֹשָׁה עָשָׂר מִדַּיָּא. שְׁנֵים עָשָׂר שִׁבְטַיָּא. אַחַד עָשָׂר
כּוֹכְבַיָּא. עֲשָׂרָה דִבְּרַיָּא. תִּשְׁעָה יַרְחֵי לֵדָה. שְׁמוֹנָה
יְמֵי מִילָה. שִׁבְעָה יְמֵי שַׁבַּתָּא. שִׁשָּׁה סִדְרֵי מִשְׁנָה.
חֲמִשָּׁה חֻמְשֵׁי תוֹרָה. אַרְבַּע אִמָּהוֹת. שְׁלֹשָׁה אָבוֹת.
שְׁנֵי לֻחוֹת הַבְּרִית. אֶחָד אֱלֹהֵינוּ שֶׁבַּשָּׁמַיִם וּבָאָרֶץ:

have assimilated into the foreign culture. This was sym-
bolized by their refusal to change their names, as the
Midrash states רְאוּבֵן נַחְתִין רְאוּבֵן סַלְקִין, *he came as*
Reuben and he left as Reuben.

12 — The twelve tribes remained distinct and
separate from the Egyptians in every significant way,
uncontaminated by the immorality of Egypt. As
Midrash Shir Hashirim relates: Hashem says that His
name יָ-ה bears witness that the children born in Egypt
were pure and deserving of redemption.

Who knows twelve? I know twelve: twelve are the tribes; eleven are the stars (in Joseph's dream); ten are the Ten Commandments; nine are the months of pregnancy; eight are the days of circumcision; seven are the days of the week; six are the Orders of the Mishnah; five are the books of the Torah; four are the Matriarchs; three are the Patriarchs; two are the Tablets of the Covenant; One is our God, in heaven and on earth.

Who knows thirteen? I know thirteen: thirteen are the attributes of God; twelve are the tribes; eleven are the stars (in Joseph's dream); ten are the Ten Commandments; nine are the months of pregnancy; eight are the days of circumcision; seven are the days of the week; six are the Orders of the Mishnah; five are the books of the Torah; four are the Matriarchs; three are the Patriarchs; two are the Tablets of the Covenant; One is our God, in heaven and on earth.

13 — In conclusion, we are given the clue to the final redemption. If we observe the lesson G-d taught Moses that even if Israel sins, it may secure G-d's forgiveness by invoking His Thirteen Attributes of Mercy — then we can speed the coming of Messiah.

חַד גַּדְיָא

חַד גַּדְיָא. חַד גַּדְיָא.
דְּזַבִּין אַבָּא בִּתְרֵי זוּזֵי.
חַד גַּדְיָא חַד גַּדְיָא:

וְאָתָא שׁוּנְרָא וְאָכְלָה לְגַדְיָא
דְּזַבִּין אַבָּא בִּתְרֵי זוּזֵי
חַד גַּדְיָא חַד גַּדְיָא:

וְאָתָא כַלְבָּא וְנָשַׁךְ לְשׁוּנְרָא.
דְּאָכְלָא לְגַדְיָא.
דְּזַבִּין אַבָּא בִּתְרֵי זוּזֵי.
חַד גַּדְיָא חַד גַּדְיָא:

וְאָתָא חוּטְרָא וְהִכָּה לְכַלְבָּא.
דְּנָשַׁךְ לְשׁוּנְרָא.
דְּאָכְלָה לְגַדְיָא.
דְּזַבִּין אַבָּא בִּתְרֵי זוּזֵי.
חַד גַּדְיָא חַד גַּדְיָא:

חַד גַּדְיָא — One kid

Three approaches ⊷§ The commentators unanimously agree that that deceptively simple 'folk story' of *Chad Gadya* is deeply meaningful. A wide variety of interpretations have been offered for this concluding song of the *Haggadah*. Here are three of the many different approaches:

A Kid

A kid, a kid,
that father bought for two zuzim,
a kid, a kid.

A cat then came and devoured the kid,
that father bought for two zuzim,
a kid, a kid.

A dog then came and bit the cat,
that devoured the kid,
that father bought for two zuzim,
a kid, a kid.

A stick then came, and beat the dog,
that bit the cat,
that devoured the kid,
that father bought for two zuzim,
a kid, a kid.

Israel survives ◄§ The tale illustrates the history of Israel, the *lone kid* which G-d, the *father*, selected for Himself. He acquired it through giving the two Tablets of the Covenant, the *two zuzim* of the song. The animals, objects, and people who successively devour one another are the nations that subjugated and oppressed Israel throughout its history. The end will be, however, that the Holy One, Blessed be He, will bring the final redemption of His beloved and unique *kid* which, alone among the nations, accepted His Torah.

Dialogue about idols ◄§ The song is a debate between a Jew and an Egyptian concerning the *one kid* which the Egyptians deified and worshiped. The Jew asks, 'How can you worship the *kid* when the *cat* can easily devour it?'

The Egyptian replies, 'In that case, I will worship the cat.'

'But the dog can overpower the cat!'

'Then I will worship the dog.'

The debate continues until the Jew concludes 'But all

וְאָתָא נוּרָא וְשָׂרַף לְחוּטְרָא.
דְּהִכָּה לְכַלְבָּא.
דְּנָשַׁךְ לְשׁוּנְרָא.
דְּאָכְלָה לְגַדְיָא.
דְּזַבִּין אַבָּא בִּתְרֵי זוּזֵי.
חַד גַּדְיָא חַד גַּדְיָא:

וְאָתָא מַיָּא וְכָבָה לְנוּרָא.
דְּשָׂרַף לְחוּטְרָא.
דְּהִכָּה לְכַלְבָּא.
דְּנָשַׁךְ לְשׁוּנְרָא.
דְּאָכְלָה לְגַדְיָא.
דְּזַבִּין אַבָּא בִּתְרֵי זוּזֵי.
חַד גַּדְיָא חַד גַּדְיָא:

וְאָתָא תוֹרָא וְשָׁתָה לְמַיָּא.
דְּכָבָה לְנוּרָא.
דְּשָׂרַף לְחוּטְרָא.
דְּהִכָּה לְכַלְבָּא.
דְּנָשַׁךְ לְשׁוּנְרָא.
דְּאָכְלָה לְגַדְיָא.
דְּזַבִּין אַבָּא בִּתְרֵי זוּזֵי.
חַד גַּדְיָא חַד גַּדְיָא:

וְאָתָא הַשּׁוֹחֵט וְשָׁחַט לְתוֹרָא.
דְּשָׁתָא לְמַיָּא.
דְּכָבָה לְנוּרָא.
דְּשָׂרַף לְחוּטְרָא.
דְּהִכָּה לְכַלְבָּא.

A fire then came and burnt the stick,
that beat the dog,
that bit the cat,
that devoured the kid,
that father bought for two zuzim,
a kid, a kid.

Water then came and quenched the fire,
that burnt the stick,
that beat the dog,
that bit the cat,
that devoured the kid,
that father bought for two zuzim,
a kid, a kid.

An ox then came, and drank the water,
that quenched the fire,
that burnt the stick,
that beat the dog,
that bit the cat,
that devoured the kid,
that my father bought for two zuzim,
a kid, a kid.

The slaughterer then came, and slaughtered the ox,
that drank the water,
that quenched the fire,
that burnt the stick,
that beat the dog,

powers on earth are subservient to the Holy One Blessed be He. Why don't you finally realize that only He is
to be worshiped?'

Forget ◆§ Since so much of the *Seder* ritual is designed to
not the symbolize the freedom and greatness that was given
purpose to Israel on this fateful night, the *Haggadah* concludes
with a song designed to restrain the potential for arrogance that can result from preoccupation with status.

דְּנָשַׁךְ לְשׁוּנְרָא.
דְּאָכְלָה לְגַדְיָא.
דְּזַבִּין אַבָּא בִּתְרֵי זוּזֵי.
חַד גַּדְיָא חַד גַּדְיָא:

וְאָתָא מַלְאַךְ הַמָּוֶת וְשָׁחַט לְשׁוֹחֵט.
דְּשָׁחַט לְתוֹרָא.
דְּשָׁתָה לְמַיָּא.
דְּכָבָה לְנוּרָא.
דְּשָׂרַף לְחוּטְרָא.
דְּהִכָּה לְכַלְבָּא.
דְּנָשַׁךְ לְשׁוּנְרָא.
דְּאָכְלָה לְגַדְיָא.
דְּזַבִּין אַבָּא בִּתְרֵי זוּזֵי.
חַד גַּדְיָא חַד גַּדְיָא:

וְאָתָא הַקָּדוֹשׁ בָּרוּךְ הוּא וְשָׁחַט לְמַלְאַךְ
הַמָּוֶת.
דְּשָׁחַט לְשׁוֹחֵט.
דְּשָׁחַט לְתוֹרָא.
דְּשָׁתָה לְמַיָּא.
דְּכָבָה לְנוּרָא.
דְּשָׂרַף לְחוּטְרָא.
דְּהִכָּה לְכַלְבָּא.
דְּנָשַׁךְ לְשׁוּנְרָא.
דְּאָכְלָה לְגַדְיָא.
דְּזַבִּין אַבָּא בִּתְרֵי זוּזֵי.
חַד גַּדְיָא חַד גַּדְיָא:

that bit the cat,
that devoured the kid,
that father bought for two zuzim,
a kid, a kid.

The angel of death then came and killed the slaughterer,
who slaughtered the ox,
that drank the water,
that quenched the fire,
that burnt the stick,
that beat the dog,
that bit the cat,
that devoured the kid,
that father bought for two zuzim,
a kid, a kid.

The Holy One, blessed be He, then came
    and slew the angel of death,
who killed the slaughterer,
who slaughtered the ox,
that drank the water,
that quenched the fire,
that burnt the stick,
that beat the dog,
that bit the cat,
that devoured the kid,
that father bought for two zuzim,
a kid a kid.

Our freedom should be utilized for the service of G-d,
not of self. The *one kid* symbolizes the soul which left
the highest spiritual world and passed through two
lower worlds [the *two zuzim*] before it finally arrived
on earth, the lowest sphere of existence. Each stanza of
the song symbolizes a different stage of life. Man goes

through a portion of his life — and then is reminded חַד גַּדְיָא, חַד גַּדְיָא, 'Unique soul! unique soul! What have you accomplished here? Have you been worthy?' But instead of seizing the opportunity to perfect himself, man procrastinates, saying that he will attend to his spiritual needs later, later. But later never comes. Finally, man is warned that his soul will be taken from him and returned to its Maker to account for its deeds. How will it explain its wasted opportunities?

תם ונשלם שבח לא-ל בורא עולם